DISCARD

| DATE DUE | |
|---|---|
| APR 2 2 2004 | |
| JUL 2 0 2004 | |
| NOV 0 3 2004 | |
| MAR 2 2 2006 | |
| JAN 1 4 2008 | |
| | |
| | |
| APR 0 7 2008 | |
| FEB 0 2 2012 | |
| | |
| May 12, 2013 | |
| APR 1 9 2017 | |

# Crime
## SCENE

### the ultimate guide to forensic science

# Crime
# SCENE

## the ultimate guide to forensic science

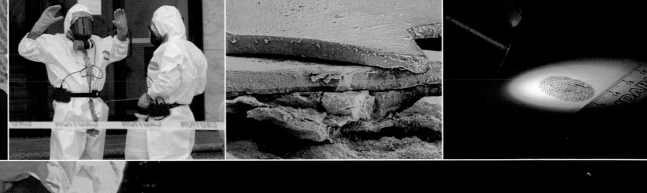

Richard Platt

DK Publishing

## Dorling DK Kindersley

LONDON, NEW YORK, MUNICH,
MELBOURNE, and DELHI

**Senior Editor** Kitty Blount
**Senior Art Editor** Stefan Podhorodecki
**Editors** Mary Atkinson, Francesca Baines, Kate Bradshaw,
Camilla Hallinan, David John, Bradley Round
**Art Editors** Darren Holt, Philip Letsu
**Managing Editor** Andrew Macintyre
**Managing Art Editor** Jane Thomas
**Category Publisher** Linda Martin
**Art Director** Simon Webb
**Picture Research** Julia Harris-Voss, Marie Osborn, Frances Vargo
**DK Picture Library** Jonathan Brooks, Gemma Woodward, Sarah Mills
**Production** Erica Rosen
**DTP Designer** Siu Yin Ho

**General Consultant**
Dr. Clive Steele, Head of Forensic Science Unit, South Bank University, London

**Subject Consultants**
Dr. Sue Black, Forensic Anthropologist, University of Glasgow; Dr. Anne-Maria Brennan,
Senior Lecturer in Biosciences, South Bank University; Superintendent Philip Carson, City
of London Police; Ron Cook, Fingerprint and Forensic Expert; Andy Day, Former Scene of
Crime Officer; Dr. Nikolas Lemos, Head of Forensic Toxicology, St. George's Hospital
Medical School; Dr. Freddie Martin, Forensic Odontologist; Dr. Neil Morgan, Senior
Lecturer in Biosciences, South Bank University; Professor Phil Nolan, Research Professor
of Explosion and Fire, South Bank University; Dr. Freddy Patel, Home Office Pathologist;
Professor Peter Vanezis, Regis Professor of Forensic Medicine and Science, University of
Glasgow; Peter Whent, Homicide Investigator; Dr. Caroline Wilkinson, Medical Artist,
University of Manchester; John Yarrow, Forensic Photographer

**US Consultant**
Frank J Rodgers, Phoenix Police Department (retired)

First American Edition, 2003
Published in the United States by
DK Publishing, Inc.
375 Hudson Street
New York, New York 10014

03 04 05 06 07 08 10 9 8 7 6 5 4 3 2 1
Copyright © 2003 Dorling Kindersley Limited

A Cataloging-in-Publication record for this book is available
from the Library of Congress.

ISBN 0-7894-8891-4

Color reproduction by GRB Editrice, Italy
Printed and bound in Italy by G. Canale & C. S.p.A.

See our complete product line at
**www.dk.com**

# Contents

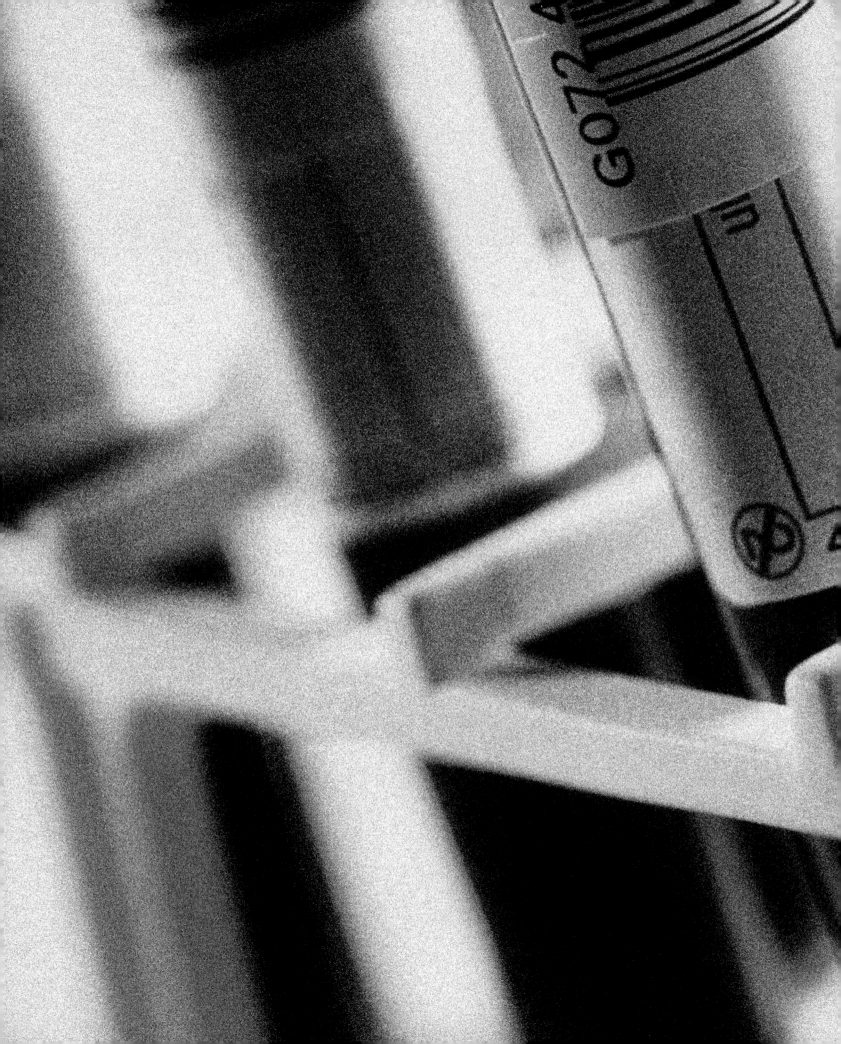

For weeks we watched the OJ Simpson criminal trial on television and were fascinated by the DNA, shoeprint, hair, fiber, serology, and other evidence that was methodically laid out by forensic scientists. Since then, as technology has advanced, forensic science (science as it relates to law) has been used more effectively to convict—beyond reasonable doubt—criminals of almost every description. Forensic science has also become a mainstay for dozens of movies and television programs. But in order to entertain their audiences, many of them get it wrong. This book, however, allows the reader to learn about all of the major forensic disciplines in an accurate, concise, well-illustrated, imaginative, and extremely entertaining manner. And, most importantly, it gets it right. Each section of *Crime Scene: The Ultimate Guide to Forensic Science* provides solid information coupled with outstanding visuals, and then follows up with an actual case study. The book explains how modern, high-tech tools and techniques, in addition to good investigation, are used to help discover the truth and provide a solution that can ultimately be used in a court of law.

Having spent over thirty years as a supervisor in the FBI Laboratory and as a private examiner, I have seen thousands of cases and been involved in numerous high-profile trials. During that time, one of the most difficult challenges has been explaining to friends, news media, students, juries, judges, and others, not only my own areas of specialty, but the many others that encompass forensic science. Now all I need to do is hand them *Crime Scene: The Ultimate Guide to Forensic Science* and I can be confident that they will have one of the best possible overviews of this fascinating subject.

**Gerald B. Richards, FBI Special Agent (retired)**
Former Chief Special Photographic Unit;
Document Operations and Research Unit
FBI Laboratory

# The investigative process

Forensic science is a versatile and enormously powerful tool in the investigation of a crime. But science alone is not enough to catch criminals. To be successful, forensic techniques must be combined with the knowledge, experience, and intuition of detectives, uniformed police, and civilian experts and administrators.

A crime is committed in a cosmopolitan city—any member of the local, or even national, population might be the culprit; they may even have fled the country. Investigators need to eliminate potential suspects systematically, to cut them down to a manageable list to interview.

There is no single way to do this. Criminal records and forensic databases can help identify similar crimes, and perhaps provide a list of known criminals who might be suspects. Also, a forensic investigation of the crime scene can provide pointers. Victims and witnesses of crimes frequently give police valuable information that can lead them to a suspect. Finally, where it appears that nobody saw the crime, publicity and a media appeal can sometimes persuade reluctant witnesses to come forward.

## Healthy skepticism

Victims and witnesses often provide information about a perpetrator's sex and age, and this can obviously reduce the size of the suspect pool by half or more. However, acting on this information is not as straightforward as it might appear. Witness statements need to be scrutinized, if not skeptically, then with an understanding of their limitations. For example, if a witness states, "I saw a woman walk away from the crime scene," then it might seem reasonable to eliminate men from the enquiry. But what if the witness noticed a man with long, blond hair, and assumed he was female? Experience has shown that witness perceptions and memory can be inaccurate in other respects, so when witnesses refer to "a 25-year-old," investigators look for suspects between the ages of 12 and 40.

## Vital assumptions

If witness or victim statements fail to eliminate suspects, investigators need to make assumptions that narrow down the initial field. For example, most crimes occur in the neighborhood of the culprit's home—so investigations tend to begin around the crime scene. Local house-to-house inquiries can often elicit apparently unconnected information that later proves crucial.

Seeking corroboration helps in this process: by asking the same question of many different people, investigators assess reliability and perhaps motives of witnesses. For example, knocking on enough doors and asking, "How many people live here?" and "How many people live next door?" can unmask incriminating lies.

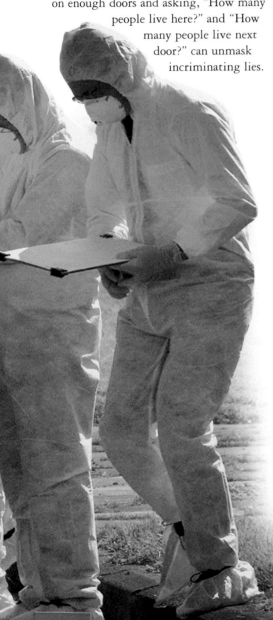

## Everyone is a suspect

The search for a suspect is comprehensive and impartial. It even includes the person reporting the crime, since murderers often turn out to be the very people who "find" the body. Nobody is ruled out, however unlikely their guilt may seem, however disturbing the implications, and however much their accusation might conflict with popular preconceptions.

The abduction and murder of children provides an instructive, if harrowing, example of this principle. "Stranger danger" attracts intense media interest— but only because such cases are rare. In the overwhelming majority of crimes, the perpetrator is known to the victim.

This knowledge led investigators to doubt Lindy Chamberlain's claim that a dingo had taken her baby (see p. 64), but this notorious Australian case also neatly illustrates the risk of preconceived ideas. Investigators who jump to conclusions are more inclined to overlook evidence that conflicts with their initial views. The longer an assumption guides an investigation, the more difficult it is to set it aside and consider alternatives. In the "Dingo Baby" case, failure to do this led to a miscarriage of justice.

Diligent detectives learn to question even apparently reliable evidence. For example, it is tempting to regard a suspect's confession as cast-iron proof of guilt, yet someone may confess to a crime they did not commit to protect the real perpetrator, or to hide a greater crime. Further probing, as well as corroborating evidence, is essential to prove that the person confessing is actually the culprit.

## Proving guilt conclusively

Proof beyond reasonable doubt secures convictions. Investigators are now learning that forensic science can provide such proof with a level of objectivity and plausibility often lacking in other forms of evidence. Today, forensic science plays a vital part at every stage in an investigation, from crime scene to court.

◀ **SHOOTING SCENE**
*By systematically cataloging evidence at the scene of a shooting, SOCOs (scene of crime officers) create a foundation on which to build the investigation.*

The chapters that follow take a thematic look at the diverse disciplines of forensic science, showing how each one helps to guide a crime investigation toward an arrest and conviction.

◀ **AT THE CRIME SCENE**
*Evidence that investigators initially overlook at the crime scene may be irretrievably lost, or inadmissible in court.*

**THE VICTIM** ▶
*Cases where a victim is killed require a special kind of investigation, in which the corpse of the victim is a major source of clues.*

◀ **HUMAN IDENTIFICATION**
*Forensic techniques, from fingerprinting to DNA, can help to discover the identity of both the suspect and the victim.*

**THE SUSPECT** ▶
*Tracking down a suspect may involve psychology, as well as the assessment of the memory and judgment of fallible eyewitnesses.*

◀ **ANALYSIS OF EVIDENCE**
*To find vital clues that could close a case, crime labs use sophisticated tests and instruments to sift through evidence.*

**LETHAL AGENTS** ▶
*Death comes in many guises, and forensic technology helps to trace the whole range—from the speeding bullet to the tiniest drop of poison.*

The final chapter of the book considers so-called "white-collar crimes," including forgery of works of art, currency, and documents, computer crime, and criminal damage to wildlife and the environment.

# AT THE CRIME SCENE

As small as a computer, or as big as a plane crash, a crime scene is the largest area that may contain valuable evidence for later investigation. By methodically protecting, searching, and documenting the crime scene, police and forensic specialists work together to ensure that nothing of importance escapes scrutiny—even the tiniest smudge on a window pane can prove useful. Without taking basic evidence-handling precautions, crime investigations are fatally compromised before they have even really begun.

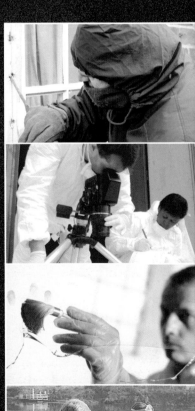

# First on the scene

With sirens wailing, the emergency services rush to the crime scene. The police officers, along with fire and ambulance crews, see what the other investigators never will: a completely undisturbed site. But before they can exploit this one chance to preserve and record evidence, they may have other, more urgent, responsibilities.

**LIFE-SAVING DASH ▲**
*Crime investigation has to wait if lives are at risk. Here, a victim of a 1998 shooting on Capitol Hill, Washington, DC, is rushed to an air ambulance.*

### PRIORITIES:

| | |
|---|---|
| 1 | *Save and preserve life.* |
| 2 | *Provide emergency first aid for those injured at the scene.* |
| 3 | *Arrest, detain, and remove any suspect present.* |
| 4 | *By cooperating with the other emergency services, ensure that the scene is safe for entry by investigators and forensic examiners.* |
| 5 | *Secure and preserve the crime scene, keeping a record of everyone who enters and leaves.* |
| 6 | *Record and preserve evidence that may be perishable, fragile, or could be destroyed, before the formal investigation begins.* |
| 7 | *Identify and locate any witnesses, and, where possible, keep them separate until their statements have been taken.* |
| 8 | *Communicate with the senior officer, who will coordinate the initial investigation and appoint an Investigating Officer.* |

**WEDGEWOOD MASSACRE**
*Emergency services arrive at a 1999 massacre at Wedgewood Baptist Church in Texas.*

## Preserving life

Whatever the type of crime scene, the priority is always to preserve life and assist any victims, ensuring that they are not in any danger. But once any injuries they have sustained are stabilized, and they are safe and composed, the importance of further assisting victims must be weighed against the risk that in doing so, evidence may be destroyed. For example, the victim of an assault is discouraged from bathing, in case they have the suspect's blood, skin, or hair on their hands.

## Suspects at the scene

After supporting victims, the next—and obvious—role of the police is to detain and remove suspects. The apprehended are searched and their condition, statements, and behavior are all documented. Items of clothing may also be seized for forensic analysis. A less obvious police task is to make sure that suspects cannot return to the crime scene. Their return may make it difficult to prove at trial that traces of their presence, such as footprints, fibers, or hairs, originated when they committed the crime, rather than when they returned to the scene under police supervision. Also, if they revisit the scene, bystanders may see them for a second time, possibly prejudicing identification evidence.

## Detaining witnesses

Part of the job of those first on the scene is to detain both willing and reluctant witnesses: people who see a crime committed are not necessarily eager to relive the experience in the pursuit of justice. Even if they are not eyewitnesses, people near the scene can nevertheless provide information that might prove valuable in the investigation. If it is impossible to take statements from them immediately, witnesses should be separated to prevent them from discussing what they saw. This not only prevents one witness's recollections from being tainted by the ideas of another, it also ensures that if a suspect is caught and tried, defense lawyers will have less opportunity to cast doubt on eyewitness evidence.

## Controlling the scene

The more people that visit a crime scene, the more difficult it is for investigators to reconstruct what happened, and to identify potential suspects. So the next priority is to seal off the crime scene and protect any evidence it contains.

Clearly the size of the area to be sealed depends on the individual circumstances, but it should be big enough to enclose not only the immediate area of the crime, but also any points of entry and exit.

In major crime investigations, the area cordoned off needs to extend well beyond the actual crime scene, which is accessible only to investigators. Excluding the public from a wider area makes it easier to manage the crime scene, and provides a secure zone for communications, incident vehicles, and for dealing with the media.

Sealing off a crime scene is not just about enclosing it in a ring of tape. An effective plan for controlling the scene must also define a single route in and out. This normally involves one exit and entry route marked off for access by all forensic and scene investigators. Personnel numbers should be kept to a minimum, and all visitors should wear protective coveralls to avoid cross-contamination. It is also important to document every visitor to the scene. An accurate log of when each arrived and left and what they removed can be used at trial to deflect defense accusations of "evidence tampering."

**ARREST AND DETENTION ▶**
*Arresting suspects prevents them from returning to a crime scene and possibly contaminating evidence.*

## Examination of the crime scene

Foresight and a methodical approach by those first on the scene can help preserve and record evidence that might otherwise be destroyed. Unthinking routines such as flushing toilets or using the telephone can dispose of vital evidence, and recording whether a door was open or closed can make the difference between a killer being jailed or walking free.

When crime scene managers reach the scene, their primary aim is to interview the police officers who arrived initially, in order to document the crime scene. By walking through the area together, investigators can collect information about transient evidence, such as dissipated odors. So those first on the scene need to register as much information as possible about the undisturbed surroundings. Further forensic investigation could hinge upon what they report.

**EYEWITNESS STATEMENTS ▲**
*Statements collected and recorded by officers first on the scene can provide the forensic specialists with direction for any later investigation.*

## TAKING CHARGE

**SENIOR INVESTIGATING OFFICER ▲**
*Here, the senior investigating officer directs his homicide investigation team.*

A call from those first on the scene mobilizes senior officers and other agencies. Major crimes may then be investigated by literally hundreds of police and civilian specialists. Their coordination is the job of the senior investigating officer, who sets about deploying inquiry teams, house-to-house teams, and scene-of-crime teams, and directs the administrators who collate, file, and analyze evidence. Scene-of-crime teams, each headed by a crime scene manager, and supervised by a crime scene coordinator, report directly to the senior investigating officer. If the investigation concerns a number of different crime scenes, then separate scene-of-crime teams are allocated to each site. This helps to avoid cross-contamination, where evidence from one location may be inadvertently transferred to another (e.g., by being carried on someone's shoe).

# The photographer

The camera can record details of crime scenes with an accuracy no detective's notepad can match. It can preserve evidence as fragile and ephemeral as footprints in melting snow. If a jury cannot visit a crime scene, photographs can vividly recreate it for them. No wonder photographers are key members of every investigating team.

## PHOTOGRAPHIC SETUP:

(1) *Larger film area of medium-format camera means pictures are sharper.*

(2) *Macro lens focuses close enough to fill the frame with evidence smaller than a playing card.*

(3) *Tripod keeps the camera steady and exactly perpendicular to the subject.*

(4) *Measuring scale or tape, part of the crime-scene kit, makes any distortion obvious, and avoids confusion regarding the size of the subject.*

(5) *Evidence on a plain background.*

(6) *Documentation includes not only the details of the exhibit and camera settings, but also a record of the time, date, and location.*

After the crime scene manager has completed an initial assessment, crime scene photographers are often the first to operate. Their priority is to "document" key elements of an undisturbed crime scene in relation to the surroundings, since such evidence may be moved to a forensic laboratory for further analysis. The photographer then makes a broader and more comprehensive record. Photographs might include: the entry and exit routes, exterior and interior shots of the building, the connection between specific rooms, and the location of any significant evidence. Images are usually taken for the prosecution case, but may also help support any explanation given by the suspect.

As a general rule, crime scene photographers shoot more images than they think they will need. Selected photographs are then presented to a court as evidence. However, the defense team has a right to see any unused photographs. Therefore, each photograph is an item of evidence, and must be systematically documented, showing the details of the photographer, camera settings, the date and time taken, the location, and the

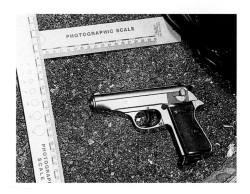

◄ EVIDENCE AS IT WAS FOUND
*Evidence, such as this gun, is first photographed in situ, both with scales and without—in case the scales hide details that later prove significant.*

processing procedures, to prove continuity of the film from the photographer to the processing laboratory.

## Equipment

Forensic photographers tend to use medium-format or 35mm cameras. These balance the conflicting demands of picture quality, economy, portability, and ease of use. The interchangeable lenses of single lens reflex (SLR) cameras make them especially adaptable, and their viewfinders show the subject exactly as film records it. For close-up pictures of evidence, a tripod-mounted camera provides the necessary quality and stability.

Digital cameras have many advantages for forensic photography: their pictures need no chemical processing, and can be instantly transferred to a computer database. Also, photographers can use the camera's display to verify immediately that the image was captured. However, the current ease of altering digital images prevents them from being used as

evidence, though a digital "watermark" system will eventually change this.

Investigators may also use video cameras to document crime scenes quickly and cheaply: panning around a room gives a jury a more realistic sense of place than showing them four still pictures taken from the corners. Crime-scene videos can also be used as briefing tools for police officers who have not visited the scene.

## Technique

General crime-scene picture-taking employs techniques familiar to any amateur photographer, but close-ups of evidence need more exact requirements. These pictures form a factual record in which reproduction of size, shape, and color balance must be accurate. In these cases, pictures are normally taken with the camera square to the subject, with two scales at right angles to each other.

## Special lighting

Conventional flash and floodlights are adequate for general crime-scene photography, but close-up evidence may

need careful lighting. For example, oblique-angled light brings out detail in textured surfaces, such as shoeprints in mud.

Forensic light sources have revolutionized the photography of special evidence. Equipped with colored filters and flexible light-guides, these lamps direct a brilliant, narrow beam at the subject. Changing the filter allows the detection of different evidence: ultraviolet makes stains and some fingerprints glow, violet makes gunshot residues and blood more visible, while blue and green light are used with enhanced fingerprints, and to show up fibers, urine, and semen.

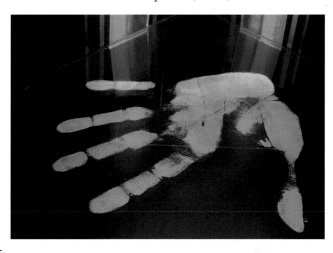

**ULTRAVIOLET ILLUMINATION ▲**
*Few fingerprints are naturally fluorescent in an ultraviolet beam, though contamination with oil or grease can make prints glow. More often, UV is used as a photographic light source after prints have been treated with DFO or superglue (see p. 19).*

## SYSTEMATIC PHOTOGRAPHY

Crime-scene photography, complete with thorough documentation, has to cover systematically both the general scene and specific details. Here, for example, the photographer started with a long shot of the crime scene (far right), and only later closed in on the spent cartridge cases (right). Important evidence gets photographed from several different aspects: pictures taken from ground level, or high above, show up clues that are not visible in images taken from normal eye level. Lighting helps capture extra detail, too: even in daylight, a flash puts extra light into shadows, so that parts of the crime scene are not hidden in shade.

**DOCUMENTING A SHOOTING SCENE**
*After a shooting near Wiesbaden, Germany, photography was a priority because the scene of the crime was a street, which could not be kept closed.*

# Searching for evidence

The quality and thoroughness of the search for evidence can make or break a criminal investigation, because there are usually no second chances. Once the search has been completed and the crime scene is released from its secure cordon, valuable clues may be destroyed, removed, or rendered worthless as evidence in court.

**MARKING OUT KEY EVIDENCE ▲**
*By placing numbered cards where they find evidence, investigators can record many items' locations in a single photograph. Documentation links the numbers to an evidence inventory and to a plan of the scene.*

## FINGERTIP SEARCH:

① *Coveralls prevent a searcher's clothing from contaminating the scene. After use, they are often examined for any residual evidence.*

② *Surgical gloves ensure that genetic material found on evidence does not come from the fingers of the searcher.*

③ *Masks are worn here to protect evidence, but searchers routinely use them for their own safety when handling biological material.*

④ *A shoulder-to-shoulder fingertip search is usually practical only for small crime scenes. In more extensive searches, spacing is often wider and searchers advance on foot.*

⑤ *Notes written at the crime scene while the search is in progress are much more valuable as evidence than information recalled from memory at a later date.*

⑥ *Photographic and video recording of the crime scene is routine.*

**SHOULDER-TO-SHOULDER**
*Police search for evidence in Yorkshire, England, where a woman's body was found in a suitcase in 2001.*

No crime scene can be secured indefinitely in order to safeguard the evidence it contains. So when an investigation begins, one of the very first tasks is to search for relevant evidence as thoroughly as possible, so that the crime scene can be released. But how do investigators know what is relevant?

### Beyond the obvious

The answer is not always clear-cut. For example, when a crime has taken place outdoors, samples of soil and dirt can help to place suspects at the scene, if matching samples are later found on their clothes or shoes. In a rural location, soil may even contain plant material, such as pollen or seeds, that can potentially pinpoint a suspect's presence in time as well as space.

If samples of dirt can provide clues, then almost anything else at the scene may potentially implicate a suspect. Collecting every single item that might possibly be related to a crime would create administrative chaos, and hide vital clues in an avalanche of irrelevant data. But equally, if investigators are too selective, they overlook evidence that could lead to the solution of the crime. Training and experience allow searchers to strike a balance between collecting too much and too little.

By using photography, video, and paper records to document clues on-site, they can control the number of objects that must be removed from the scene.

## Search methodology

Crimes and crime scenes are so diverse that every search demands an individual approach. A murder that occurred indoors, for example, may require a very localized search, but an explosion or major accident can scatter evidence over a very wide area. Nevertheless, there are general rules that guide all crime scene managers when planning a search.

The nature of the crime scene often dictates the search order. Outdoor areas are searched first, because weather can damage or destroy evidence. Public areas are a higher priority, because they are more difficult to secure than private spaces. If the removal of a body cannot take place until the area around it is searched, then that search is the priority. Searches of a suspect's entry and exit routes are more likely to produce results than searches of peripheral areas.

## Search patterns

In a similar way, search patterns are tailored to the crime scene. Large open areas, such as parks and fields, lend

themselves to a line search, in which investigators stand in a straight line and move forward together. A grid search covers the same area twice, with the searchers crossing first in one direction, and then again at right angles to their original route. However, these methods are usually impractical indoors, where a room-by-room search is more appropriate.

## Recording evidence

When artifacts or traces are found that may be linked to the crime, their location and position are crucial. Before they are moved they are photographed, and their position logged relative to fixed points of reference. This helps to reconstruct the crime scene as a sketch, a solid model, or—increasingly—a virtual model on a computer.

## Preventing contamination

Finally, investigators methodically pack and record evidence for storage and later analysis. This handling and labeling, and the painstaking isolation of evidence, has taken on a new importance with the

evolution of analytical techniques. The most advanced DNA analysis methods can match a subject's identity from a microscopically small biological sample recovered from the scene. But the match is useless if the sample is contaminated by the DNA of the searcher who found it.

**SPECIAL SEARCHES ▲**
*Poor underwater visibility makes evidence hard to find in ponds, lakes, and rivers. Searches for buried evidence on dry land may require metal detectors, magnetometry, and ground-penetrating radar, as well as sniffer dogs, who also help to find drugs.*

## REMOVING EVIDENCE

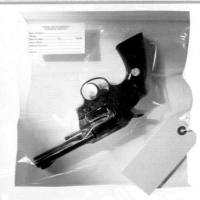

There are two main reasons for packing and recording evidence methodically. Not only do the containers protect the contents from contamination and natural decay, but they also help prove that evidence has not been deliberately removed, added to, or altered. Evidence containers are sealed in such a way that tampering is obvious. Coupled with careful record-keeping, this helps establish the "chain of custody"—a list of everybody who handled the item between crime scene and courtroom.

# Recovering fingerprints

Few things define our identities as precisely as a fingerprint. But the power of fingerprints as evidence lies not just in their uniqueness, but in their simplicity and familiarity. Collecting and analyzing them at a crime scene does not require costly, complex technology, and juries understand and trust them without explanations from expert witnesses.

**◄ VISIBLE PRINTS**
*If hands were dirty or bloodstained, or surfaces they touched were dusty, visible fingerprints may have been left at a crime scene. These prints are first photographed, and are then often enhanced to improve contrast and visibility.*

The swirling patterns on our fingertips are unique—even identical twins, with identical DNA, can be distinguished from one another by looking at the ridges on their fingers. It is these ridges, and the secretions from the sweat glands that line them, that leave telltale traces on everything we touch.

At a crime scene, finger marks on shiny surfaces may be obvious, but many more may be too indistinct to be seen with the naked eye. Using a variety of treatments, such as powders, chemicals, and lighting techniques, these latent fingerprints can be revealed and enhanced. Although fingerprints are the most common marks found at crime scenes, palm prints, bare footprints, and even ear prints can also be recovered using the same methods. However, these additional prints are of limited use, since police only have database records of fingerprints.

## Prints on nonporous surfaces

The best-known technique—and still the most widely used—is dusting. Examiners use soft brushes to apply a powder, such as finely ground aluminum, to nonporous surfaces that a suspect might have touched. The powder sticks to the moist, greasy lines left by the sweaty skin ridges. Light, dark, and colored powders can be used to make the prints stand out on different colored backgrounds. Once powdered, the mark can be "lifted" from the surface using low-tack adhesive tape, and mounted on an acetate sheet to be preserved as evidence.

## Porous surfaces

If marks are on porous surfaces, such as paper or cardboard, the sweat residue is absorbed by the material. Dusting with most powders does not work, though magnetic powders can achieve results. For most porous surfaces, examiners tend to use chemical reagents, such as ninhydrin and DFO (1,8-Diazafluoren-9-one), that react with the chemicals present in sweat. Porous objects are dipped in, or sprayed with, the solutions, then warmed in an oven. Ninhydrin-treated prints appear purple, and DFO makes fingerprints glow when they are lit by laser or blue-green light.

**DUSTING FOR PRINTS**
*It is impractical to dust every surface at a crime scene, so examiners are guided by information from the victim or the investigating police officer. The examination is restricted to specific areas or objects that may have been touched, and particularly to entry and exit routes. If a window has been broken, investigators also search for and dust missing pieces.*

**◄ MAGNETIC POWDERS**
*Magnetic "wands" can be used on certain porous surfaces to avoid the need for chemical treatment. They have no bristles, and apply a dust containing iron filings that adheres to the greasy sweat deposits.*

## SPECIAL TREATMENTS

In the laboratory, technicians can develop fingerprints with methods that are tricky to use at the crime scene, or that require toxic reagents. The most commonly used technique is superglue (cyanoacrylate) fuming. In moist conditions, the vapor from superglue bonds with the sweat residue of latent prints and makes them visible, even on difficult surfaces such as flexible plastics. Developed marks can then be dyed, and powders and special lighting can improve contrast.

Vacuum metal deposition (VMD) is the most sensitive of all lab techniques. Objects bearing latent prints are enclosed in a pressure vessel, the air is pumped out, and the chamber filled with metal vapor: first gold, then zinc. The metals condense on ridge patterns, making prints visible, though further treatment with superglue is sometimes necessary. VMD is time-consuming and expensive, but can reveal old prints and those exposed to water.

There are several other widely used chemical treatments. Physical developer (PD), a solution of silver and iron compounds, can reveal prints on porous surfaces that have been soaked in water. Fuming with iodine vapor gives prints a brown color that fades rapidly, so prompt photography is needed to record the image. (Iodine fuming also enhances prints on nonporous surfaces.)

Some enhancement techniques are potentially destructive, and some will not work if preceded by another. Examiners at the crime scene and laboratory technicians use their knowledge and experience in deciding which methods to use. As a precaution, they photograph the developed marks at each stage of the process, before applying further treatments that could obliterate them.

### Lighting and photography

Anyone who opens a window to clean it or turns a glass to catch the light will know that doing this can make formerly invisible fingerprints stand out clearly. This is the most basic lighting technique used by forensic photographers to record fingerprint evidence. They train a powerful white light on the mark, and then move the camera or the light until the print appears. Faint prints on very shiny surfaces sometimes stand out with coaxial illumination. This uses a diagonal

semi-transparent mirror in front of the camera lens to reflect a shaft of light at the print, which appears as a dark pattern against a white background.

Most of the other photographic techniques for enhancing fingerprints use special illumination rather than white light. Shining brilliantly colored light at a print often makes it stand out, especially if it has been treated with ninhydrin or DFO. Ultraviolet radiation is used in combination with fluorescent dusting powders, and after superglue fuming (see right-hand box). Argon-ion (blue-green) laser light can exceptionally reveal fingerprints that do not respond to other treatments. The FBI used this technique in 1984 to reveal prints left on a postcard sent by war criminal Valerian Trifa to the head of the Nazi SS 42 years earlier.

**◄ LIGHTING TECHNIQUES**
*Here, monochromatic light is directed at a print using a fiber-optic light guide. Chemical treatments can make prints glow under certain light sources, and sometimes prints can fluoresce without treatment—if the fingers are contaminated with oils.*

### Elimination and matching

Examination of crime scenes does not just produce the perpetrator's marks. Prints of innocent people, such as the owners of a burgled home, are obviously far more numerous. To eliminate these people from the investigation, their fingerprints are recorded by inking and pressing on cards.

The process of matching prints with those of suspects, and of known criminals, is explained on pages 46–47.

**LIFTING PRINTS ►**
*Low-tack tape peels up easily but is sticky enough to make a permanent record of fingerprints. Lifting saves photographing the print at the crime scene.*

# Shoeprints and tire tracks

I n fiction, trails of footprints lead the detectives straight to a criminal's hiding place. In reality, however, shoes and tires rarely create such an obvious trail. More often, they can help prove that an individual, or their vehicle, visited a crime scene. And shoeprints may also indicate a criminal's height and gait.

**TWO TYPES OF PRINTS**
*"Footwear marks" are tracks of dust or dirt that a shoe leaves on a hard surface (above). Prints in soft ground (left), called "depressed marks," often provide greater detail of the shoe's sole and instep.*

How do crime-scene examiners deal with shoe marks? Well, it depends on the surface on which the marks are printed, and whether any material has transferred from the shoe to the surface. The classic "footprint" in soft ground leaves a clearly indented pattern of the sole that can be photographed and cast. Forensic photographers use oblique lighting to emphasize the indentation, with a camera held perpendicular to the ground. A measuring scale next to the print means that full-size photographs can be compared to the shoes of a suspect.

Filling a print with plaster or dental stone often records more detail than a photograph can capture. Examiners may first spray the print with fixatives, which stabilize fragile materials such as sand, or with a release agent, which helps the cast lift freely from the print. Footprints in snow are coated with a wax spray, and then filled with chilled casting material.

### Prints without impressions

Visible prints on solid floors, hard ground, and carpets can be photographed just like impressed prints. Oblique lighting provides no benefit, but high-intensity forensic light sources can sometimes enhance detail.

Wet shoes leave clear trails of prints that are easily photographed. Dry prints in dust are harder to find. They can be lifted from a surface using two different methods. The first is a gelatin lifter, a thick layer of sticky gel on a fabric backing that lifts shoeprints in a way similar to fingerprint-lifting tape. The second is an electrostatic lifter, a foil sheet coated in black plastic that connects to a device generating a high static-electric charge. It lifts dust from the print on to the black surface, where it is more clearly visible.

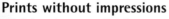

**◀ MUDDY BOOTS**
*Traces of materials caught in a shoe's tread, and left behind in a shoeprint, can suggest where the wearer has been before reaching the crime scene.*

**COMPARING SOLES ▶**
*Simple measurement (top right) can quickly link a cast or photograph of a footprint with a shoe taken from a suspect. Copying prints on to an acetate overlay (bottom right) allows a direct comparison of every detail.*

When shoeprints are not so obvious, examiners may use the same treatments that bring out fingerprints, such as dusting and superglue fuming. On porous surfaces, ninhydrin and DFO (see p. 18) may be used to enhance bloody shoeprints.

## Using shoeprint evidence

A recovered print can be compared side-by-side to a suspect's shoe. If the soles have matching patterns and wear marks, it strongly suggests that the shoe's owner was present at the crime scene.

Footprints can also demonstrate a link between otherwise unconnected crimes, and provide a new direction in a suspect hunt. Matching a print using shoe databases can identify the footwear's make and style. Also, shoe size is roughly proportional to stature, and a trail of prints can suggest a suspect's gait, such as a limp.

## Tire tracks

Investigators treat tire tracks in much the same way as footprints, using the same techniques to photograph, cast, and lift them. However, the length of tire tracks can cause practical problems. Recording the track of a large truck may require several photographs or casts.

Like shoes, tires have identifying tread patterns. Similar treads can be distinguished by tread-wear gauges and subtle variations that manufacturers introduce to the tread to reduce noise or improve grip. By comparing a tire track with a standard reference, such as Tread Design Guide,

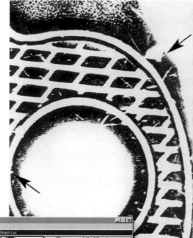

**WEAR MARKS ▶**
*Manufacturing defects may be the same on many shoes, so they are not enough on their own to match a print found at the crime scene (near right) to the sole of a suspect's shoe (far right). But distinctive cuts (arrowed) are unique to a single sole.*

**◀ SHOE DATABASE**
*A footprint index, such as SICAR, allows prints to be manually compared with those found at other scenes. Footwear manufacturers supply patterns of new sole styles for inclusion in the database.*

investigators can identify most tire types. As with shoes (above), tread damage produces unique marks that can tie a track to a particular tire.

Although the distance between tire tracks or the radius of a tight turn do not provide conclusive information, they may be enough to eliminate a vehicle from an investigation, or to narrow a search.

**TIRE CAST ▼**
*If an initial comparison between a cast from a trail roughly matches a tire from a suspect vehicle, investigators will examine the tire's whole circumference for points of similarity.*

## CASE STUDY

Police in the town of Torquay, southwest England, were convinced of the value of a shoeprint database when they gave the Treadmark system a trial run in 2001. In one case, a customer slipped into the stock room of a Torquay sports store, stole a Nike jacket, and escaped through a second-floor window. The police had little to go on until three weeks later, when store staff opened a shoe box to find a pair of old shoes inside. The criminal who had stolen the jacket had also swapped his shoes for a new pair. Detectives scanned in the soles of the old shoes, and the Treadmark system matched them to the shoes of a man who had been previously arrested for an unconnected crime. Confronted with the evidence, he pleaded guilty to both offenses.

## CASE STUDY

# Incriminating marks

No witnesses. No fingerprints. No footprints. No DNA. A skilled, smart, and methodical criminal knows just what investigators are looking for, and works hard to stop them from finding it. However, even the tools used and the gloves worn can leave subtle marks behind. Investigating these marks can help police link a suspect with a crime scene.

Tools feature in many different crimes. They can be used to force open a door or window, break a padlock, or even to cut up a corpse. By cutting, striking, and scraping, tools can leave marks on every surface they touch. These marks, if clear enough, have identifying features that can be matched to the tools that made them.

## Types of tool marks

There are two basic kinds of tool marks—multiple and single contact marks. Multiple contact marks occur when a surface is repeatedly sawed. They have limited value as evidence, and may only demonstrate what class of tool was used, such as a saw or knife, and its general size and shape. Single contact marks occur when a surface is struck once. They can be either impressions, such as when a hammer dents a metallic surface, or striations, such as when a screwdriver scrapes against a window frame to prize it open. Striation marks are parallel indentations left on a surface, as shown in the above right-hand image. Their unique pattern can provide proof that a particular tool produced a mark. However, the tool's owner may not have committed the crime, since tools may be stolen, borrowed, or simply found at the crime scene.

## Making their mark

Tool marks may show tiny surface imperfections of a tool's working edge. These imperfections are created both during manufacturing and through general wear and tear while the tool is in use. Manufacturing defects may appear on every tool of the same batch, so although they can help to trace a tool's source, they cannot necessarily provide investigators with a positive match.

By contrast, wear on a tool can make it unique—impressions in soft materials faithfully reproduce some of the tiniest chips, dents, and scratches. Though this is

**BREAKING THE CHAIN ▶**
*Here, a chain link has been cut using bolt cutters. By examining the cut at a microscopic level, marks from the tool can be seen.*

**BOLT CUTTER MATCH ▲**
*Microscopic ridges, known as striae, are left on a cut chain link at the scene (A). The suspect's bolt cutters, pressed into soft lead, match these marks exactly (B).*

one of the principal advantages of tool marks, it can also be a limitation. If a tool is in regular use, its value as evidence falls with each day that passes after the crime is committed. Eventually, new marks obliterate old ones, so many crime bureaus delete tool-mark evidence from their databases after six months.

If imperfections in a tool are very pronounced, they can leave clear traces even on multiple contact marks. For example, a saw with a broken tooth will leave a characteristic gap when it cuts.

## Finding and recording tool marks

By their very nature, tool marks occur where force has been used. Investigators look for them at a crime scene's point of entry—a forced window or door, or a cut padlock on a perimeter fence. They also find them wherever damage has been done or a tool was obviously necessary—such as on the limbs of a dismembered corpse, or in the slash in a vandalized car tire.

The ideal method of collecting tool-mark evidence is to remove the mark itself from the crime scene—for example by removing a forced door, or a portion of it, for later examination. If this is not practical, investigators photograph the mark, lighting it from an oblique angle to highlight the surface detail. They may also cast it using an opaque resin, which retains microscopic detail much better than the plaster or dental stone usually used when casting footprints (see p. 20).

## Examination and comparison

Examiners compare tool-mark evidence with corresponding implements recovered from a suspect. An initial examination and measurement using a low-power stereo microscope (see p. 89) is usually enough to eliminate tools that clearly could not have made the mark. But if there are conspicuous similarities, these can be confirmed by using the tool to duplicate the marks found at the crime scene. For example, examiners might cut a lead or aluminum rod with the bolt cutters they suspect a criminal used to open a padlock. (By cutting a soft metal, they reduce the risk of marking the tool itself, but since damage is always possible, this is the last test examiners carry out.) The more points of similarity there are on the two marks, the more compelling the evidence that the same tool made both.

Investigators rarely study tool marks in isolation. Instead, they analyze the marks in conjunction with other trace evidence from the scene that may have transferred to the tool. This helps to interpret the marks and often results in a more convincing case. For example, when bolt cutters shear through a chain, only a small portion of the blade actually cuts the metal. Using trial and error it would be difficult to find the correct portion of the blade to match with marks on the chain. However, chemical spot tests can reveal traces of the chain's metal, and pinpoint a region of the blade for comparison. Other traces left on tools can help to prove guilt. Pliers used to cut telephone cable, for instance, may retain traces of the plastic insulation.

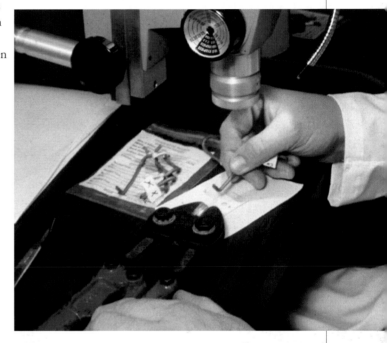

**LAB ANALYSIS ▲**
*Bolt cutters recovered from a suspect are analyzed in the lab. As well as looking for striation marks, technicians examine the tool for any trace evidence.*

## FABRIC PRINTS

Marks from fabrics can be collected and compared in ways similar to fingerprints and footprints—by dusting, tape lifts, and electrostatic lifts (see p. 20). Marks are more distinctive if the material is coarse, and are commonly made from gloves. The prints of brand-new gloves at a crime scene provide few clues. However, like tools, gloves accumulate unique features with use. In this image, a glove is compared to a mirror-image of a print. The rips and dried paint on the glove's fingers help match it to the distinctive print. Fabric prints also occur in hit-and-run road accidents. The textured weave of a victim's clothing can leave a patterned imprint on the vehicle's hood.

*Glove prints left on a window pane are recovered using fingerprint powder.*

*The paint on this finger leaves a distinct pattern break in the glove's print.*

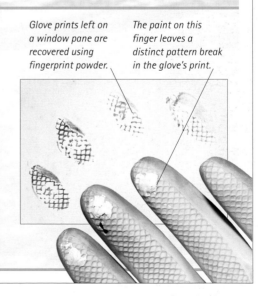

# OJ Simpson on trial

**ACQUITTED**

W hen Nicole Brown Simpson was found dead at her Los Angeles home, suspicion fell on former husband OJ Simpson. But at his hugely publicized trial, the faded sports celebrity was not the only one accused. Police procedures and evidence handling were also on trial.

**POLICE MUGSHOT ▲**
*OJ Simpson's arrest at age 46 for his ex-wife's murder wasn't his first brush with the law. He was convicted of beating her six years earlier, and sentenced to community work and probation.*

**IT'S IN THE BAG ▼**
*The defense team claimed investigators didn't change their gloves between handling Simpson's blood sample and bagging crime-scene evidence. So Simpson's DNA may have contaminated this glove.*

It was Nicole's dog who raised the alarm on the night of June 12, 1994. Neighbors had heard howling from 10:15 PM onward, and eventually found the white Akita covered in blood. It led them to the gate of 875 South Bundy Drive, in the desirable LA suburb of Brentwood. Through the gate, they saw a row of bloody footprints. Beyond, highlighted by the porch light, Nicole's body lay slumped in a spreading pool of blood.

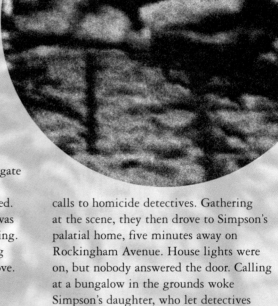

## Police on the scene

An LAPD squad car arrived just after midnight, and patrolmen opened the gate to take a closer look. Nicole had been ferociously attacked, almost decapitated. Nearby, her friend Ronald Goldman was also found dead from a frenzied stabbing. Scattered around were items including a hat and a bloodstained left-hand glove. Inside the house they found Nicole's sons, age six and nine, fast asleep.

The uniformed officers telephoned their report and triggered wake-up calls to homicide detectives. Gathering at the scene, they then drove to Simpson's palatial home, five minutes away on Rockingham Avenue. House lights were on, but nobody answered the door. Calling at a bungalow in the grounds woke Simpson's daughter, who let detectives into the house. A guest, Kato Kaelin, had been sleeping in another bungalow. He told detectives that Simpson had taken a night flight to Chicago. Kaelin had helped to load luggage into an airport limo just before 11 PM. While buzzing the intercom, detectives noticed blood on Simpson's Ford Bronco parked outside. They then saw a trail of drips leading from the car to the mansion's front door. Detective Mark Fuhrman also found another bloodstained glove that matched the one found near Nicole's body.

**"THEY'RE TOO TIGHT" ▶**
*Simpson had trouble wearing a key piece of evidence. The prosecution claimed the gloves had shrunk, but the jury believed the defense slogan "if it doesn't fit, you must acquit."*

Dawn broke as police called Simpson at his Chicago hotel. He sounded distraught but strangely incurious about his ex-wife's death. He agreed to catch the next flight back, and by lunchtime detectives were interviewing him. As they talked, they noticed a bandage on his hand. He'd cut it some time before, he told them, and a broken glass in his Chicago hotel room had reopened the wound.

The detectives photographed his hand, and fingerprinted him. The nurse then took his blood for DNA tests, squirted the sample into a vial containing a preservative, EDTA, and handed it to the detectives. Simpson was then free to go.

Meanwhile, the investigation had been continuing at the two crime scenes. To try to preempt defense challenges, the search of Simpson's house was videotaped. By mid-afternoon, the detectives who had interviewed Simpson joined the rest of the investigating team at Rockingham Avenue. At 5:20 PM they handed over the vial of blood to be logged and packed away with the other crime-scene evidence.

## Mass media attention

In the four days that followed, the case became a media circus: Simpson's arrest was famously preceded by a slow-motion police car chase around the LA freeway system. It was clear that the trial was going to attract immense news interest.

When it began seven months later, the State seemed to have a compelling case against Simpson. He had no alibi, and hair and fiber evidence linked him to the hat found at the murder scene. DNA analysis showed that blood on a sock found in Simpson's bedroom was Nicole's, and that the car and the right-hand glove were stained with blood from Simpson and both victims. As the Deputy District Attorney put it, "That trail of blood from Bundy through his own Ford Bronco and into his house on Rockingham

**NOT GUILTY!** ▶
*Lawyer F. Lee Bailey, Simpson, and attorney Johnnie Cochran (l-r) celebrate the verdict. But a civil court found him guilty, and awarded $33 million in damages,*

is devastating proof of his guilt."

However, Simpson had hired a crack legal team. From the start, they painted a picture of a white racist detective trying to frame an innocent, if bullying, black defendant. Detective Mark Fuhrman's evidence was fatally compromised when the jury heard a tape recording in which he used racial slurs 41 times. In addition, the defense alleged that the detectives had both the means and opportunity to frame Simpson.

About a quarter-teaspoonful of his blood sample had vanished before being logged as evidence. The defense suggested that detectives had ample time to smear it around the crime scene. Worse, some of the crime-scene samples contained traces of EDTA. The glove could have been planted—and didn't even fit Simpson. Finally, there was the video of the search. Far from preempting defense objections, it showed certain police procedures that reinforced them (see box).

However, the prosecution could explain many apparent shortcomings in their case: small traces of EDTA, for example, occur naturally in blood. But the jury, exhausted by a nine-month trial in the news spotlight, and baffled by much of the expert testimony, was not convinced. They took just six hours to clear Simpson of the murder.

Certain police procedures undermined the prosecution case. Uniformed officers used Nicole's telephone to report the homicide, possibly destroying fingerprint evidence. When detectives arrived, one covered Nicole's corpse with a blanket, to hide it from news cameras, thus potentially compromising fiber evidence. The above image of an investigator pointing to the bloodstained leather glove shows that he hasn't taken basic precautions of wearing sterile coveralls and gloves. The police video captured more blunders, showing a junior investigator dropping blood swabs and wiping tweezers with soiled hands. Detectives also missed bloodstains on Nicole's gate, noticed by uniformed officers. The gate wasn't swabbed until nearly three weeks later.

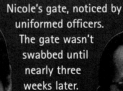

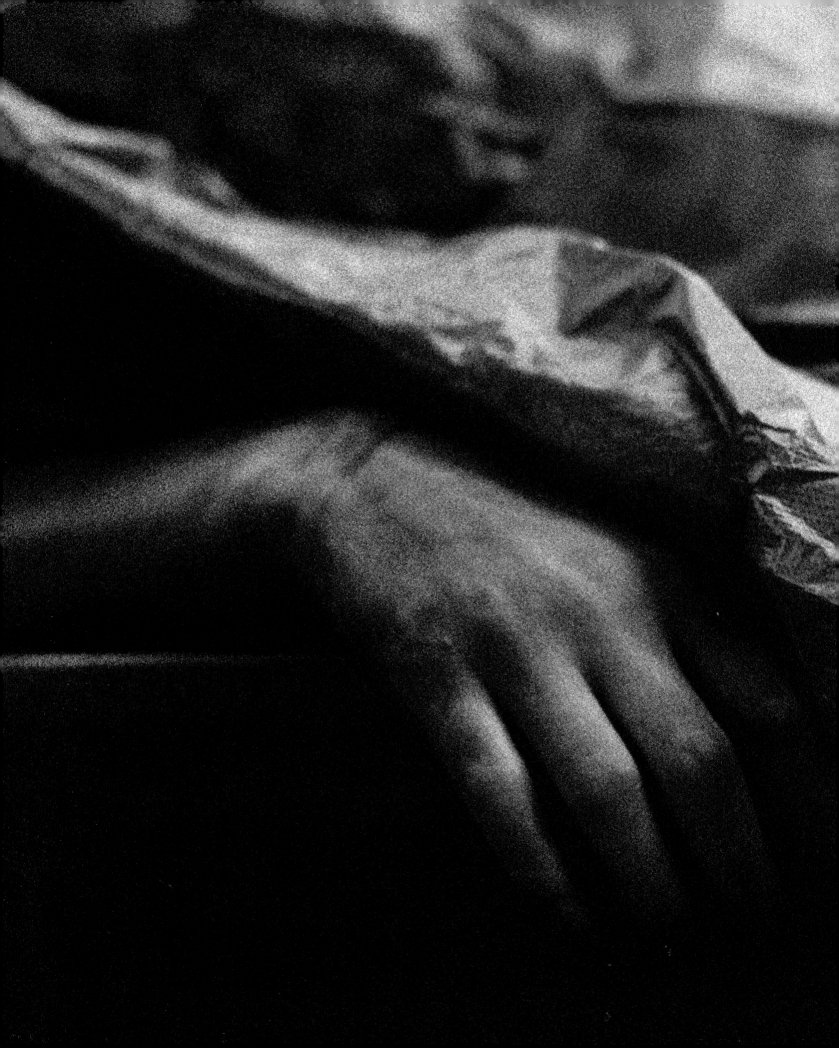

# THE VICTIM

Crimes of all types blight the lives of their victims, leaving behind misery, destruction, and loss. For the victims of homicide, though, the loss is absolute. Because of this, and because society has a particular horror of these crimes of extreme violence, their investigation is more than usually exhaustive and probing. Uniquely, a homicide victim's body is itself a scene of crime. Its condition, and the marks and traces on it, may provide valuable clues to the identity, methods, and motives of the killer.

# Investigators of death

W hether it is a warm corpse in a spreading pool of blood or a heap of dry bones, the discovery of a human body triggers a special kind of investigation. Its organization, progress, and participants depend on how the death happened—was it natural, accidental, suicide, or homicide? If there is doubt, the death is treated as suspicious.

No matter what its condition, the discovery of a corpse brings a medical examiner to the crime scene. Medical examiners are public officials that investigate all sudden, unexplained, unnatural, or suspicious deaths. They also perform autopsies and assist in criminal cases. These physicians, trained in forensic medicine, advise police on situations where law and medicine meet. Often, they can answer crucial questions at the earliest stages of an investigation, such as, was it a sexual assault, is the assailant right- or left-handed, and has the body been moved after death?

### Checking for life

At the crime scene, though, the main responsibility of the medical examiner is to certify death. Even when a victim is obviously dead, such as where the body is decapitated or decomposed, official certification of death is still required.

For recent deaths of between a few hours and a few days, medical examiners measure the ambient (air) temperature, since this affects the rate at which the body cools—an important clue to the time of death. They also make an initial assessment of the manner of death (see facing page).

### Medical detectives

Forensic pathologists are specialists who combine medical and legal skills. Like clinical pathologists, they are experts in injuries to and diseases of the human body. Unlike their colleagues, forensic pathologists focus on the dead

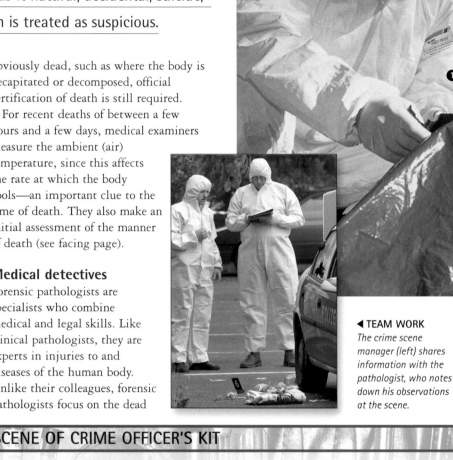

◀ TEAM WORK
The crime scene manager (left) shares information with the pathologist, who notes down his observations at the scene.

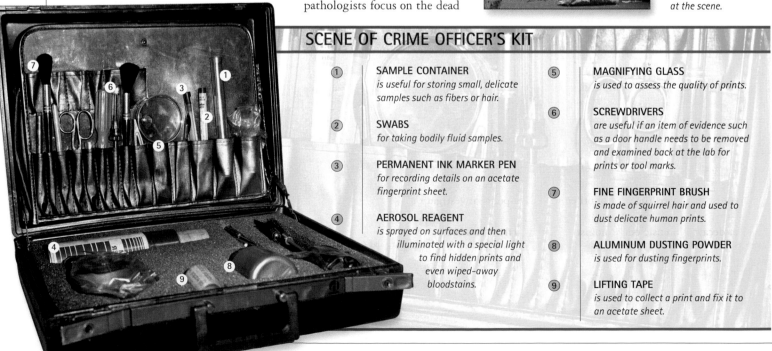

## SCENE OF CRIME OFFICER'S KIT

① **SAMPLE CONTAINER**
is useful for storing small, delicate samples such as fibers or hair.

② **SWABS**
for taking bodily fluid samples.

③ **PERMANENT INK MARKER PEN**
for recording details on an acetate fingerprint sheet.

④ **AEROSOL REAGENT**
is sprayed on surfaces and then illuminated with a special light to find hidden prints and even wiped-away bloodstains.

⑤ **MAGNIFYING GLASS**
is used to assess the quality of prints.

⑥ **SCREWDRIVERS**
are useful if an item of evidence such as a door handle needs to be removed and examined back at the lab for prints or tool marks.

⑦ **FINE FINGERPRINT BRUSH**
is made of squirrel hair and used to dust delicate human prints.

⑧ **ALUMINUM DUSTING POWDER**
is used for dusting fingerprints.

⑨ **LIFTING TAPE**
is used to collect a print and fix it to an acetate sheet.

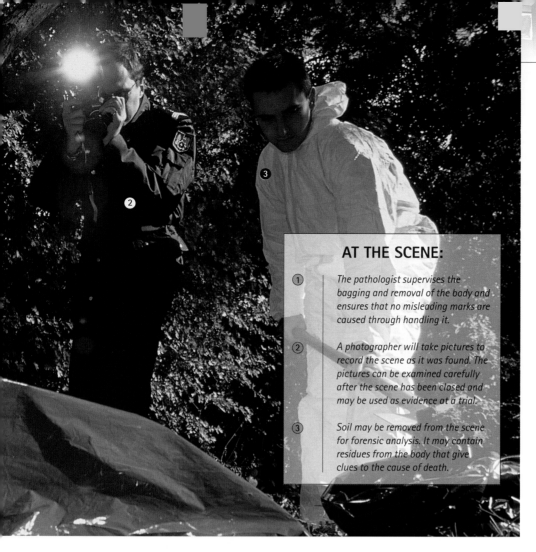

## AT THE SCENE:

① *The pathologist supervises the bagging and removal of the body and ensures that no misleading marks are caused through handling it.*

② *A photographer will take pictures to record the scene as it was found. The pictures can be examined carefully after the scene has been closed and may be used as evidence at a trial.*

③ *Soil may be removed from the scene for forensic analysis. It may contain residues from the body that give clues to the cause of death.*

▲ **AVOIDING CONTAMINATION**
*Protective clothes worn at the crime scene are disposable, but some police forces retain them in order to demonstrate that they took appropriate care to protect the scene from contamination.*

rather than the living—and, in particular, how the cause of death may affect a criminal investigation and trial. If a suspect is caught and tried, the pathologist may be called to give evidence as an expert witness.

The work of the pathologist at the crime scene involves examining the body and its surroundings (see p. 30). Later, an autopsy at the morgue (see p. 34) will give the pathologist the chance to make a more thorough study. At the crime scene, though, the pathologist works alongside the team of investigators, which is supervised by a crime scene manager (also called a scene of crime officer or SOCO).

As the investigation moves forward, the pathologist may need the help of other specialists. If the body is in an advanced state of decay, a forensic odontologist (see p. 50) can often establish identity by examining dental records. A forensic anthropologist may also help with establishing age and gender. And, if the later autopsy suggests that the subject was poisoned, the pathologist might require

the expertise of a forensic toxicologist.

The pathologist's objectives are to discover the cause of death from an analysis of organ failure. They may also be able to give an indication as to what instrument or mechanism would have caused organ failure. With any death that raises questions, including accidental and some natural deaths, a coroner will hold an inquest, which may give a verdict of nonaccidental death, prompting a police investigation.

### The inquest

Coroners' investigations conclude with an inquest (inquiry). After listening to the evidence, the coroner returns a verdict on the manner of death—natural, accidental, suicide, or homicide—and on how, when, and where the death occurred.

## THE MANNER OF DEATH

In discovering the cause of death, the forensic pathologist contributes valuable information about the circumstances surrounding a death. This information will determine the nature of the police investigation and also helps the coroner decide whether the death was natural, accidental, suicide, or homicide.

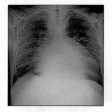

**NATURAL ▶**
*Most people die of natural causes, such as heart failure (shown in this X-ray). However, a death may still be the subject of a coroner's inquest if it happened suddenly or unexpectedly, or if the person was chronically ill and had not seen a doctor within the previous two weeks.*

**◀ ACCIDENTAL**
*Coroner's inquests also examine accidental deaths, but coroners may start criminal investigations if they find that accidents could and should have been avoided—for example, because a safety guard was not in place on a dangerous machine.*

**HOMICIDE ▶**
*Literally "killing a human," homicide usually means either murder, where it was the killer's deliberate intention to cause someone's death, or the lesser crime of manslaughter, where death was not the intention.*

**◀ SUICIDE**
*Helping someone to end their life is against the law. A suicide pact in which one person survives may also lead to manslaughter charges.*

# The body at the scene

Though no two deaths are exactly alike, the examination of every corpse follows a similar routine. Standard procedures ensure that nothing is left to chance; that treatment of the body complies with the law; that no evidence is lost or overlooked; and that the dead receive the respect and dignity to which they are entitled.

If there is even the slightest sign of life, the primary concern of those first on the scene is resuscitation. Clearly, the importance of this far outweighs the risk that it will destroy evidence that might be useful if the attempt fails.

## Checking for vital signs

If resuscitation fails, or if death is very recent, the medical examiner's first task is to make an exhaustive check for vital signs. These include looking for a pulse; listening for a faint heartbeat by using a stethoscope; holding a mirror to the nose and mouth to see if breath condenses on it; and checking whether blood is moving in the veins of the eyes. The medical examiner certifies death only if all these tests are negative or obviously unnecessary.

## Preserving evidence

The work of the forensic pathologist may involve moving the body. Since this can disturb evidence, the crime scene is first photographed, sketched, or videotaped to document the substantially undisturbed situation. Crime scene managers direct general photography of the body and its surroundings, though pathologists may also request specific pictures before the body is removed. The crime-scene manager also controls access to the body, by deciding which route to it is likely to cause the least disturbance.

## Pathologist at the scene

At the crime scene, the pathologist's examination is necessarily superficial—a comprehensive study of the corpse can only

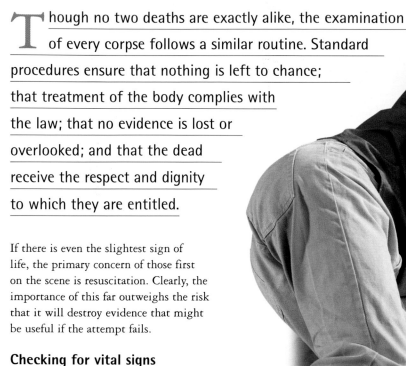

### PROCEDURE:

① The medical examiner checks for vital signs by looking for a pulse, a faint heartbeat, and breathing.

② Photography records evidence by using numbered cards as references.

③ The pathologist examines the body before it is removed from the scene.

④ Blood splatters are analyzed to help understand the preceding events.

**CHECKING TEMPERATURE ▶**
*In the first 24 hours, temperature drop is the most reliable guide to the time of death.*

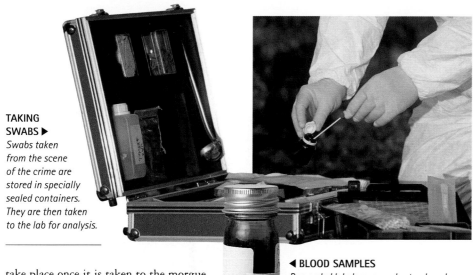

**TAKING SWABS ▶**
*Swabs taken from the scene of the crime are stored in specially sealed containers. They are then taken to the lab for analysis.*

take place once it is taken to the morgue. Pathologists take only a notepad and a pen to the corpse. Everything else they need, such as a fresh swabs, empty containers for samples, or a thermometer to measure body core temperature, is handed to them by the medical examiner or the crime-scene manager.

## Pathological examination

The pathologist's examination of the body focuses on those elements most likely to change once the body is moved to the morgue. Many of the indicators of time of death (see p. 32) fall into this category. For example, if the body has stiffened, bagging and moving it destroys rigor mortis. So the pathologist will check for stiffness by trying gently to bend the limbs and move the jaw, neck, and eyelids.

Clothing may be removed— to look for lividity (discoloration of the skin), for example, or to insert a thermometer in the rectum. The photographer takes pictures of the body. Each item is bagged, labeled, and logged.

If there are fluids or marks on the body or clothes that might be disturbed when they are moved, the pathologist takes swabs from them. Swabbing and sampling is more comprehensive if there is any suspicion that the killer had a sexual motive.

**◀ BLOOD SAMPLES**
*Bar-coded labels on samples track and record their progress after leaving the scene.*

### Examining surroundings

Although investigators will later search the crime scene exhaustively, pathologists also look at the body's immediate surroundings. Their training, and their medical perspective, sometimes enables them to notice details that others miss. They will also want to compare marks on the body, such as abrasions or lacerations, with corresponding marks on surfaces nearby, or with makeshift weapons. If the body is tied up, or has been strangled with a tied rope, the cords are photographed before they are removed. The knots are themselves

## SURROUNDING MARKS

Investigators will exhaustively document marks at the crime scene, but pathologists also record them in their own notes, especially when they correspond with marks on the body. These blood splatters, for example, were thrown from the tip of a weapon as the killer swung it to strike his victim.

**◀ BLOOD SPECKS**
*Marks on surrounding walls are photographed and analyzed by a blood pattern analyst (see p. 84) to explain the nature of the murder.*

**◀ DIRECTION GUIDES**
*Bloodstains may appear to travel in a particular direction. Noting this can help deduce where in the room the murder took place.*

**◀ POINTS OF EXIT**
*Important areas to check are doors and windows, where traces may have been left on exiting or trying to exit the room.*

evidence, as the way they are tied can suggest a link between otherwise unconnected crimes. So they are kept knotted, and the cords are cut to allow removal of the body.

This is done with care to ensure that the body arrives at the morgue in an unchanged condition. The crime scene manager covers the head, feet, and hands with individual bags, loosely fixed with tape, and then the whole body is bagged for removal. The pathologist oversees even this last detail, since careless handling can cause misleading marks on flesh.

**◀ BODY BAG**
*Police take the bagged body to the morgue for further examination.*

# Time since death

Estimating how long someone has been dead is an inexact science. However, even a rough idea of when death occurred is vital if it is known that a suspect was at or near the crime scene at a certain time.

The temperature and stiffness of the body provide the first clues.

A more precise assessment of time since death is made by careful observations at the crime scene combined with laboratory tests.

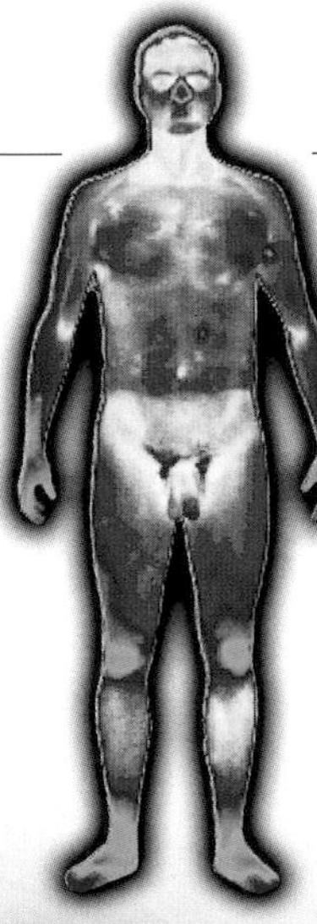

## ◢ BODY TEMPERATURE

A simple way of estimating time since death is to measure the temperature of the body's core (not the extremities, which are cooler, as this thermal image shows). Core temperature falls roughly 1.5°F (0.8°C) each hour, though clothing, ambient temperature, humidity, air movement, and the size of the body may speed up or slow down the cooling process.

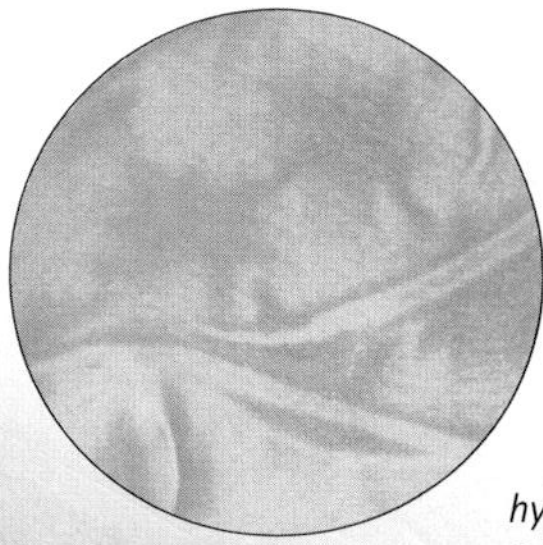

## ◢ BLOOD POOLING

When blood stops flowing, it settles to the lowest parts of the body, turning the skin pink-red. This process, which pathologists call lividity or hypostasis, is complete within 6 hours (it does not affect the very dark-skinned). Slight pressure reduces it.

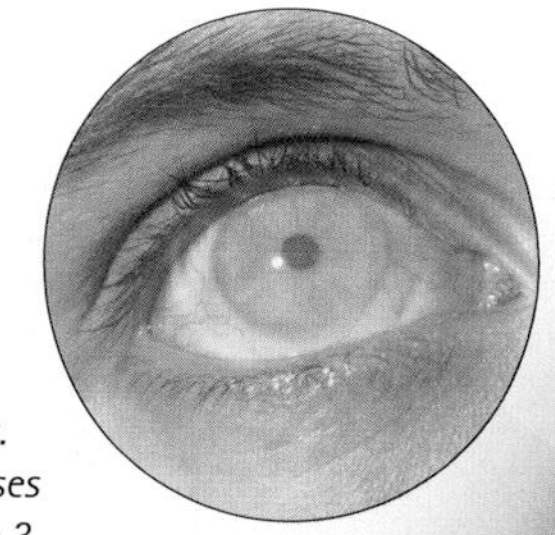

## GUT CONTENTS ▶

Food in the guts of a homicide victim provides important clues to the time of death, especially if the time of the victim's last meal is known. But it cannot fix the time precisely. Heavy foods such as meat stay in the stomach for longer than lighter meals, and speed of digestion is affected by factors such as illness, fear, alcohol, and drugs.

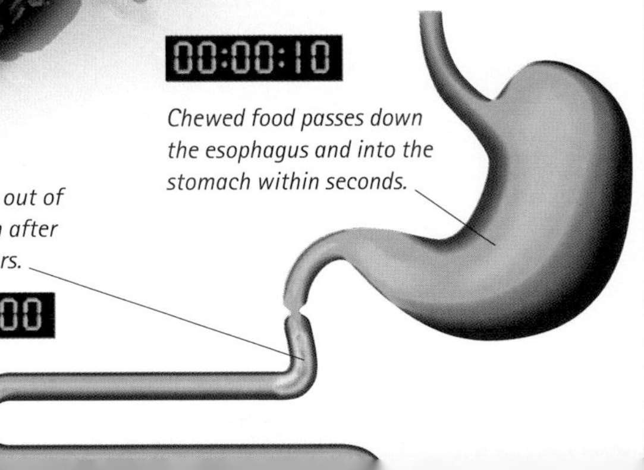

**00:00:10**

Chewed food passes down the esophagus and into the stomach within seconds.

**03:00:00**

Food passes out of the stomach after about 3 hours.

## EXAMINING THE EYES ▶

Within minutes of death, a thin film forms over the eyes, and the eyeballs become soft as the pressure of the fluid inside them falls. If the eyes are open, the lenses may turn cloudy in less than 3 hours. An opthalmoscope reveals a subtler change— red cells in the veins of the retina (the light-sensitive area at the back of the eye) continue moving for several hours.

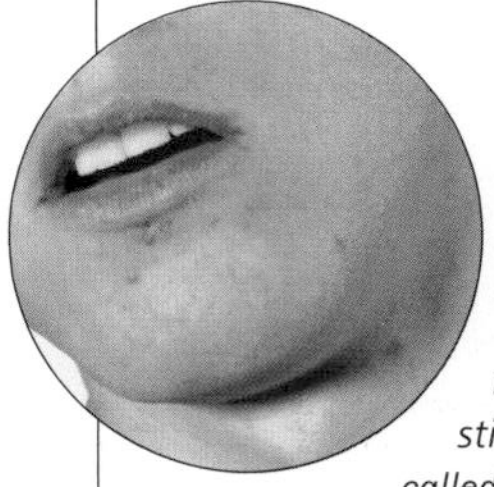

## ◢ STIFFENING

Between 30 minutes and 3 hours after death, the muscles begin to stiffen, in a process called rigor mortis. This is first noticeable in the eyelids and jaw, and rigor mortis spreads to the whole body in 6–12 hours. It stays for another 6–12 hours, then disappears over the following 6–12 hours. Many factors affect stiffness. It may not develop at all at low temperatures, and muscles that were very active before death stiffen more quickly than others.

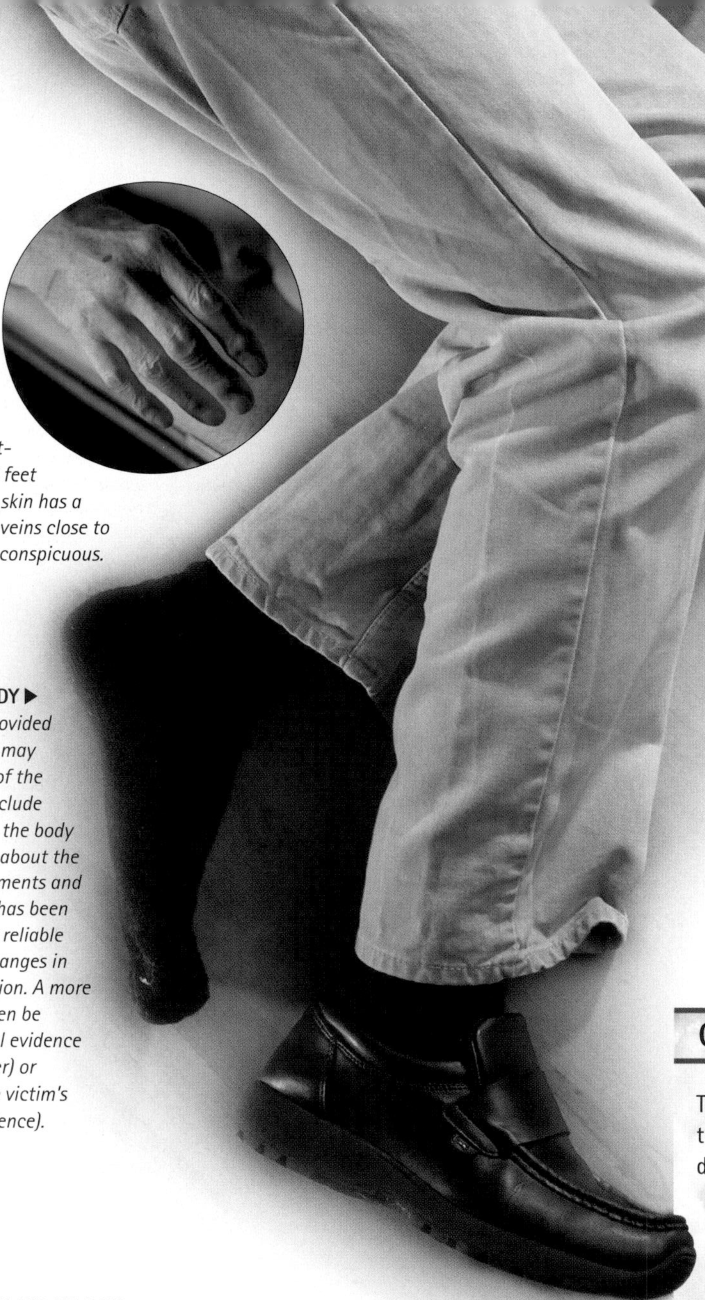

**09:00:00**

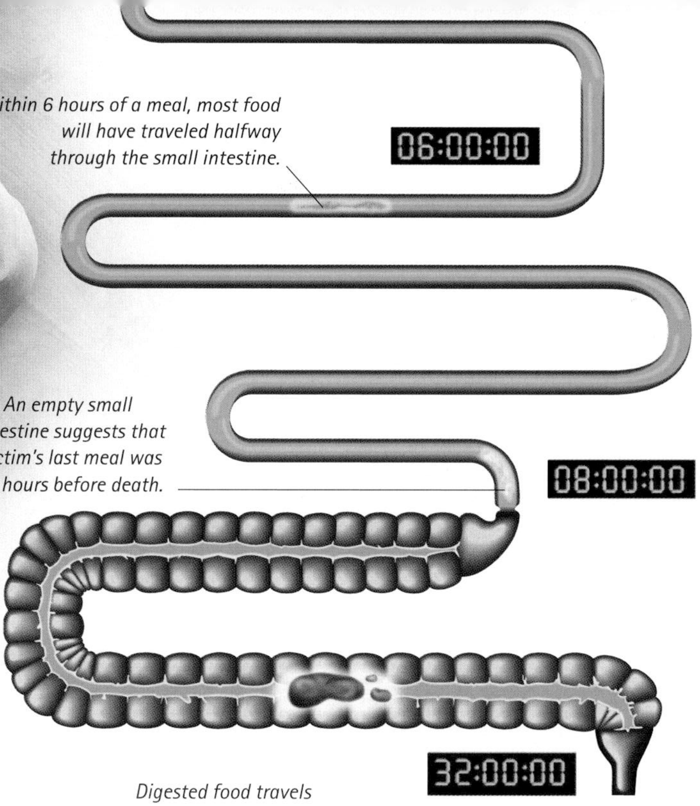

*Within 6 hours of a meal, most food will have traveled halfway through the small intestine.*

**08:00:00**

*An empty small intestine suggests that the victim's last meal was at least 8 hours before death.*

**32:00:00**

*Digested food travels more slowly through the large intestine.*

*In all, the process of digestion may take more than a day.*

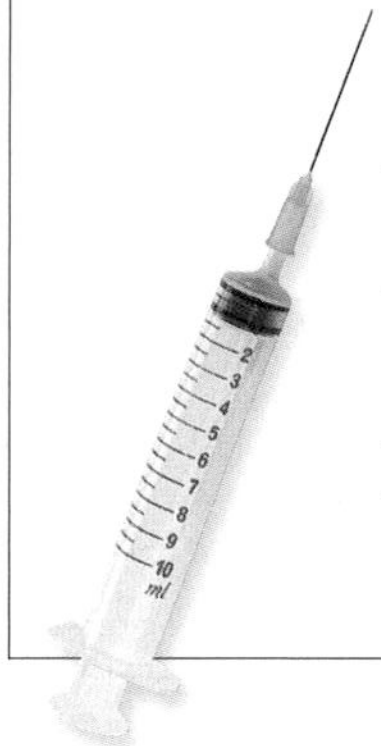

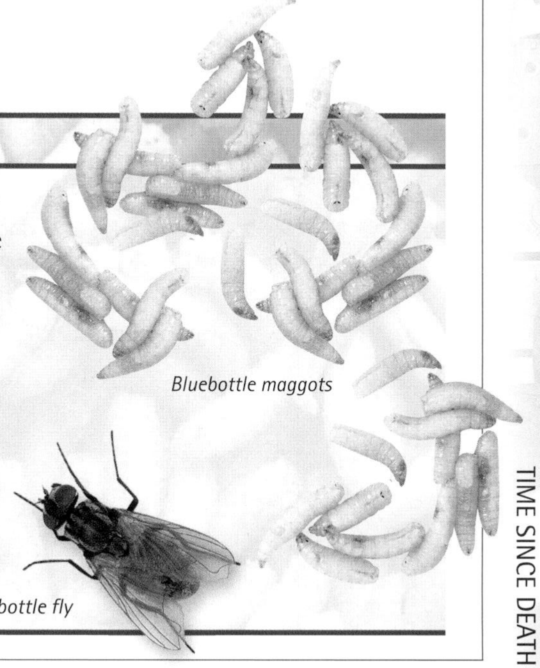

*Bluebottle maggots*

*Bluebottle fly*

## CLUES FROM CORPSE FLIES

Though decay erases much of the evidence that pathologists use to estimate time since death, it also introduces new clues. Of the millions of insect species, only a hundred or so scavenge on corpses, and the different infestations follow each other in a fixed and predictable order. So by identifying the maggots, flies, and beetles on a body, and by knowing the pupa stages of each, forensic entomologists can narrow down the time since death to within a day or so if a body has been left undiscovered for 3–4 weeks.

**GREEN SKIN COLOR ▶**

About 48 hours after death (depending on ambient temperature) bacterial action gives the corpse's skin a greenish tint, except in the very dark-skinned. This starts at the lower abdomen, and spreads outward, reaching hands and feet last. Within 4–7 days, the skin has a marbled appearance, and veins close to the surface become more conspicuous.

**CLUES BEYOND THE BODY ▶**

In addition to the clues provided by the body, other factors may yield important evidence of the time since death. These include the environment in which the body is found, and information about the victim's day-to-day movements and habits. The longer a body has been left undiscovered, the less reliable are estimates based on changes in the body's physical condition. A more accurate estimate may then be provided by environmental evidence (such as insects or weather) or personal details about the victim's activities (associated evidence).

**▼WHEN DID HE DIE?**

Besides the physical signs shown here, chemical analysis can help a pathologist to determine time since death. The most common test is of the vitreous humor—a transparent jelly that fills the eyeball. Potassium is low in the living eye, but rises at a known rate after death. Biochemical testing seems more objective than other methods, but this precision is misleading. All techniques of estimating time since death are approximate, and responsible pathologists recognize this by giving investigators an interval of confidence that reflects the uncertainty of even the best methods.

# The autopsy

The goal of any autopsy is to discover the cause of death. But when forensic pathologists wield the scalpel, they have special legal responsibilities. Their findings, and the conclusions drawn from them, may help to guide the police investigation and provide crucial evidence needed to bring a killer to justice.

The dissection of a body is just one part of a wider postmortem examination that includes identification of the body, the photography of the exterior of the body, and possibly an X-ray examination.

## Mortuary team

A pathologist is not alone in the mortuary. An anatomical pathology technician prepares the body and also assists in the postmortem; an exhibits officer samples material stuck to the skin before the body is washed; and a photographer records the entire process. In murder cases, a police witness may also be present.

Photography is thorough: the body is photographed from front and back, full length, and in detail. If the corpse was found fully dressed, it is photographed while clothed, then again each time the pathologist removes a layer of clothing.

Before the autopsy begins, the pathologist cuts samples of hair, and either clips the fingernails or scrapes under them. DNA analysis of these samples may help to identify an assailant, and can also reveal traces of poisons or drugs. Swab samples from the mouth, rectum, and sexual organs are also taken before dissection, and the pathologist notes all external marks on the skin—not just injuries, but tattoos and scars as well. External marks can help to identify the body, if identity is unknown (see p. 44).

Though the dissection usually begins with the opening of the chest cavity (shown below), the order varies. For example, if there are signs of strangulation, the autopsy starts with the head and neck. In a stabbing case, though, the pathologist's scalpel follows the track of the knife blade through the flesh.

Sometimes toxicology testing or histology (microscopic study of tissues) is needed before it is possible to say with certainty what the cause of death was. And in writing up their reports, pathologists are not simply documenting a procedure carried out in isolation. They must put their findings in the context of the police investigation, and ensure that the report will stand up as evidence in a court of law.

(see p. 44)

### THE AUTOPSY ROOM:

①　Hygiene is essential both for health reasons and to avoid contamination of evidence.

②　A lip around the stainless-steel dissection table directs all bodily fluids to the drain at one end.

③　A place for the pathologist to examine and section individual organs as they are removed.

④　A scale used for weighing organs.

⑤　Blackboard for recording weights of major organs.

⑥　Samples taken from major organs are stored in a refrigerated cabinet until they can be sent for analysis.

## THE PROCEDURE

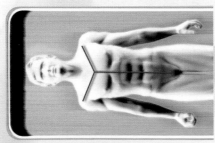

**EXTERNAL INSPECTION ▲**
External injuries, marks, and stains may dictate the order of the autopsy, so the pathologist first carries out a careful external examination. The wounds of violent deaths are usually obvious, but subtle signs can also suggest an unnatural death.

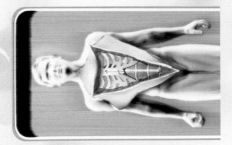

**SIMPLE INCISION ▲**
Where the death seems natural, the pathologist makes one cut up the torso, and removes internal organs for examination. This procedure is similar to a medical autopsy, which charts the progress of disease as well as establishing the cause of death.

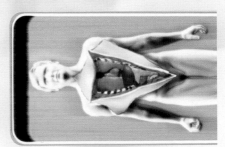

**SUSPICIOUS DEATHS ▲**
With a victim of crime, the pathologist makes a T- or Y-shaped cut that allows better access to the body cavity. If there are any injuries to the neck or head, the pathologist will start there before opening the chest and abdomen.

## TOOLS FOR THE JOB
A pathologist needs a range of tools and equipment to complete the full procedure. Here is a sample of some of the instruments used.

### SCALPEL ▶
*Different shaped, interchangeable blades adapt the scalpel for a diverse range of small cutting tasks.*

### BONE CUTTERS ▶
*These cut through the ribs so as to lift the chest plate and allow access to the internal organs. Pair A are used for the smaller ribs. Pair B have been designed with a compound action, which applies more pressure on the blades for the same effort, and are used on the larger ribs.*

### HAND SAW ▶
*Sturdy stainless steel hand saws are used for amputations and a variety of cutting tasks.*

### BRAIN KNIFE ▶
*Used to cut sample slices of all large organs, not just the brain.*

### CRANIUM CHISEL ▶
*After scoring the skull with a saw, the chisel gently finishes the separation and gains access to the brain.*

### EVIDENCE SOURCING ▲
*The autopsy room is where the pathologist painstakingly pieces together the facts behind a suspicious death. A corpse may hide many valuable clues, both inside and out, that can only be uncovered by meticulous examination.*

### MAJOR ORGANS ▲
*Cutting the ribs allows the removal of the chest plate. Some pathologists remove the heart, lungs, trachea, and esophagus together, others individually. Abdominal organs are treated similarly. Samples of fluids are removed for analysis.*

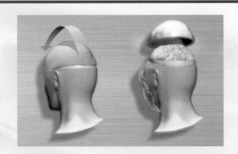

### THE HEAD ▲
*Cutting the skull, nerves, and blood vessels allows the pathologist to remove the brain. Studying it with the naked eye rarely reveals much. However, microscopic examination of very thin slices of brain tissue can show tearing and tiny blood clots.*

### WEIGH AND MEASURE ▲
*The pathologist weighs organs as they are removed. Depending on suspected cause of death, samples may be cut from every organ for microscopic analysis of the tissue. This allows for a more complete study of the body.*

# Marks of violence

Murder leaves marks: no matter how cunning killers are, they cannot hide telltale traces of violence on the bodies of their victims. At an autopsy the pathologist follows the marks of death like symbols on a map to locate the cause, and confirm—or refute—suspicions of homicide.

**◄ STRANGULATION**
*Both ligatures (cords, ropes, and similar weapons) and hands can produce distinct bruise patterns on the neck. Most ligatures leave obvious lines, but soft fabrics such as scarves may scarcely bruise the skin. When the skin is not marked, dissection shows clear signs of bruising in the tissue beneath.*

**BRAIN HEMORRHAGE ►**
*At an autopsy there may be no external signs that brain hemorrhage (bleeding) caused death, but an internal examination or, as here, a scan reveals the fatal clots.*

Every method of killing leaves characteristic traces on the body, but not all marks are equally distinct and obvious. Some poisons and drugs, for instance, leave no clearly visible marks, and can only be detected by analysis. At the other extreme, signs of a violent death are immediately apparent from an external examination. These injuries are usually divided into blunt-force trauma, gunshot, and sharp-force trauma. Attacks that leave such obvious signs on the body make up by far the majority of murder cases: instances where the cause of death leaves no obvious sign are much rarer in reality than they are in detective novels. Some of the most common signs of death are explained below. There are fuller accounts in Chapter Six: Lethal Agents.

## Color changes
Some fatal agents cause alterations to the appearance of the body, such as a color change—though not in the very dark-skinned. Carbon monoxide poisoning, for example, causes a characteristic "cherry pink" color change in the skin. And the pinhead-size patches of bleeding in the face caused by smothering or crushing of the chest can be so extensive as to make the whole face blue. Other color changes not directly linked to the cause of death are nevertheless relevant to an investigation.

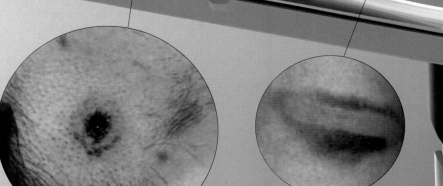

**GUNSHOT ▲**
*Details of gunshot wounds provide information about the circumstances of death: they can rule out suicide—but cannot prove it; their size is a guide to the caliber of the weapon; and burn marks on the skin show the victim was shot at close range.*

**BRUISING ▲**
*Often called contusions, bruises are small blood vessels broken by blunt-force trauma. Their shape can show the direction of impact, and color indicates how long ago the injury happened. As bruises heal, they change from red or purple through brown, green, and yellow. Interpreting bruises is not straightforward; people bruise at different speeds, and bruising continues after death.*

## Burn marks

Extensive burns to the body can themselves cause death, but even tiny burns are significant when there are no other obvious signs on the skin because they may suggest electrocution. Lethal electric current can, in some cases, cause blistering at the point of contact, though where contact is extensive—as it is when the victim was in the bathtub—the skin is often unmarked. A lightning strike may leave no external marks on the body, but the intense electrical current can heat metal objects in clothing, such as clasps and zippers, and these can burn the skin.

## Internal injuries

It is rare for fatal internal injuries to leave no external marks: more often, dissection confirms what a pathologist suspects from the first inspection of the body. This is hardly surprising: a blow that is strong enough to cause fatal damage to internal organs usually leaves bruises on the skin.

One exception to this general rule is brain damage. A blow to the head, or violent shaking of a baby's head, may leave no bruise or graze but can nevertheless be sufficient to cause death by bleeding within the skull.

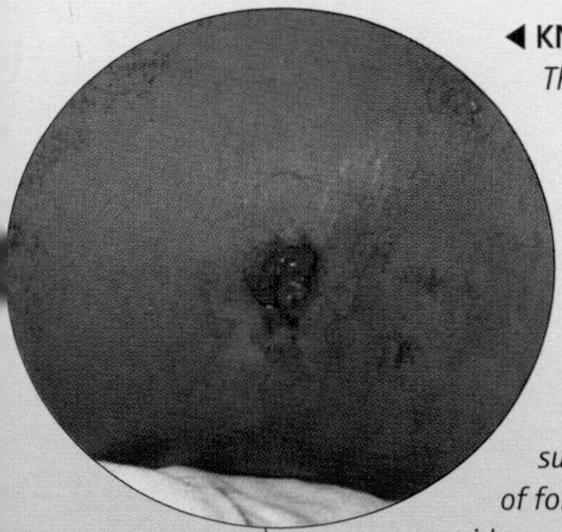

**◄ KNIFE WOUNDS**
*The shape of cuts in flesh can reveal whether the weapon had one cutting edge or two. The angle of entry may indicate direction to rule out accidental death, and depth suggests the amount of force used—important evidence of intent to kill.*

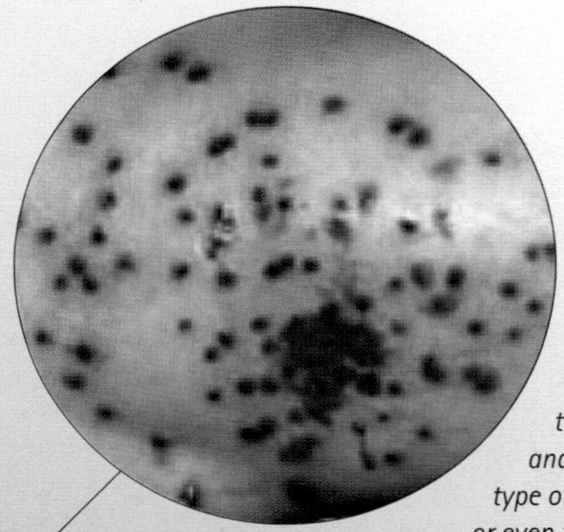

**◄ SHOTGUN**
*Fired at close range, shotguns make a single large wound. At a greater range, pellets make individual wounds, as shown here. Investigators often ask pathologists to use wound distribution to estimate the distance between the killer and victim, but many factors, such as the type of weapon, the batch of ammunition, or even the temperature, make such estimates unreliable.*

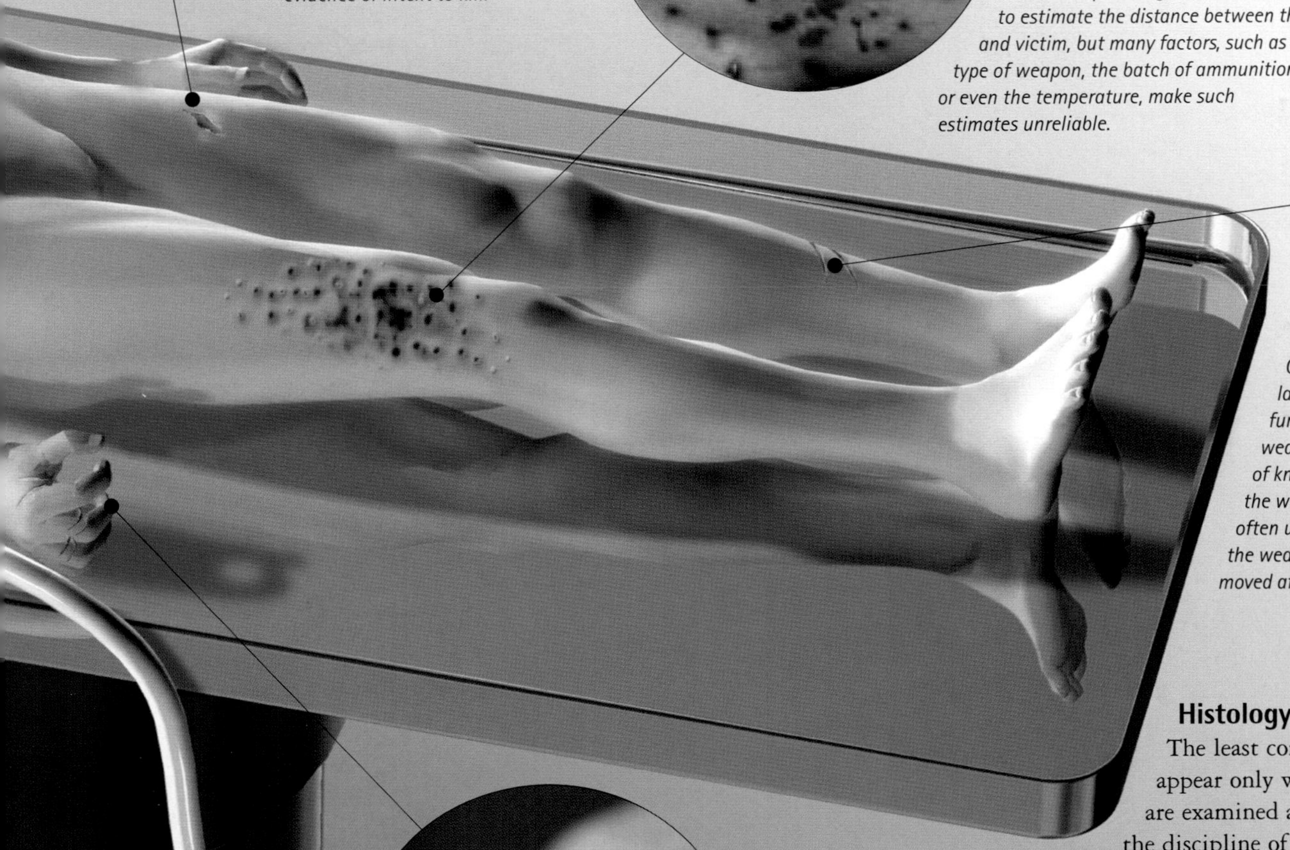

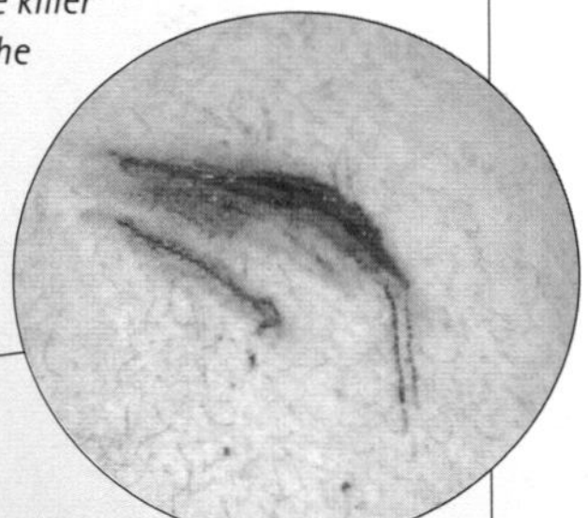

**LACERATIONS ▲**
*Close inspection of a laceration can reveal further details of the weapon used. In the case of knives, information on the width of the blade is often unreliable because the weapon may have been moved after the initial cut.*

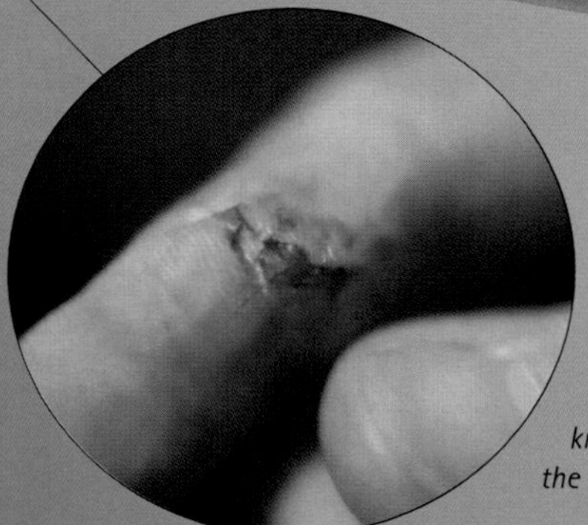

## Histology

The least conspicuous signs may appear only when the body's organs are examined at high magnification— the discipline of histology. A precision device called a microtome is used to pare off a transparently thin slice of tissue, which is mounted on a microscope slide. The slide is then chemically stained to enhance any tissue abnormalities. If any aberrations are found, further chemical stains may be carried out in order to indicate specific damage or disease.

**◄ STRUGGLE WITH A KNIFE**
*If a victim of a stabbing has cut hands, the pathologist carrying out the autopsy could conclude that there had been a struggle for the knife—which would suggest that the killer might also be wounded.*

# Cause of death

**BODY FOUND AT SCENE OF FIRE**

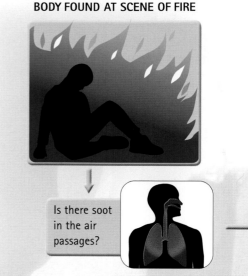

The circumstances in which a body is found may clearly indicate how the victim died. But what happens if the superficial evidence is inconclusive? In these cases, an autopsy may help the coroner to decide the cause of the fatality, and to discover whether a seemingly innocent death was in fact a disguised homicide.

Deciding the manner of death—suicide, natural, accidental, or homicide—is not the pathologist's responsibility. However, in seeking the cause of death—such as a gunshot wound to the head—pathologists uncover evidence that points to the manner. The three examples on this page show how a pathologist is a detective of sorts. He uses a process of deduction to discover the facts surrounding a death.

Is there soot in the air passages?

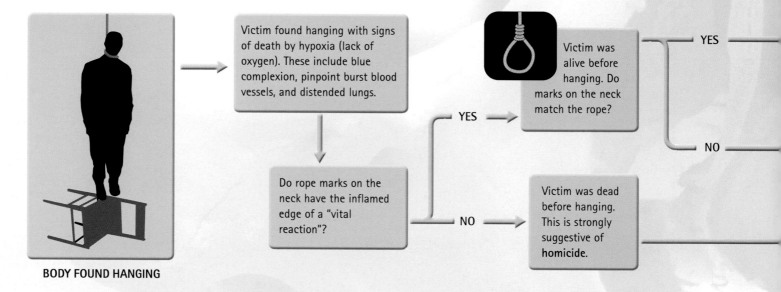

**BODY FOUND HANGING**

Victim found hanging with signs of death by hypoxia (lack of oxygen). These include blue complexion, pinpoint burst blood vessels, and distended lungs.

Do rope marks on the neck have the inflamed edge of a "vital reaction"?

YES

NO

Victim was alive before hanging. Do marks on the neck match the rope?

YES

NO

Victim was dead before hanging. This is strongly suggestive of **homicide**.

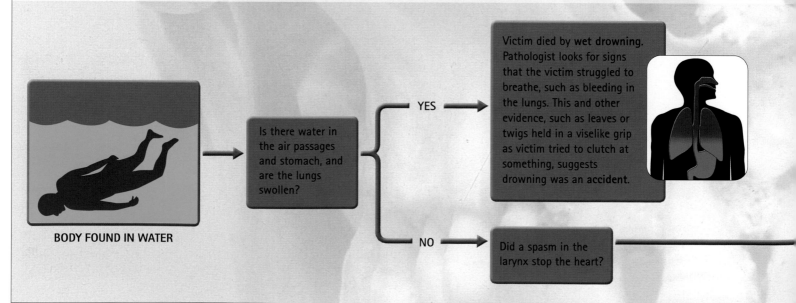

**BODY FOUND IN WATER**

Is there water in the air passages and stomach, and are the lungs swollen?

YES

NO

Victim died by **wet drowning**. Pathologist looks for signs that the victim struggled to breathe, such as bleeding in the lungs. This and other evidence, such as leaves or twigs held in a viselike grip as victim tried to clutch at something, suggests drowning was an accident.

Did a spasm in the larynx stop the heart?

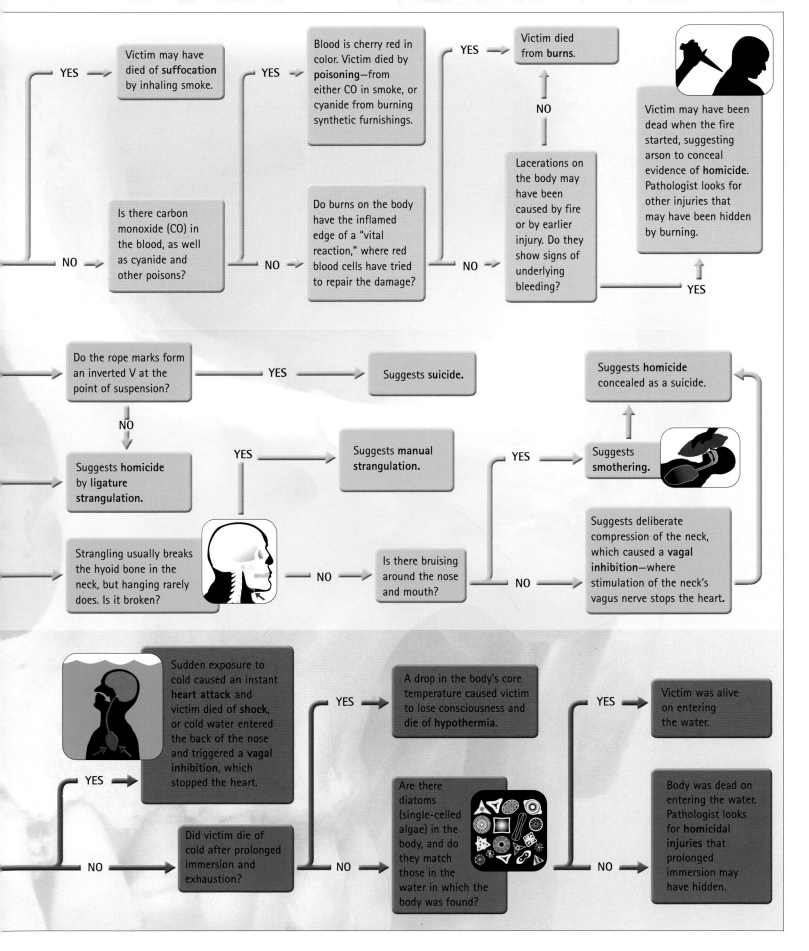

YES → Victim may have died of **suffocation** by inhaling smoke.

YES → Blood is cherry red in color. Victim died by **poisoning**—from either CO in smoke, or cyanide from burning synthetic furnishings.

YES → Victim died from **burns**.

Victim may have been dead when the fire started, suggesting arson to conceal evidence of **homicide**. Pathologist looks for other injuries that may have been hidden by burning.

Is there carbon monoxide (CO) in the blood, as well as cyanide and other poisons?

NO →

Do burns on the body have the inflamed edge of a "vital reaction," where red blood cells have tried to repair the damage?

NO →

NO

Lacerations on the body may have been caused by fire or by earlier injury. Do they show signs of underlying bleeding?

NO →

YES

Do the rope marks form an inverted V at the point of suspension?

YES → Suggests **suicide**.

Suggests **homicide** concealed as a suicide.

NO

Suggests **homicide** by ligature strangulation.

YES → Suggests **manual strangulation**.

YES → Suggests **smothering**.

Strangling usually breaks the hyoid bone in the neck, but hanging rarely does. Is it broken?

NO →

Is there bruising around the nose and mouth?

NO →

Suggests deliberate compression of the neck, which caused a **vagal inhibition**—where stimulation of the neck's vagus nerve stops the heart.

Sudden exposure to cold caused an instant **heart attack** and victim died of **shock**, or cold water entered the back of the nose and triggered a **vagal inhibition**, which stopped the heart.

A drop in the body's core temperature caused victim to lose consciousness and die of **hypothermia**.

YES →

YES → Victim was alive on entering the water.

YES →

Did victim die of cold after prolonged immersion and exhaustion?

NO →

Are there diatoms (single-celled algae) in the body, and do they match those in the water in which the body was found?

NO →

Body was dead on entering the water. Pathologist looks for **homicidal injuries** that prolonged immersion may have hidden.

NO →

39

# Trapped by flies

Alton Coleman was a terrifying, brutal rapist who killed those he preyed on as casually as you might swat a fly. As it happens, it was a fly—a fat, shiny bluebottle—that led to his execution. Knowledge of insect life cycles led to the crucial pinpointing of the time of death of one of his victims, one month after she had been murdered.

**EXECUTED**

**ALTON COLEMAN ▲**
*Born in 1956 in Waukegan, just north of Chicago, Alton Coleman was in trouble with the police even as a teenager. Arrested several times for rape, he escaped conviction by threatening witnesses.*

You couldn't expect to meet a nastier character than Alton Coleman. Plausible and sly, he won the confidence of the people he met, then ruthlessly exploited it to satisfy his voracious, violent, and perverse sexual appetite. Indiscriminately carnal, he was attracted equally to men, women, and children. He so terrified those he raped that he often escaped conviction because they did not dare testify against him.

In the summer of 1984, Coleman's sporadic sequence of petty crime, rapes, and sexual assaults suddenly accelerated. With his girlfriend Debra Brown, he went on a frenzied spree of rape and murder that crossed five states. When police caught up with the pair in July, Coleman and Brown were wanted for eight murders, seven rapes, and 14 armed robberies.

Securing convictions against the pair should have been easy, but Coleman had wriggled out of apparently straightforward cases before. He knew just how to behave in court, with a confident manner that oozed bogus innocence. So when prosecutors began planning to try him, they looked first at crimes where the evidence was strongest—and in the states where the punishment would be harshest.

## Vernita Wheat

One of the cases they picked was a murder in Illinois, a state that retained the death penalty. It was as gruesome and heartless as any that Coleman had committed. He had spent a month befriending a single mother in Kenosha, Wisconsin. Then, on May 29, Coleman persuaded her to let him take her nine-year-old daughter Vernita to pick up a used stereo as a belated Mother's Day present, and then go on to a local carnival. They never returned.

### Gathering evidence

Vernita's body was found three weeks later in the bathroom of a derelict building in nearby Waukegan, Illinois. Her body was little more than a fly-blown shell. Investigators combed the bathroom for evidence, unscrewing the whole door so that they could examine it in the lab for fingerprints. They found one of Coleman's prints on the door, but this alone was not enough to convict him. What they needed was proof that the girl had died between the afternoon she was abducted and early the following morning. Brown had admitted that Coleman had been out all night, and that when he returned to the apartment they shared at 8 A.M., he told her he had done something "real bad."

◀ THE ACCOMPLICE
*Coleman's accomplice Debra Brown was judged to be retarded and dominated by him, but was nevertheless sentenced to death. It is unclear whether she will be executed.*

The FBI turned to forensic entomologist Bernard Greenberg to supply the link. To get him started, they sent him the flying, buzzing, creeping, and wriggling inhabitants of Vernita's corpse, and the heaps of pupae that surrounded the body. Greenberg, they hoped, would in return give them a time of death.

It wasn't an easy task. The empty cocoons were from black blowflies that had hatched from eggs laid on the corpse soon after death, and the cloud of flies that hummed around the corpse when it was found was the second generation. Since black blowflies complete their life cycle in little more than two weeks, they didn't give Greenberg the precision he needed, so he turned to the unhatched, unidentifiable cocoons that the FBI had collected from the bathroom floor.

These he gently incubated in laboratory cages. As the days went by, more black blowflies emerged. Sheep blowflies followed, but were equally worthless—they also had too short a life cycle.

◀ GREENBERG
*A pioneer of forensic entomology, Bernard Greenberg turned crop sprayers' calculations upside down to work out how long Vernita Wheat had been lying dead.*

## Hatching hope

Finally, a month and a day after Vernita was abducted, Greenberg got what he wanted. A baritone hum from the cages signaled that a squadron of fat bluebottles had emerged from their cocoons. He knew that at a constant 59°F (15°C), bluebottles take 33 days to metamorphose from newly laid egg through grub and cocoon to adult fly. But June temperatures in Illinois are higher than this. They rarely drop below 61°F (16°C), and the average in the daytime is 77°F (25°C). At these higher temperatures, the life-cycle would be shorter.

A scientific estimate taking these variables into account had always been used at this point, but Greenberg knew that it could be made to seem like a "guess" in a court of law. He wanted

a much more precise resolution, something mathematical. He turned to an unusual source: agricultural entomology.

## Pinpointing time

He knew that entomologists told farmers when to begin crop spraying so that they hit insect pests at the most vulnerable point in their life-cycle. They did this by using a concept called "accumulated degree hours." The agricultural entomologists had discovered that the temperature-dependent growth of insects could be distilled into a simple formula of growth per unit of heat. So if it takes a hypothetical insect 100 hours at 59°F (15°C) to reach a certain stage, then it would take 50 hours at 86°F (30°C).

Armed with more than 700 hourly weather reports from a weather station near the crime scene, Greenberg set to work, "winding back the clock" from the moment the bluebottles started to hatch. When he had finished, he had what he believed was an objective estimate for the moment the eggs were laid. It was midnight on May 30th. Bluebottles, however, aren't active at night, so when Greenberg appeared as an expert witness at the trial of Alton Coleman, he explained that the eggs had probably been laid early the following morning.

It was enough to convince the jury, and Alton Coleman was sentenced to death for Wheat's murder. Another state beat them to it, though, and he was executed on April 26, 2002 for the murder of Marlene Walters, 44, from Ohio.

EXECUTION ▶
*Coleman was eventually executed not for killing Vernita Wheat, but for another of his murders. Here, jailers remove his bagged body.*

## INSECT TIMES

As a corpse rots, time of death indicators (see p. 32) become useless. Forensic entomologists look at the insects that colonize the body in a known succession.

| STAGES OF DECOMPOSITION | INSECT FOUND |
|---|---|
| **FRESH**     0–3 DAYS<br>Adult blowflies are among the first to colonize a fresh corpse, as carbohydrates and proteins break down. | <br>Bluebottle |
| **BLOATED**     4–7 DAYS<br>Fly larvae and beetles move in as the body begins to putrefy, producing gases that inflate the abdomen. | <br>Rove Beetle |
| **DECAY**     8–18 DAYS<br>When the abdominal wall breaks, the body starts to decay. Ants, cockroaches, and beetles dominate. | <br>Ants |
| **POST-DECAY**     19–30 DAYS<br>In damp sites the corpse is still wet and sticky, but in dry places, it's desiccated, attracting different species. | <br>Springtail |
| **DRY**     31 DAYS +<br>After just a month in warm summer conditions, the remaining bones, hair, and dry skin smell only of soil. | <br>African Ground Beetle |

# HUMAN IDENTIFICATION

Who are you? Can you prove it? In crime investigation the issue of identity is central—and not just the identity of a suspect. In trying to locate and prosecute the perpetrator of a crime, detectives may first need to identify the victim—and then eliminate innocent bystanders. Famously, the gold standard of ID is analysis of an individual's unique DNA, but numerous other techniques, including traditional fingerprinting, forensic dentistry, and blood analysis, still have an important role to play.

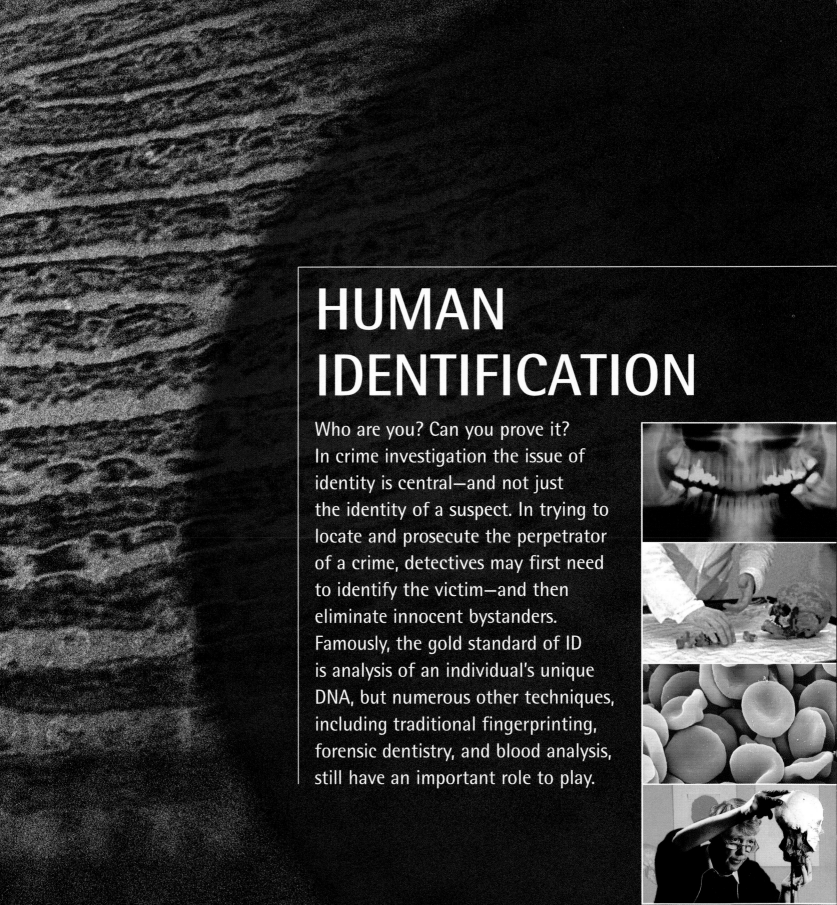

# Identifying the body

The ebbing tide gives up an anonymous corpse. A plummeting aircraft scatters bodies. A murder investigation turns up a shallow grave. The circumstances of death are never quite the same, but "who was this person?" is always the first question investigators ask. Finding out the answer demands ingenuity, patience, and sometimes sheer luck.

**A WATERY GRAVE ▲**
*Here, police officers remove a body from the River Thames, England. Immersion in water can make the skin swollen, wrinkled, and distorted, so it can be more difficult to identify the victim.*

The identity of most bodies is either immediately apparent or reasonably simple to establish. Often the discovery of a corpse marks the tragic end to a missing persons investigation. Identification can also concern the remains of accident victims. Plane crashes, for example, are fairly straightforward for investigators, because bodies can be matched to a passenger list. This type of self-contained investigation is known as a "closed" case. "Open" cases, such as washed-up bodies or train crashes where no list of travelers exists, can be more difficult to solve.

## Plastic and gold

But even in open cases, there are usually some indications of the identity of the deceased. Few adults leave home without any identifying documents, such as a credit card or driver's license. However, in major transport accidents, linking the ID to the victims can have its difficulties. Men present fewer problems, because they generally carry their ID in their pockets. Women's possessions, usually kept in purses, are more easily scattered.

Clothes and jewelry can help to confirm identity when coupled with other evidence, but are of limited value on their own because most garments and cheaper jewelry pieces are mass-produced. Also, jewelry's value, as well as its size and ease of removal, makes it an attractive target for looters, particularly when an aircraft comes down in a remote and impoverished region.

### THE TOP TEN IDENTIFIERS:

| | |
|---|---|
| 1 | Dental evidence—fillings, missing teeth, bridgework, and crowns |
| 2 | Physical description |
| 3 | Jewelry and other personal effects |
| 4 | Documents, such as passports and credit cards |
| 5 | Fingerprints |
| 6 | Visual identification by a relative |
| 7 | Details of clothing |
| 8 | Medical records |
| 9 | Age assessment |
| 10 | Tattoos |

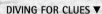

**DIVING FOR CLUES ▼**
*When a car is seen plummeting into the water, the police divers are quick to reach the scene. Thorough searches of the surrounding area can help to recover, and identify, any victims.*

## IDENTIFIABLE EXTERNAL MARKS

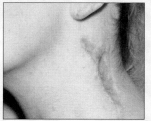

**◀ BIRTH MARKS**
*Children's "strawberry" birthmarks usually disappear by school age, but "port-wine" stains, caused by abnormal distribution of blood vessels, are permanent marks on the skin. Photographs of these, and descriptions from relatives, help in making an identification.*

**SCARS ▶**
*Accidents, burns, and medical treatment all leave distinctive marks on the skin that can aid investigators in ID cases. However, relatively few people have large scars, and damage to the skin in fires can eliminate traces of even extensive scarring.*

**TATTOOS ▲**
*Once the mark of sailors and criminals, tattoos are now commonplace and fashionable. Their permanence, and the individuality of the designs, means they can be a valuable guide to identity, as long as the skin remains intact.*

### Are you sure it's him?

Surprisingly, the most obvious ways of identifying bodies are not always the most reliable. Visual identification by relatives, for example, provides a definitive answer less often than you might imagine. In major disasters, grief, as well as the sheer number of bodies, makes recognition harder. But there can be other difficulties. Death erases character—few of us realize how much we rely on gestures, expressions, gait, and voice to recognize our friends and family. Fraud can be a factor, too. People have been known to "identify" the bodies of complete strangers in order to make false insurance claims.

### Distinguishing marks

When a direct visual identification may be unreliable or impractical, descriptions and photographs are useful. In particular, details such as birthmarks, scars, and tattoos are easy to identify, and are often very distinctive. Dental records can also be helpful (see p. 50). Fingerprints can confirm a tentative identification if relatives can produce personal objects bearing a set of prints.

If all these routes fail, the next step is a closer inspection of the body at the morgue. X-rays reveal old fractures, which may match relatives' descriptions of past accidents. Even implants can provide clues. When a dismembered, headless torso was found in a garbage bag in London, in January 2003, the body was identified by serial numbers on its breast and buttock implants. Blood tests are also useful, and can be quick, cheap, and easy to perform. But blood type is only helpful when blood is from one of the less common groups. Drugs in the bloodstream, or medical conditions that can be detected by serology, can also help confirm an identity. If a close relative can provide a DNA sample, then DNA tests can confirm a match with near certainty.

### Matching the clues

All of these procedures can assist in matching a body to a shortlist of possible identities. Few, however, are any help for anonymous, unclaimed corpses. In these cases, investigators trawl through lists and databases in the hope of finding a match.

Convicted criminals can be identified by matching their fingerprints or DNA to police records. Local, national, and international missing persons bureaus may be able to resolve other "identity unknown" cases.

If these sources fail, the chances of investigators identifying the body are slim, especially in large cities that attract people who seek anonymity. For example, in New York City, around 1,500 people leave the city morgues each year anonymous, unnoticed, and unmourned.

## CASE STUDY

In Connecticut, in the winter of 1986, blonde Pan Am flight attendant Helle Crafts disappeared. Police had a murder suspect—her violent, adulterous husband—but no victim. When they discovered that he'd rented a wood-chipper, they realized the body hunt was going to get difficult. Witness reports led them to a nearby river. A search of the river banks turned up roughly one thousandth of a human body, including 59 slivers of bone, part of a finger (shown below), five droplets of blood, two tooth caps, and 2,660 human hairs—all blonde. Over 50,000 forensic tests were carried out on this tiny amount of material. They showed that the remains matched Helle's blood type, and the capped tooth matched her dental records. This led to Richard Crafts' arrest and subsequent conviction of her murder.

**FINGERTIP TEST ▶**
*The largest body part found by the police was Helle Crafts' fingertip, complete with painted nail. The nail polish was analyzed and compared to a sample recovered from the Crafts' home.*

## CASE STUDY

**ORTHOPEDIC EVIDENCE ▼**
*The metal implants that surgeons use to replace worn or weak bones provide a very distinctive identifying mark, which survives even ferocious fires.*

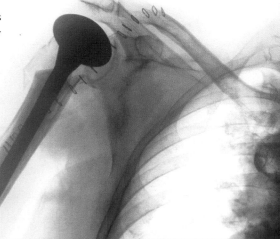

# Fingerprinting

Ancient Babylonians used fingerprints to "sign" contracts as long ago as 2000 BC, but the forensic use of fingerprints only dates back to the late 19th century. Despite more modern methods, such as DNA profiling, fingerprint identification is still widespread, thanks to the unique pattern of raised ridges on our fingertips.

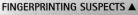

**FINGERPRINTING SUSPECTS ▲**
*The traditional way to record fingerprints is to ink each fingertip and roll it across the card (above left). Increasingly, hands are scanned electronically (above right) to add prints directly to the database.*

Fingerprint evidence relies on the classification of fingertip patterns. Without an organized system, police could only prove that a suspect was at a crime by directly comparing crime-scene marks with the suspect's prints. With classified files, however, police can compare the marks they find with the stored fingerprints of thousands, or even millions, of known criminals.

## Classification

Systematic fingerprint records began in 1891 in Argentina (see box below). Five years later, English fingerprint expert Edward Henry developed a "ten-print" classification system—the most widely used method until computers took over in the late 20th century.

Henry separated fingerprint patterns into two groups—value patterns (whorls) and nonvalue patterns (loops and arches). A finger with a whorl pattern was given a numerical value that depended on the finger's position. For example, a whorl on the right thumb had a value of 16, but on the left little finger had a value of 1. By grouping together values from certain fingers, Henry formed a fractionlike code for each set of ten prints. He created 1,024 different codes. Any set of prints could be easily filed using their code.

This system worked well for identifying criminals working under aliases. Newly arrested suspects were fingerprinted and coded. Comparing their prints with those of known criminals filed under the same code meant searching for a match was much faster than searching through the whole collection. But because a complete set of ten prints was required, the system was of limited use for matching finger marks found at crime scenes. Single-print systems, introduced in the 1930s, got around this by classifying and filing separately the prints of individual fingers.

## Comparison

Single-print systems did not avoid the task of comparing a crime-scene mark with every similar print on file. In this time-consuming and skilled procedure, fingerprint examiners look at the characteristic shape of ridges. They compare where the ridges start and end, and where they join and split. Also noted are the positions of short ridges and dots, as well as any areas enclosed as "lakes." Examiners look for points of similarity between mark and print to decide whether the two patterns match.

## Computer databases

If a print found at a crime scene shows a complete fingertip with an unusual pattern, it can be quickly matched. However, crime-scene finger marks are rarely perfect, and their quality often restricts a search.

As fingerprint collections began to grow, the task of searching through them mushroomed. But from the 1960s

**WILLIAM JAMES HERSCHEL** first used fingerprints to identify Indian pension claimants in the 1860s. He demonstrated that the pattern did not change with age. Over the next 30 years, Henry Faulds suggested that fingerprints were unique, and Francis Galton published a scientific study of prints and their value in identification. These three pioneers were all British, but it was an Argentinian police official, Juan Vucetich, who developed the first criminal fingerprint ID system, in 1891. The system was used to convict a murderer the following year.

**William James Herschel
1833–1917**

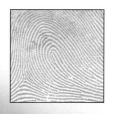

**◄ LOOPS**
*Ridges can fold back on themselves to form a loop. Radial loops originate at the thumb side; ulnar loops travel in the opposite direction.*

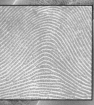

**◄ WHORLS**
*When ridges revolve around a point on the finger, a whorl is formed. Along with ulnar loops, these are the most common types of prints.*

**◄ ARCHES**
*Formed when the finger's ridges lie above one another in an arch-like shape. These are the least common of the three main patterns.*

onward, computers began to help. For thirty years automated fingerprint identification systems (AFIS) were developed, until they were sufficiently fast and dependable to be widely adopted.

The computerized systems in use today scan prints retrieved from the scene and plot the relative positions of individual ridge characteristics, such as bifurcations (where the ridges divide into two). They also record the direction of the ridge at each of these points. The computer then compares this data with similar information from prints in the database, and presents a ranked list of the most likely matches. Fingerprint examiners then compare the crime-scene print with this "shortlist" in the traditional way to confirm any match.

The main advantage of this approach is with partial prints. An incomplete whorl pattern looks just like a loop, so a manual search would begin in the wrong part of the database, and would fail. AFIS systems do not need to divide prints into the traditional pattern categories, so they can process "mark against print" searches very quickly and suggest possible matches.

AFIS has revolutionized fingerprint searches: the FBI's system can perform 40,000 searches a day. Until the introduction of AFIS, suspects were often released without being charged because manual searches took so long.

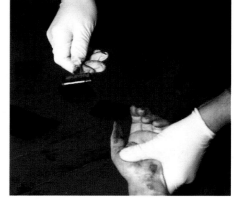

**PRINTS FROM THE DEAD ▲**
*Taking fingerprints from the recently dead is not generally difficult once rigor mortis has passed, but older corpses present problems. Skin often peels from drowning victims, and forensic technicians may have to wrap it around their own fingers to take prints.*

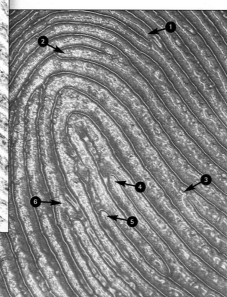

**PRINTING A FINGER**
*An inked finger prints a mirror image of its ridge patterns. The above print has been reversed to help compare it with the original finger (right). Note their unique ridge endings (points 1, 2, 4, and 5) and bifurcations (points 3 and 6).*

# CASE STUDY

"I've got him! He's here!" With a triumphant shout, a fingerprint searcher in Blackburn, England, marked the end of one of the biggest manhunts in British history. It began in May 1948, when three-year-old June Devaney disappeared from her hospital crib. After a two-hour search police found her battered corpse nearby. Fingerprints on a hospital bottle did not match those of hospital staff, or known criminals, so police fingerprinted every male voter in Blackburn—more than 40,000 people. None of them matched the prints on the bottle. Desperate to find the killer, police checked numbers on ration cards, which Britons needed to buy food during and after World War II. They found 200 Blackburn men who were not registered voters, and took their prints. One set matched: those of Peter Griffiths (pictured). Confronted with the evidence, this 22-year-old former soldier confessed to the killing and was hanged on November 19. The other citizens' fingerprint records were destroyed.

# CASE STUDY

# The Docklands bomb

**CONVICTED**

**FACE OF THE BOMBER ▲**
*Sentenced to 25 years, terrorist James McArdle served only two—he was released in a prisoner amnesty aimed at restarting the peace process.*

**FAINT FINGERPRINTS ▼**
*These police photographs show the actual meal voucher and rain-soaked copy of Truck and Driver on which the bomber's thumbprints were found.*

**W**hen a massive IRA bomb ripped through Canary Wharf, it shattered not only windows in London's Docklands, but also a fragile Northern Ireland peace process. The detectives who spent two years on the trail of the bomber nicknamed him the "Triple Fingerprint Man" after the forensic evidence that eventually led to his conviction.

"We were working late, tapping away at our terminals, when there was a tremendous flash and a huge boom and we were all knocked down onto the floor. The water pipes exploded, shards of glass went everywhere, and the office filled with dust and smoke."

The blast that threw George Sparks across his office came from a huge bomb in a truck parked 1,650 feet (500 m) away. It exploded at 7 PM on February 9, 1996, killing two and injuring nearly 40 people.

It ended a ceasefire that had kept mainland Britain free of Irish Republican bombs for 17 months.

London's Canary Wharf was a prime target for the IRA—it was a symbol of corporate wealth, and Europe's second-tallest office building. It lay just outside a security cordon that protected London's financial district. Nevertheless, the blast wrong-footed British security forces. "We were taken completely by surprise," one of their spokesmen confessed.

Scotland Yard's antiterrorist squad had little to go on. The scene of crime was just a huge crater alongside the South Quay train station. The only obvious lead was a uniformed police officer's description of the vehicle. He had spotted it while helping to clear the area after telephoned warnings. From his account, forensic artists drew a picture of the truck—a Ford flat-bed that had been modified to carry cars. When newspapers

**◄ THE HUNT FOR EVIDENCE**
*After receiving a tipoff, police searched nearby waste ground. They found a discarded trailer, piles of garbage, and a tire full of evidence.*

published the picture, 850 people called the police with information. The 199th caller had seen the truck parked at an industrial estate 10 miles (16 km) away, in the days before the blast. He said that two men had unloaded a trailer it had been carrying, and the trailer was still parked in the same spot.

Investigators rushed to the patch of waste ground. Beside the trailer they found a tire containing tachograph charts, magazines, a set of Northern Ireland license plates, and other bits of garbage. The tachograph chart gave them a vital early lead. It had recorded speeds, stops, and starts, and enabled police to trace the truck's movements back to Carlisle, in the north of England. Bought at an auction there four months earlier, the truck had then been driven to Northern Ireland. Helped by the license plates, as well as

**GANTRY CAMERA** ▲
*Surveillance cameras mounted over British highways enabled police to retrace the truck's route from the Irish ferry to Canary Wharf.*

tapes from CCTV cameras on highway bridges, investigators learned that the transporter had made a return trip to the mainland a month before the bombing. They also discovered that the bombers had stayed twice at the same Carlisle motel.

Though its rooms had been cleaned many times since their stay, fingerprint officers dusted them anyway. They collected 100 fingerprints, and took prints from the motel staff to eliminate them. After fuming an ashtray with superglue (see p. 19), one print stood out—it didn't match those of any of the cleaners.

270 miles (435 km) south of Carlisle, technicians in Scotland Yard's fingerprint lab had been minutely scrutinizing

garbage found near the trailer. After two months of work, they at last got a result. They had used DFO and ninhydrin (see p. 18) to treat a meal voucher from the ferry that brought the truck over from Northern Ireland. It bore the faint print of a thumb—the same thumb that had gripped the ashtray in the Carlisle motel.

Physical developer (see p. 19) revealed another thumbprint, on a magazine that had been left out in the rain for two weeks. This print matched the other two. The bomber was no longer such an enigma, and investigators nicknamed their suspect the "Triple Fingerprint Man." Elated by the discoveries, they ran a computer comparison with fingerprint records. It was negative. The IRA had chosen their bomber with care—he had no criminal record. The investigation stalled.

Then, in April 1997, an SAS raid in South Armagh, Northern Ireland, captured an IRA active service unit who had been carrying out sniper shootings. One of the arrested men was James McArdle, a bricklayer and driver from the village of Crossmaglen. In a routine check, his fingerprints were compared with those of the Docklands bomber. They matched— McArdle was the Triple Fingerprint Man.

His trial, in June 1998, made public the details of the deadly plan. The car transporter had traveled to England in January 1996 to visit a used-car auction. This had established an alibi for the bombers as legitimate motor traders, and was also a dry run for the bombing. The tachograph that led investigators to Carlisle was a prop, added to help them look convincing.

On the bombing trip itself, empty spaces in the transporter were packed with more than a ton of explosives— mostly a ground-up mix of fertilizer and sugar, with a small trigger charge of Semtex plastic explosives.

The fingerprint evidence was enough to convict McArdle, and on June 25, 1998, the Triple Fingerprint Man received 25 years for conspiracy to cause explosions.

**DOCKLANDS DEBRIS** ▶
*The IRA bomb caused $225 million worth of damage to Docklands' buildings. Store owner Inam Bashir and his assistant John Jeffries died in the blast.*

# Dental identification

Drilled, filled, bridged, and pulled, there is more to teeth than an innocent smile. The bite marks they leave behind give clues to their owner's identity, appearance, and health. And because teeth do not burn or rot, they are sometimes the only method of identification when the face, fingerprints, and possessions have all been destroyed.

Forensic dentists, or odontologists, feature in many of the world's worst disasters. "The victims were identified from dental records" evokes the scale of fire, explosion, crash, or grave, while sparing television viewers the grisly details.

Recognizing the dead from their teeth is not a recent practice. Even as far back as AD 59, when Roman emperor Nero had his mother Agrippina murdered by a slave, her corpse was identified from her teeth. In 1776, Paul Revere identified Joseph Warren's body, ten months after his anonymous burial at the battle of Bunker Hill, Massachusetts. Revere recognized a bridge that he had made for Warren the previous year.

## Long-lasting jaws

Dental evidence is a valuable aid to identification because teeth are extraordinarily hard and resilient. They survive fires that melt glass and copper and reduce ordinary bones to ash. They can also resist the most determined murderers' attempts to hide the evidence of their crimes.

At a crime scene, forensic dentists confirm identification by comparing the teeth of an unrecognizable corpse with a set of dental records. They carry out a postmortem dental examination, and then, if necessary, take X-rays using a portable machine.

If the jaws are complete, and the records are recent, then confirming a match is a skilled but straightforward task. Dentists routinely chart which of their patients' teeth are missing, which have been filled, and all details of bridges, crowns, and other treatment.

The task becomes more difficult when records or X-rays are very out-of-date, or when the skull has been severely damaged. Under these circumstances, forensic dentists use their knowledge of tooth development, and look for points of similarity between the records and the skull they are examining. If there are no dental X-rays, then full-face X-ray records can be used as a substitute. The unique shape of the frontal sinuses above the nose

◀ THE JAWS OF DEATH
*Identification of a corpse is very reliable when dental office notes exist, because dentists record details of all the surfaces of each of the 32 adult teeth.*

### BAZAAR DE LA CHARITÉ
Modern forensic dentistry began on May 4, 1897, when a fire at a charity bazaar killed 126 wealthy Parisians. Three-quarters of the victims were recognizable from clothes or possessions, and though the identities of the remainder were known, they were too badly burned to be easily distinguished. At the suggestion of a diplomat, dental records were used to sort out the remains. This proved successful, and helped the pioneers of forensic odontology, Davenport and Amoedo, establish guidelines that are still followed today.

An 1897 newspaper illustration of the fire

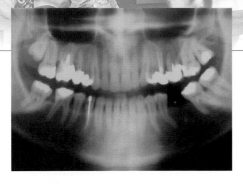

**X-RAY EVIDENCE ▲**
*Extensive fillings and root canal treatment (shown as white on the X-ray), and a missing tooth in the lower jaw, made the mouth of this victim unmistakable.*

can help to accurately identify a victim.

When there are no surgery records or X-rays, valid deductions are limited. But there are some useful guidelines. For example, a child's age can be determined by the stage of development of their teeth, and, in older people, the roots become more transparent with age. Also, the pattern of wear on an adult's teeth can help to indicate both age and diet. In addition, the materials and techniques used in fillings, bridges, or dentures can point to the country where the victim received dental treatment.

## Bite marks

Dentistry also has a vital role in the analysis of bite marks. The teeth of both humans and animals can leave distinct impressions. In flesh, they make pronounced bruises or puncture wounds, and certain foods, such as fruit or hard cheese, can retain their impressions.

Whether these marks are of any value for identification purposes depends on how distinct they are, and the individual characteristics of the teeth that made them. If a gap or irregularity in a suspect's teeth matches corresponding features in a

bite mark, then it is reasonable to infer that the suspect's teeth made the mark. When the teeth are very distinctive, and the bite marks very clear, identification can be near-certain.

To match suspect and bite mark, dentists first document the mark, typically using photography. In the case of bitten food, preservation is necessary. The apple in the right-hand case study, for example, was preserved in alcohol, glycerol, and formaldehyde.

The next stage is to obtain a record of the suspect's teeth. Forensic dentists take a dental impression of a suspect, much as a clinical dentist makes an impression of a patient needing a bridge or crown. Once this impression has set, filling it with a plaster material makes a near-perfect replica of the teeth and gums.

Printed on a transparent overlay, scans or photographs of a suspect's teeth can sometimes correspond directly with a bite mark. More often, though, the marks are subtle and unclear in photographs. In these cases it is the opinion of the forensic dentists who give evidence as expert witnesses, and the responses they give under cross-examination, that convince a jury of a suspect's guilt or innocence.

**SHOULDER BITE ▼**
*In leaning over his victim's shoulder and biting her, a rapist left this bite mark, which was distinct and individual enough to help convict him of the attack.*

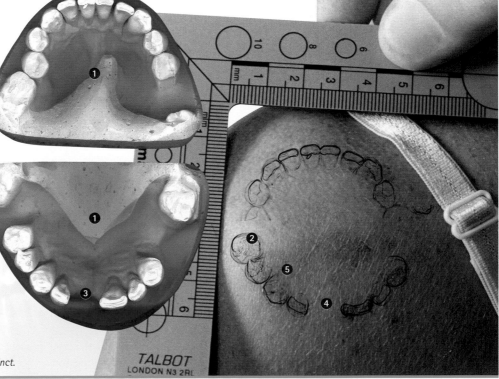

## BITE MARK ANALYSIS

① *Upside-down cast of upper and lower jaw taken from the suspect.*

② *Print of jaw cast on transparent overlay matches bite mark.*

③ *Noticeable gap in upper front teeth.*

④ *Gap in bite mark matches cast.*

⑤ *Bruising of victim makes marks indistinct.*

TALBOT
LONDON N3 2RL

# Forensic anthropology

Skeletons are crime's mute witnesses, and it is the job of the forensic anthropologist to make dry bones talk. By careful examination, including measurement and comparison, specialists can determine the age, gender, stature, and ethnicity of human remains. Often the bones can reveal much more, including medical history and manner of death.

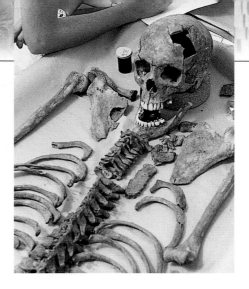

**A VIOLENT DEATH ▲**
*The hole in the skull suggests blunt-force injury as a cause of death. These are the remains of someone murdered during Argentina's military rule, 1976–83.*

When bones are discovered—either by chance or because they are unearthed in a police investigation—it is the job of the forensic anthropologist to help identify the victim, and determine whether the death was crime-related. The first step is to find out whether the bones are human. This sounds strange, but bones of certain animals can resemble a range of human bones. For example, a horse's tail bones look similar to human finger bones.

### Age at time of death
Next, the age of the victim is assessed by examining the growth and decay of certain bones. Emerging teeth, for example, can help determine the age of a child's skeleton, from the first milk teeth up to about age 18, when wisdom teeth often appear.

Throughout the teenage years, children's bones become denser and bigger, uniting in a process called "ossification." The 800 centers of ossification in the body are among the best guides to the age of a youngster's skeleton. For example, by age six, two bony plates called epiphyses have formed at either end of the outer forearm (radius). By up to age 17 for males and 20 for females, the lower epiphysis and radius have fused. The upper epiphysis and radius fuse soon after.

The last of the bones to finish growing is the collarbone, at up to 28 years of age.

In the skeletons of older people the anthropologist looks for degeneration. Tiny spikes of bone begin to appear around the edges of the vertebrae; the teeth wear down; and joints may show signs of arthritis. All this deterioration increases with age.

### Marks of gender
To distinguish male from female anthropologists look first at the skull and hips. Clues to sex are at three points on the skull: the ridge above the eyes, a bone

### READING THE BONES

① *Facial injuries like this are strongly suggestive of brutal homicide.*

② *The thigh bone (femur) is the longest bone in the body, and gives a good indication of body height.*

③ *The pelvis can determine sex even when damaged or incomplete.*

④ *Crushed vertebrae can indicate osteoporosis—a condition that mainly affects older women.*

**EXAMINATION OF A CZAR**
*The exhumed bones of the last Russian czar, Nicholas II, his wife the czarina, and her chambermaid, Anna Demidova, are examined in a Russian forensics lab in 1998.*

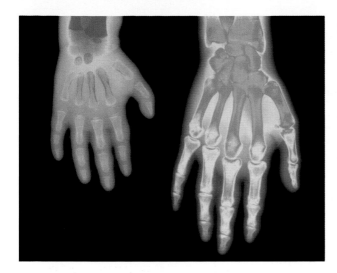

◄ **AGE DETERMINATION**
*These hand X-rays from a three-year-old and an adult show the process of ossification. Wide spaces of cartilage in the child's hand have been replaced by bone in the adult's.*

## DETERMINING ETHNICITY

The racial origins of a body are a crucial clue in establishing identity. It is the skull that provides this information. When studying a skull to determine ethnicity, anthropologists look for some of these key features:

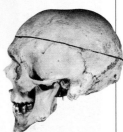

**MONGOLOID ►**
*People of Asian descent have long skulls, broad and conspicuously flat faces, and projecting cheekbones. The eye sockets are rounded, and the nose bridge is moderately low with straight sides.*

**NEGROID ►**
*Afro-Caribbean skulls are recognizable by the wide nose opening. Teeth are larger than other races, and the skull tends to be long and narrow. Cheekbones project moderately.*

**CAUCASOID ►**
*The skulls of white people are generally high and wide in appearance. The cheekbones do not project, nor does the jaw—it falls behind a line dropped vertically from the forehead.*

below the ear, and the occiput—the bone at the lower back of the skull. The latter two are muscle attachment sites, and all are more prominent in men.

The difference in the hips is clear even to laypeople: men's are substantially narrower, but there are more subtle differences as well, as shown below.

If the skeleton includes neither hips nor skull, establishing sex is much more difficult. Anthropologists are forced to rely on the difference in size and strength between men and women. In skeletons of males, the points on the bones to which muscles are attached are more pronounced, indicating greater strength.

## How tall?

The most straightforward way of estimating height is to assemble the skeleton, or total the length of the relevant bones. Adding 4 in (10–11 cm) accounts for the missing connective tissue in adults—more for children, depending on age. If the skeleton is incomplete, individual bones are a guide to stature. The longer the bone, the better the estimate, so the thigh bone (femur) is usually measured first. Most people measure two-and-two-thirds times their femur length, though the precise ratios depend on race and sex.

## Diseases and injury in life

In life, some medical conditions, including birth defects such as spina bifida, a few infectious diseases, inadequate diet, and cancers, can damage the bones. However, only chronic cases have any noticeable impact on the skeleton. This is not true of injury: when broken bones heal, the mending process is clearly visible, so a healed fracture can help confirm identity.

Work can leave clues, too: occupational arthritis causes easily visible changes to the affected joints.

**ARTHRITIC ELBOW ▼**
*The elbow joint of a worker who operated a hammer drill shows signs of arthritis in this X-ray. The bone ends, normally smooth, have been roughened by the constant shock of the pneumatic tool.*

**BUILT FOR BABIES**
*Because women's pelvises are built to accommodate babies, they are visibly wider than men's. The female sacrum—the wedge-shaped bone consisting of five fused vertebrae—is wider too, and the cavity is roomier.*

*Male pelvis*

*Sacrum*

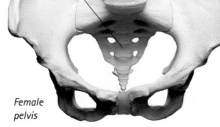
*Female pelvis*

## Cause of death

The skeletons of people who died violently frequently bear the marks of the weapon that killed them: bullets leave characteristic holes, and sharp-edged weapons cut and chip the bone. Fractures also suggest violence. The challenge for the anthropologist is to distinguish between fractures that occurred before and after death. There are clues: dry bone breaks in a different way from live bone, and signs of early healing at the edge of a fracture indicate injuries in life.

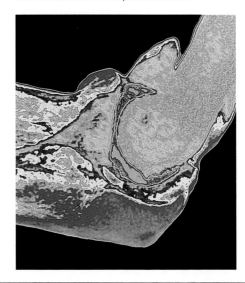

# Facial reconstruction in clay

To create a recognizable likeness from nothing but the bare skull of an unknown crime victim demands a rare combination of skills. To keep their creations accurate, sculptors need the objectivity of the forensic anthropologist. But to create a resemblance of a living person also requires the imaginative flair of an artist.

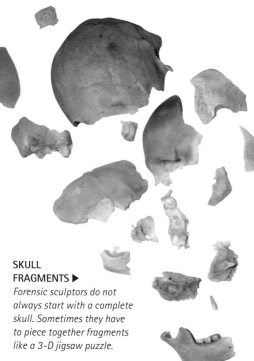

**SKULL FRAGMENTS ▶**

*Forensic sculptors do not always start with a complete skull. Sometimes they have to piece together fragments like a 3-D jigsaw puzzle.*

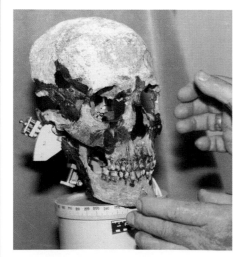

**MAKING HEADWAY ▲**

*If enough skull fragments remain, they can be built into a reasonably complete skull. This skull can then be cast and used as a basis for facial reconstruction.*

When skin and muscles decay from a human head, all semblance of character disappears with them. Few of us can look beyond the hollow eye sockets and rictus grin and make the imaginative leap that is necessary to picture a living face. Yet it is the skull that gives the face form and structure, and using its contours as a starting point, forensic sculptors use clay to build up a likeness that can be uncannily realistic.

## Pegs and strips

The most common reconstruction method relies on knowledge of the depth of the tissue that overlays every part of a skull. This technique has been dubbed morphometric, from the Greek words for "form" and "measure." It was pioneered in the United States, so it is also known as the American method. Researchers began measuring flesh depth at the end of the 19th century, though the data they compiled was not used for the purposes of forensic reconstruction until around the 1930s.

Initially, the measurements were taken during the dissection of corpses, but recently ultrasound scanning techniques have allowed the measurement of soft tissue depths from living subjects.

Sculptors generally work from between 20 and 35 anatomical landmarks—key tissue depths. Their locations are scattered around the face, but are most densely concentrated around the mouth and between the eyes. Measurements are available for different sexes, ages, and ethnic groups, and for faces that range from emaciated to obese.

Reconstruction starts with depth indicators—typically small pegs. Fixed

**Mikhail Gerasimov 1907–1970**

Systematic forensic facial reconstruction began with the work of Russian anthropologist Mikhail Gerasimov. Working at Moscow's Third Medical University College, he measured the tissue depth on the faces of cadavers awaiting dissection there. When he had enough information, he made his first attempts at reconstruction. As a scientific technical assistant at Irkutsk Museum in the late 1920s, he recreated faces from the fossil skulls of early humans. His reconstructions first helped to solve a murder case in 1939, when human bones were found near Leningrad, Russia. However, the work for which he became famous was the facial reconstruction not of a crime victim, but of Tamerlane, the Mongol king.

to the skull (or to a cast of it) at each landmark, these indicate the average flesh depth. Sculptors then apply strips of clay between the pegs. The strips are graded in thickness to match the height of the pegs. Once these strips are in place, clay fills the gaps between them, and the sculptor starts on the eyes, nose, mouth, ears, chin, and jowls.

These are the aspects of the face that give an individual character, but unfortunately they are the features that disappear rapidly as a body decomposes. Though sculptors need experience and judgment to reconstruct them, they also rely on rules of thumb.

## Ahead by a nose

The width of the nose, for example, is roughly the same as the distance between the inner corners of the eyes. The corners of the mouth lie directly below the inner borders of the iris, and lie over the back edge of the canine teeth. Also, ears roughly equal the nose in length—though older people have proportionately longer ears.

Once these features are complete, the sculptor adds finishing touches, and smooths the clay to make it resemble skin, before making a mold from the head in plaster of Paris and silicone rubber. A cast made from this can be painted to resemble a living face, to aid identification.

## Building muscle

Not all sculptors work this way. Some use the Russian method, also known as morphoscopic, from the Greek words meaning "form" and "looking at." This approach is guided not by tissue depth measurements, but by the form of the skull itself. For example, the cheek's chewing muscles are fixed to horizontal arches of bone at the sides of the head just in front of the ears. The shape and size of these bones directly affect the shape of the attached muscles.

Using features like these, sculptors build up the face muscle by muscle, shaping each one from clay before fixing it into place on the skull. The final step is then to cover the clay "muscles" with a skin of clay. In other respects, reconstruction is similar to the morphometric technique.

Both approaches have merits. Advocates of the first system, based on average measurement of flesh depth, argue that it is more objective and scientific. But morphoscopic sculptors claim average measurements are a poor starting point because a face's character relies on features that are different from the average, such as a big nose or protruding ears.

## Approximate likeness

Whichever approach is used, there are limits to the accuracy of facial reconstruction. Sculptors can only guess at hairstyles, and cannot simulate the animated expressions that bring a face to life. However, a perfect likeness is not always necessary. A facial reconstruction is a success if it jogs someone's memory, or—by excluding people whose faces do not resemble the clay model—narrows down a search.

**◄ RICHARD NEAVE**
*Like Gerasimov, Richard Neave worked with archeological remains before beginning forensic reconstruction. He is shown here working on Karen Price's face.*

**◄ DEPTH PEGS**
*To identify a young girl whose skeleton was unearthed in Wales in 1989, medical illustrator Richard Neave begins reconstruction by fixing wooden pegs to a cast.*

**◄ JAW MUSCLES**
*He next fleshes out the temples and neck with clay "muscles," using the pegs as a guide to the depth at each landmark.*

**FULL FACE ►**
*Once the underlying tissue has been completely remodeled, the pegs disappear from view, and it only remains to give the model a young woman's complexion.*

**STRIKING RESEMBLANCE ▼**
*The completed face was so lifelike that the young girl was recognized as Karen Price by her social worker. Two men were later charged with her murder.*

# Computer facial reconstruction

Slowly turning on a computer screen, a reconstructed face seems eerily lifelike. Forensic scientists and computer programmers cooperate to build these digital recreations of crime victims. To achieve the extraordinary realism, they "wrap" computer tomography (CT) scans and photographs of the living around the skulls of the dead.

To recreate faces from skulls using clay requires great artistic skill. To do the same thing on a computer screen is equally skillful, but in a different way. The programmer or technician works in a more abstract medium, indirectly manipulating data to produce a convincing likeness.

### Scanning the skull

Though there is no standard method of reconstruction, the initial data always comes from a 3-D scan of the skull itself.

This technique is nondestructive, so the original skull can be used where available, rather than a plaster cast. Typically the skull rotates on a turntable, while a laser scanner illuminates a narrow vertical strip. Mirrors on either side of the turntable reflect images of the illuminated area to sensors. An analysis of the data that they produce

allows the controlling program to calculate the distance of each point on the skull from the axis of rotation—and thus create a digital model of the skull that can be freely rotated on screen.

### From skull to face

To put flesh on the bones, most computer reconstruction techniques use data captured from computer tomography (CT) scans of living people. Unlike X-rays, which effectively show the shadows cast by bones, CT scans record both hard and

---

**CT SKULL SCAN ▼**
*Overlapping the CT scan (colored blue) with the victim's skull (colored red) shows how much the CT scan must be "warped" to match the skull exactly.*

**◀ SPINNING SKULL**
*The laser scanner is similar to those used to build digital models of faces for plastic surgery, or for burn masks. A powerful computer workstation captures the data.*

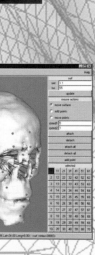
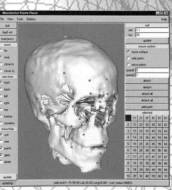

**ADDING LANDMARK PEGS ▲**
*Software drops the standard facial reconstruction "landmarks" roughly into position on the skull, and their positions are carefully fine-tuned by the operator.*

**WARPING THE CT SCAN ▲**
*The process of warping the CT scan, with its corresponding soft tissue, onto the victim's skull may take several attempts. Regions colored purple show where the warped CT scan exactly matches the skull.*

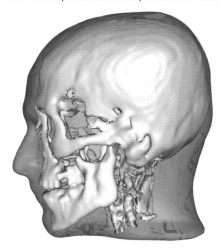

**TISSUE DEPTH ▲**
*Once the CT scan has been successfully warped, the CT scan's soft tissue is added. This "skin" (blue) envelops the victim's skull (white) precisely.*

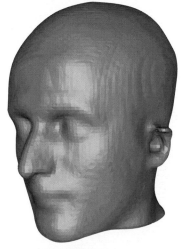

**RECONSTRUCTED HEAD ▲**
*At this stage a computer visualization of the head without a realistic skin color or texture resembles a traditionally sculpted reconstruction in blue clay.*

soft tissues (both bones and flesh) in three dimensions rather than two. So CT scan data files include both the shape of the skull and the depth of the overlying tissue.

To help choose an appropriate CT scan, forensic anthropologists must use the skull and other remains to estimate the age and race of the subject. Any clues to the subject's build—such as the size of clothing found with a corpse—can help, too, by allowing tissue depth adjustment to account for obesity or emaciation.

By merging the two scans, the CT head is superimposed on to the digital model of the skull (see main image). At this stage, the two skulls are different shapes, so the next step is to "warp" (distort) the CT in a controlled way so that corresponding landmarks on the two skulls match exactly. As the CT skull is stretched and squashed to make it fit, its facial tissue is also distorted, creating a face shape that approximates that of the victim.

## Hair and skin

Because CT scans penetrate human tissue, they do not record superficial detail. So at this stage, the reconstruction resembles a plaster cast of the victim's head. To make it look lifelike, textures and colors of human skin, eyes, and hair must be added. To do this, technicians "borrow" the appearance of a living individual and digitally paint it on to the model.

To produce a 3-D rendering, a "color map" of the whole head is needed. This is usually done by photographing a full-face and both profiles of someone whose age, race, and build match the victim. Software merges these three views into a continuous strip that is rendered on to the computer model to complete the reconstruction.

The result can be viewed and rotated on screen, and can be distributed in one of a number of standard viewing formats, such as virtual reality markup language (VRML) or Quicktime VR.

Though computer reconstruction can look more lifelike than a face created in clay, it must be remembered that both methods share the same limitations. In particular, the shapes of the nose, mouth, ears, and eyes are largely guesswork. However, the ability to create views of the victim's face under varying lighting conditions, and from virtually any angle, makes this method of reconstruction especially vivid.

In the future, computer animation techniques may be applied to the facial reconstructions to manipulate the features, raising the possibility that these models could smile, laugh, or talk on screen.

**◄ ADDING THE FACE**
*Photographing a living face in flat lighting provides the skin detail that "wraps" the finished model. The computer creates the realistic highlights and shadows.*

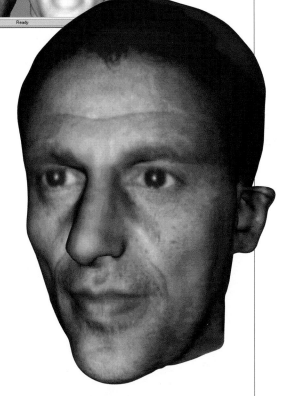

**FINISHING TOUCHES ▲**
*Eyes—added from a library—have a lifelike shine. Hair is kept as simple as possible unless there is evidence to suggest how the victim wore it.*

# Blood analysis

By defining identity in a single drop, blood and other bodily fluids can link a suspect to a victim, a crime scene, or a weapon in a potentially undeniable chain of proof. Though DNA profiling is the best-known procedure for establishing such an incriminating link, it is simply the most exacting test of the much wider discipline of forensic serology.

If DNA analysis can identify with near-certainty whether or not a sample came from a particular individual, why bother with less precise tests? The answer is simple. DNA testing is still relatively slow and expensive. Less sophisticated tests are cheap and almost instantaneous, and some are so straightforward they can be carried out at the crime scene, with enormous cost and efficiency benefits.

## Is it actually blood?

Whenever a suspicious-looking stain is found at the crime scene, investigators first carry out a simple presumptive test—one that gives reasonable grounds for supposing that the sample is blood if the result is positive. Most tests are solutions that change color when they come into contact with either hemoglobin or a blood enzyme called peroxidase. One common presumptive test is a luminol spray (see p. 84), which makes blood residues glow in total darkness. Luminol is also sensitive enough to reveal traces of scrubbed-away blood.

These presumptive tests are not absolutely specific for blood: horseradish and potato contain the same enzyme, so a spilled shrimp cocktail would test positive.

## Is it human blood?

The most common test for confirming that a sample is blood also establishes whether it is human. German biologist Paul Uhlenhuth devised the test in 1901. He took protein from a chicken egg, and injected it into a rabbit. The rabbit's immune system produced antibodies to protect it against the chicken antigens. (An antigen is a toxin or enzyme capable

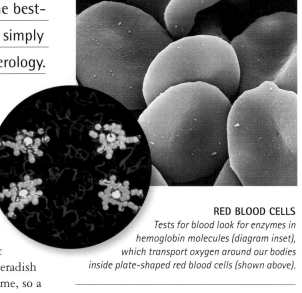

**RED BLOOD CELLS**
*Tests for blood look for enzymes in hemoglobin molecules (diagram inset), which transport oxygen around our bodies inside plate-shaped red blood cells (shown above).*

of stimulating an immune response.) When Uhlenhuth mixed the rabbit's blood with egg white, the antibodies in the blood reacted with antigens in the egg, making it separate in a cloudy deposit, which he called precipitin. Injecting human cells into the rabbit made the test specific to humans.

As used in today's forensic labs, the precipitin test is more complex. Serologists

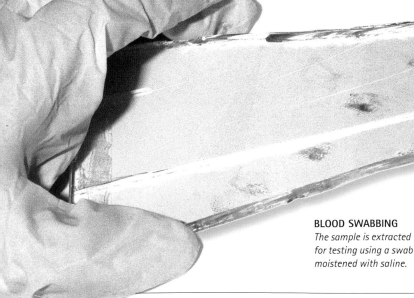

**BLOOD SWABBING**
*The sample is extracted for testing using a swab moistened with saline.*

put the sample and the testing solution containing antibodies into wells on a gel-covered glass plate, and the two diffuse toward each other. If the sample is human blood, it will contain appropriate antigens, and where the two solutions meet on the plate, a distinctive precipitin band forms. Applying a voltage turns the test into electrophoresis (see p. 60), driving antigen and antibody together to hasten the result.

The recent development of monoclonal (synthetic) antibodies has made possible a field test that provides immediate confirmation that a sample is human blood.

## Whose blood is it?

Human blood contains around 100 different antigens, but not every individual has them all. By determining which are present, it is possible to show whether blood found at the crime scene might have come from a suspect. Testing for every antigen is possible, but it would hardly be practical. Instead, serologists check for just a few. There are more than a dozen such blood-typing systems in use, but by far the most common is the ABO system, which also tests for transfusion compatibility between donor and recipient. The system is explained in detail in the box below.

## Other fluids

Blood is not the only bodily fluid tested in the serology lab. Investigators also send semen, saliva, urine, vaginal secretions, and excrement. DNA extracted from some of these may prove a match between a suspect and a crime scene sample. However, before running a DNA test serologists first confirm that what is actually on the swab corresponds to what is on the evidence label.

In rape cases, they often need to verify that a swab or stain contains semen. Presumptive color-change field tests show the presence of several components of semen—seminal acid phosphatase (SAP), spermine, and choline. Serologists confirm the test by using a microscope to spot sperms, though semen will not contain any if a rapist has had a vasectomy or is sterile. The most common alternative is to test for a protein, P30, that is produced by the prostate, using an antigen/antibody test that is similar to the precipitin test.

**Karl Landsteiner 1868–1943**

Working in Vienna, Austria, immunologist and pathologist Karl Landsteiner demonstrated in 1901 that there were at least three types of human blood, which he called A, B, and O, distinguished by the presence of antigens on the red cells. The year after, he identified AB. Landsteiner received the Nobel Prize in Physiology or Medicine for his discovery and for his development of the ABO system of blood typing, which made blood transfusion a safe practice.

## TESTING FOR BLOOD TYPE

The ABO blood-typing system checks for two antigens, A and B, on the surface of red blood cells. The test usually uses two solutions, containing antibodies to either type A or type B antigens. The first makes blood containing A antigens clump together, thus identifying A and AB groups. The second reacts the same way to B antigens, identifying AB and B groups. O blood clumps with neither. This example (right) includes a third solution that reacts with both A and B. (These substances have been colored for easier distinction.)

Blood groups are not distributed evenly: 45% of white Americans, for example, are O, 41% A, 10% B, and 4% AB. These proportions perhaps suggest that blood typing is futile: most white suspects will be either O or A. However, the test is quick and cheap, and if suspect and crime scene samples do not match, further investigation is pointless.

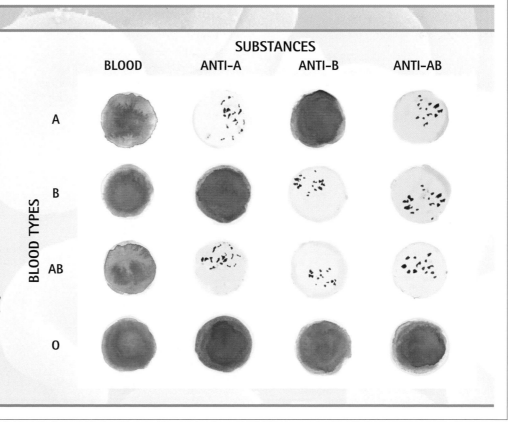

# DNA analysis

Coiled inside the nucleus of most of our cells is a 6-ft (2-m) long spiral. Parts of it encode who we are, and what we look like. The remainder contains patterns that repeat a unique number of times for each individual. The ability to count these "stutters" has revolutionized crime investigation.

**◄ DNA**

*The double helix, or spiraling spiral, shape of the DNA strand makes it very compact. The entire 6-ft (2-m) length fits inside the minute nucleus of a cell.*

This crucial spiral is deoxyribonucleic acid, or DNA. Portions of this long molecule form our genes, or the "genetic code," from which all our characteristics are derived. The structure of DNA is like a curled-up, spiraling ladder with three billion rungs. The rungs are pairs of simple organic chemicals called "bases." There are four kinds of bases (see box below), and the exact order in which they occur along a strand of DNA is different in every individual, except identical twins. This unique character of our DNA is the main reason why it is such an important tool for identifying individuals. It is also readily available—it exists in every living cell that has a nucleus, including hair roots and bone marrow—and only tiny amounts are needed for analysis.

## Crucial "junk" DNA

By examining carefully selected sections of DNA taken from a crime scene, we can compare them to a sample taken from a suspect. A match strongly suggests that the suspect was the source of the DNA found at the crime scene. DNA can also be used to help identify a victim. We

*In this graphic representation of DNA, (I) marks the start of the repeated section. The sequence between (I) and (II) is repeated many times as the strand spirals toward us.*

inherit half our DNA from each parent, so a part match from a missing person's parent can demonstrate a blood relationship to an otherwise unidentified body.

Only a small portion of our DNA actually provides the blueprint for who we are and what we look like. The remainder, so-called "junk" DNA, seems to perform no useful function that we know of. But it is this "junk" DNA that is crucial for identification purposes. This is because much of it consists of short sequences of base pairs that repeat end to end, called "short tandem repeats" (STRs). Though these sequences occur in everybody's DNA, the number of times they repeat varies dramatically between individuals. Counting the repetitions of a number of different sequences (up to thirteen) allows us to identify people uniquely. Locating the repetitions and separating them for analysis is possible because on either side of them there are always characteristic sequences of base pairs that are the same in everybody's DNA.

**James Watson b. 1928 and Francis Crick b. 1916**

## KEY:

*Four kinds of bases make up the DNA "ladder." Two of them, adenine (A) and guanine (G), are purines; the other two, cytosine (C) and thymine (T), are pyrimidines. Bases always occur in pairs of purine and pyrimidine bonded together, A with T, and G with C.*

G GUANINE
T THYMINE
C CYTOSINE
A ADENINE

**ADDING PRIMER ▲**
*PCR starts with the addition of primers to the samples of DNA in plastic reaction tubes. These are then heated and cooled in a thermal cycler.*

◀ **COLORED SPIRALS**
*Attached to each primer is a different colored fluorescent dye. Because the primer has bonded to the DNA, it makes the different sequences easy to recognize at the next step.*

## Extraction

Analysis begins with extraction of the DNA from the sample. This is usually done using a chloroform and phenol mixture, or a salt solution that separates DNA from the other material in the cell nucleus. This extraction process does not usually produce enough DNA for analysis, so the next step is to artificially increase the quantity of DNA in the sample using a technique called polymerase chain reaction (PCR).

## Amplification

Polymerase is an enzyme in our cells that can copy or repair DNA. The "ladder" of DNA splits apart at the middle of each "rung" to create two strands. Since each base can only combine with a complementary base, each strand of DNA forms a template for its other, now missing, part. The polymerase enzyme works down each strand and adds the complementary bases as it goes, and thus reconstructs each strand into a complete, double-stranded DNA molecule.

PCR reproduces this process of synthesis in a test tube. Technicians mix the DNA sample with buffer (salt water), polymerase, the four bases, and primers. Primers are short, ready-made fragments of DNA that attach to either side of a chosen

sequence. Different primers find different repeating sequences of base pairs—so as to analyze up to thirteen STRs.

Heating this mixture to just below the boiling point of water "unzips" the two strands of DNA. When the solution cools, the primers bond to the start and end of the target sequences. Warming the mixture allows the polymerase to reconstruct the second, complementary strand of DNA between the primers. The process is repeated 25–40 times. Each cycle replicates the target portions—those containing the short tandem repeats—while leaving the remainder of the DNA unchanged.

PCR can increase the size of a DNA sample millions of times over. This makes it possible to analyze samples as small as a couple of nanograms of blood—roughly one forty-millionth of a drop.

## Analyzing the sample

The product of PCR is a mass of DNA fragments. Their lengths vary according to the number of times the chosen sequences of base pairs are repeated. Each sequence will have two lengths, one from each of the parents. To analyze them, the fragments are sorted out using the process of electrophoresis—a kind of electrical race. DNA has a negative electrical charge, and is pulled toward a positive

electrode, just as north and south poles on magnets attract each other.

In electrophoresis, the movement of the fragments is artificially slowed by forcing them to travel through a stiff jelly, or down a very narrow tube. The smallest bits speed along, but longer pieces move more slowly, so the process neatly ranks the DNA fragments according to length.

A race is pointless if you cannot tell who has won, so each bit of DNA must have a unique marking. The primers added during the PCR "amplification" phase provide this. Each primer is tagged with a different fluorescent dye.

In the most automated form of DNA analysis, a powerful electric charge drives the DNA fragments along a tube. At its end, they move between a laser and a color-sensitive detector that is connected to a computer. The laser beam makes each of the dyed fragments fluoresce with its primer color. The detector captures the flashes of light, and software plots the fluorescence as peaks on a graph.

To evaluate the test results, the peaks from the suspect's sample are simply compared with those from the crime scene. However, in the absence of other evidence, an exactly matching profile does not amount to proof of guilt, as you can read on the next page.

**THE FINISHING LINE**
*A high voltage drives the fragments of DNA along a capillary tube and past a photodetector, producing characteristic peaks (left) for comparison on a computer screen. Running a parallel control sample containing fragments of known length makes it possible to determine how many repeats are in the test samples.*

# DNA matching

Hyped as a "magic bullet" for solving crime, DNA analysis has not disappointed. Samples taken from suspects are often compared with DNA databases to solve crimes committed years—sometimes decades—earlier. However, DNA matching has not escaped criticism, and convicting on DNA evidence alone makes for questionable justice.

In December 2000, Stephen Snowden was arrested for stealing a bottle of whiskey. Police swabbed his cheek for DNA and analyzed it. When they ran a routine comparison with a computer database of DNA taken from the scenes of unsolved crimes, they found a surprising match. The man they thought was just a petty criminal was actually a rapist. Ten years earlier he had attacked a woman whose car had broken down on a remote country road. Snowden received a 12-year jail sentence for the vicious assault.

## Building databases

As Snowden's conviction demonstrated, the power of a DNA database stems from the ease with which it can be searched. A DNA profile encodes the identity of an individual in a series of digits no longer than four telephone numbers. Comparing such numbers to match criminal and crime-scene samples is straightforward and quick.

The first DNA databases were set up in the US in the 1980s, with the FBI's combined DNA index system (CODIS) now integrating the data nationally. Although advocates of DNA profiling argue that the innocent have nothing to fear from DNA databases, they do not enjoy universal support. Many people dispute the collecting and storing of the data, fearing that it erodes civil liberties. In addition, the validity of DNA evidence itself is constantly questioned in court due to the possibility of contamination—despite stringent precautions to prevent this.

**◄ COMPUTER MATCHING**
*DNA databases all maintain at least two indexes: one for crime-scene DNA and one for offenders. Some countries also store missing persons' DNA.*

**INDIVIDUALS IN A CROWD ▼**
*There is just a 200 billion:1 chance that the DNA of two randomly chosen individuals will match perfectly when 13 different sequences are counted.*

**MATCHING ▼**
*Modern DNA scanners make it easy to compare DNA by plotting the short tandem repeats as peaks on a graph (see p. 60). This graphical representation shows the basic principle of how the samples are matched. There would be up to 13 different sequences (colors) to compare for each sample in a real-life case.*

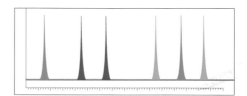

**CRIME-SCENE SAMPLE ▲**
*A sperm stain found at a rape scene contains the assailant's DNA, which can be used for comparison.*

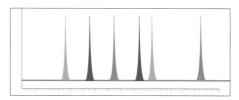

**VICTIM ▲**
*Peaks in the crime-scene sample that match peaks in the victim's DNA profile can be ignored.*

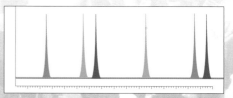

**SUSPECT 1 (NO MATCH) ▲**
*Few of the peaks in this profile of an innocent suspect coincide with the peaks of the crime-scene sample.*

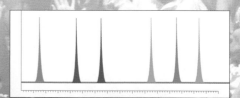

**SUSPECT 2 (MATCH) ▲**
*The profile of the suspect subsequently found guilty is an accurate match with the crime-scene sample.*

## MITOCHONDRIAL DNA

Most DNA analysis uses nuclear DNA, but this is not always present in a crime-scene sample, and deteriorates rapidly. An alternative is to analyze DNA from another part of the cell: the mitochondrion. Unlike nuclear DNA, where 50% is inherited from each parent, mitochondrial DNA (mtDNA) is passed on intact from just the mother, which makes it ideal for tracing ancestry. It is also more resistant to decay, surviving for many centuries in bone material. For these reasons, mtDNA was used in 1993 to analyze the suspected remains of Nicholas II. The last czar of Russia, Nicholas was executed along with his family by revolutionaries following the 1917 revolution that brought communist rule to the country. If the bones were genuine, mtDNA extracted from them would be similar to that of a direct descendant of the czar's family. Forensic scientists confirmed the identification by comparison with the mtDNA of Prince Philip (see below).

**CZAR'S DESCENDANT ▶**
*Prince Philip, husband of Queen Elizabeth II of England, is a direct descendant of the czar's sister-in-law.*

## Will it stand up in court?

There are also concerns about the interpretation of DNA evidence in court, after guilty verdicts that relied heavily on it have been overturned on appeal. The so-called "prosecutor's fallacy" formed the grounds for many of these appeals. To understand this, imagine a case in which investigators find a stain at the scene of the crime in a country with a population of 10 million. DNA analysis suggests that the profiles of just 1% of the population would match the crime-scene sample. Police arrest a suspect, and a DNA test reveals a perfect match with the stain found at the scene. At the trial, the prosecution argues that, since only 1% of the population share the same DNA profile, there is just a 100:1 chance that the prisoner is innocent. But the defense successfully argues that this is a fallacy, and is true only if there is a presumption of guilt. If 1% of a population of 10 million share the same DNA profile, then there are 99,999 others who could be placed at the crime scene. If there is a presumption of innocence, then the odds are nearly 100,000:1 against the accused man being the man at the crime scene.

This theoretical example illustrates the danger of relying too heavily on DNA evidence. Effectively, a closely matching DNA profile multiplies the suspicion of guilt. If there is enough corroborating evidence, then a DNA match makes the prosecution case very compelling indeed. But if there is little or no other evidence, then matching DNA profiles prove little.

## The future of DNA analysis

Identifying suspects potentially represents a small part of the utility of DNA analysis in the context of crime investigation. Scientists completed the task of sequencing the human genome in 2001, and subsequent analysis is revealing which parts of it are responsible for inherited traits. For example, DNA analysis of a crime-scene sample can already reveal whether or not a criminal has red hair. Just 6% of the British population have red hair, so this drastically narrows a search if a UK crime-scene sample is from a redhead. Many geneticists believe that further analysis will enable them to predict many more aspects of physical appearance, including race and height. The possibility of building a suspect's photofit picture from a single drop of blood is still a fantasy, but it is clear that the value of DNA analysis will continue to grow as researchers further unravel the genetic code.

## ALEC JEFFREYS

DNA fingerprinting was the discovery of British geneticist Alec Jeffreys in 1984. The idea came to him in "a Eureka moment" one fall morning. By the afternoon he had worked out how to apply it forensically. The method was first used—to acquit a suspect—the following year.

Alec Jeffreys
b. 1950

# Dingo attack or murder?

Tragedy struck a family camping trip in Australia's barren outback when a dingo—a wild dog—snatched nine-week-old Azaria from a tent. Public sympathy turned to anger when the police accused Lindy Chamberlain of her baby's murder after finding traces of blood on a pair of scissors and in the family car.

"A dingo has my baby!" Lindy Chamberlain's panic-stricken scream sent a surge of alarm through the outback campsite. It just didn't seem possible. Everything was so normal. With hundreds of other Australians, Michael and Lindy Chamberlain were camping at the site, in August 1980, to visit nearby Uluru. They were cooking dinner when, at around eight o'clock, they heard a cry from the tent where their four-year-old son and baby daughter were sleeping. Lindy spotted a dingo near the tent and broke into a run. Only as she got inside did she realize with horror that her daughter had disappeared. There was

**ACCUSED OF INFANTICIDE ▲**
*After she had served six years in prison, Lindy's conviction was quashed in September 1988, and she eventually received $765,000 compensation.*

**ULURU ▼**
*Revered by Aboriginal Australians for its unique place in their mythology, Uluru or Ayers Rock attracts half a million tourists every year.*

a pool of blood on the floor of the tent. Soon, the police arrived and organized a search. Aboriginal trackers followed the dingo's trail until its prints disappeared, but they didn't find Azaria. At eleven o'clock the distraught Chamberlains left the campsite and moved to a motel.

## The police make up their minds
The next morning a local police officer interviewed them. He took away several bloodstained items, but left many more. Later the same day a police inspector flew in from Alice Springs. Lindy's description of the previous night's events made him suspicious— dingoes just didn't take children. Also, how far could a dingo carry a 10-lb (4.5-kg) baby?

A week passed with no further leads, but then a tourist found Azaria's romper and undershirt at a dingo lair close to Uluru. Again, the police response was desultory. They did not seal the scene, or conduct a thorough examination of the clothes.

The lack of a systematic evaluation of the crime scene and the potential evidence it contained, together with a few persuasive clues, led police to believe Lindy was lying. There were no bite marks or dingo saliva on Azaria's romper, but there were cuts and bloodstains. The baby's bootees were still tied in the feet of the romper, but her undershirt was, inexplicably, inside out.

**JAWS OF DEATH ▼**
*Canine expert witnesses testifying against Lindy based their evidence mainly on studies of domestic dogs; none knew anything about the bites of wild dingoes.*

## The inquest verdict
In February 1981 the police expressed their doubts at an inquest into Azaria's death, but the coroner dismissed their suspicions, and was highly critical of police procedures. He concluded that a

dingo had indeed taken baby Azaria. With the inquest ended, Michael and Lindy believed they could at last get over the shock of losing their third child, and get on with their lives.

But the Australian media had different ideas. The "Dingo Baby" story was sensational, and the press had fed the controversy to boost sales. Journalists focused on the fact that the family were Seventh-Day Adventists, which led to bigoted and fanciful rumors. It was even suggested that Azaria was killed in a religious ritual. Nor were the police satisfied. Seven months after the inquest verdict, they returned to the Chamberlains' home, with a search warrant. They told Lindy they had new evidence. Further forensic examination of Azaria's clothes had revealed a bloody print in the shape of a woman's hand.

## The second inquest

More dramatic evidence came out during the second inquest. A forensic biologist had examined stains in the Chamberlains' car, and on a pair of scissors found there. She concluded that the marks were the blood of a baby. Other expert witnesses testified that the pattern of stains and cuts on Azaria's clothing looked like scissor stabs, not dog bites. The police trap was starting to close around the Chamberlains.

It snapped shut on February 2, 1982, when the coroner concluded that Lindy Chamberlain had killed her baby in the car with a pair of scissors. Lindy was charged with murder.

## The trial

At her trial the police presented a closer analysis of the same evidence that they had given to the coroner, and put forward more expert witnesses. Despite evidence that Lindy was a caring mother who had no motive to kill, the jury found her guilty. She was sentenced to life. When two appeals failed, Lindy Chamberlain faced many years of imprisonment.

## Freedom

Then, in February 1986, Azaria's jacket was found part-buried at Uluru. Five days later, Lindy was released, and the

following year a Royal Commission completely exonerated her. They decided that "bloodstains" in the car weren't blood at all—they were probably sound-absorbing material sprayed in by the car's manufacturer—and concluded that the bloodstains and marks on the romper were consistent with a dingo attack after all. The Commission's report censured the police for prejudice and bias, for burying expert evidence that didn't fit the case, for failing to preserve evidence, and for inadequate forensic work.

**AZARIA'S JACKET ▶**
*Azaria's bloodstained jacket acted as a catalyst for Lindy Chamberlain's release from prison, even though its discovery added little to the weight of evidence pointing to her innocence.*

**LINDY AND MICHAEL ▼**
*The stress of the case, and Lindy's imprisonment, eventually ended her marriage to Seventh-Day Adventist minister Michael, who was charged as an accessory to the murder.*

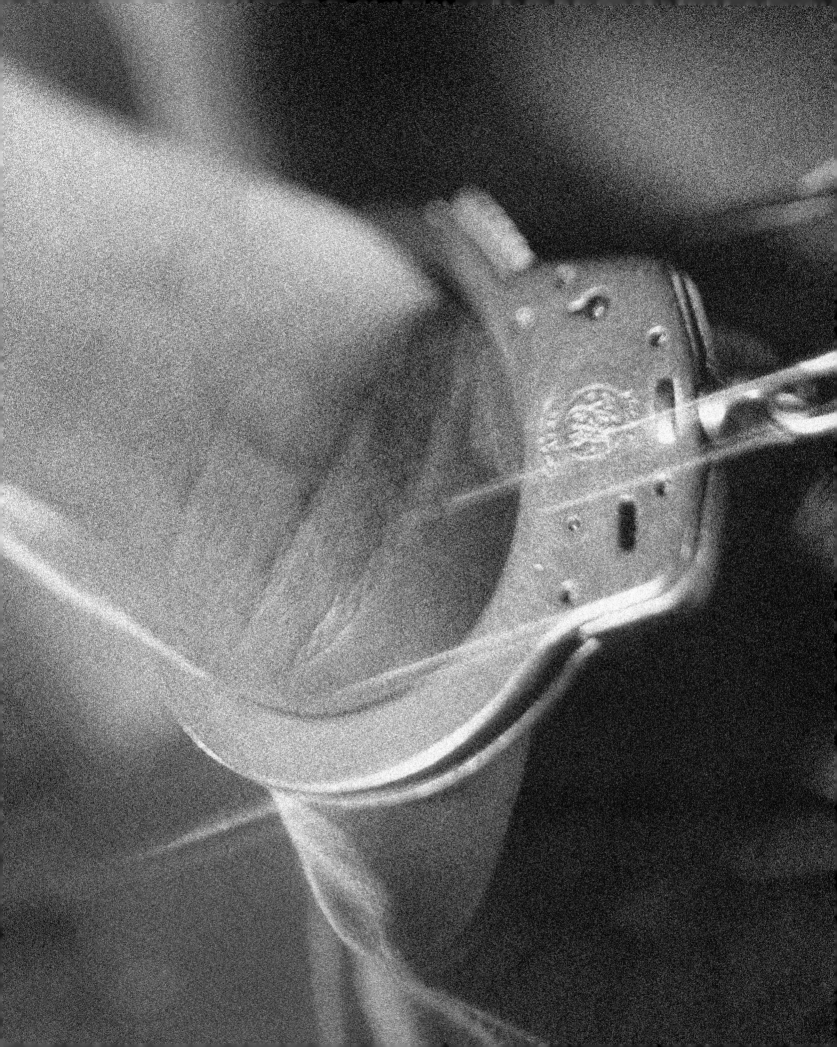

# THE SUSPECT

Like a jigsaw puzzle's missing piece, an unidentified suspect is defined by the outlines of the surrounding pieces. Descriptions of witnesses, grainy photographs, jerky CCTV footage, as well as the suspect's voice on the telephone, their habits, and how they committed their crimes—these, and other details, help give shape to the absent, yet central character. Offender profiling, ID procedures, and other emerging technologies can help to group all these details together.

# Psychological profiling

In harrowing rape and murder cases, profiling can be a valuable way of focusing investigations. It uses offenders' behavior to model their lives, motives, and backgrounds. But the public image of profilers bears little resemblance to the reality: they are not psychics, and their work involves much more science than glamor.

Studies suggest that a strange and ugly compulsion drives criminals who kill or rape repeatedly. It makes the public fear them, the press sensationalize them, but it also affects their behavior in a way that can ultimately lead to their capture.

Psychological profiling (also known as offender profiling, criminal profiling, or just profiling) analyzes habits and rituals of serial criminals. Forensic psychologists use behavioral science to study common factors that link serial crimes. They speculate on peculiarities of the offender's lifestyle that, when made public, may be recognized by colleagues or neighbors.

## History

Basic profiling began over a century ago (see box below). But it emerged as a distinct discipline in the 1950s. Former FBI employees began to interview imprisoned offenders to look for common factors that linked their crimes.

Intriguing patterns emerged from the studies of serial killers. They were often victims of child abuse. This could then lead to abnormal behavior such as fire-starting and cruelty to animals or other children, then to petty crime and defiance of authority. Most embark on an escalating pattern of serious violent crime in their mid- to late twenties.

Manipulation and domination drive them, and their motives may be sexual, even if no sexual element appears in their crimes. They find murder fulfilling; it gives them a sense of control and success previously lacking in their lives. Some revel in notoriety, collecting cuttings and taking trophies such as clothes, jewelry, or body parts to relive their triumphs.

## Profiling in practice

Methodologies differ, but profilers use either inductive or deductive approaches. Inductive profiling assumes that criminals will have backgrounds and motives similar to those of other serial offenders who have behaved in the same way. For example, a serial rapist targeting white women is unlikely to be black, because similar past crimes rarely crossed racial lines. Such

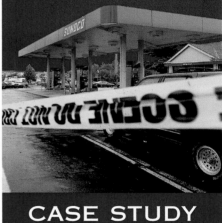
assumptions are widely challenged, and inductive profiling has suffered some well-publicized setbacks (see case study box).

Deductive profiling, though still based on likelihoods, avoids averages and generalizations. Instead, it studies subjects in great detail, adapting deductions with each fresh piece of evidence.

Usually, deductive profiling follows the strategy established by the FBI (see above right-hand box). An offender profile is built based on their actions before, during, and after the crime. For example, if a murderer uses an improvised weapon, it suggests that the crime was impulsive.

Deductive profiling builds on inductive knowledge and couples theories from past studies with evidence found at the scene.

**Artist's impression of the murderer Jack the Ripper**

**JACK THE RIPPER** was the nickname of the serial killer who murdered seven prostitutes in London's Whitechapel neighborhood in 1888. His grisly signature was the partial dissection of his victims, and this triggered the first attempt at psychological profiling. George B. Philips, a police surgeon, noticed the neat removal of the organs of Annie Chapman, the third victim. Philips concluded that only someone with medical training could have made the incisions so precisely. This observation did little to help the investigation. Despite police receiving taunting notes signed "Jack the Ripper," the killer was never caught.

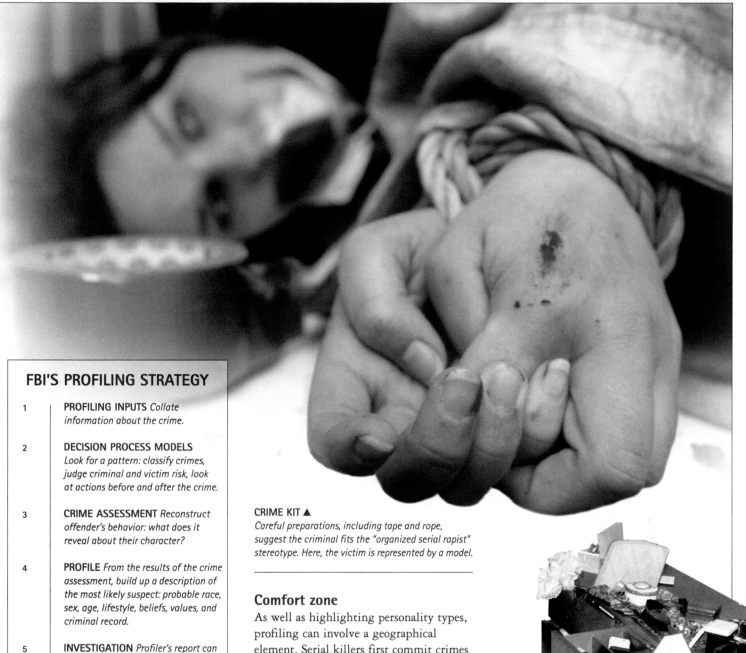

## FBI'S PROFILING STRATEGY

| 1 | **PROFILING INPUTS** *Collate information about the crime.* |
|---|---|
| 2 | **DECISION PROCESS MODELS** *Look for a pattern: classify crimes, judge criminal and victim risk, look at actions before and after the crime.* |
| 3 | **CRIME ASSESSMENT** *Reconstruct offender's behavior: what does it reveal about their character?* |
| 4 | **PROFILE** *From the results of the crime assessment, build up a description of the most likely suspect: probable race, sex, age, lifestyle, beliefs, values, and criminal record.* |
| 5 | **INVESTIGATION** *Profiler's report can be used to help police narrow their search for the suspect.* |
| 6 | **APPREHENSION** *Good interview technique may elicit a confession.* |

**CRIME KIT ▲**
*Careful preparations, including tape and rope, suggest the criminal fits the "organized serial rapist" stereotype. Here, the victim is represented by a model.*

For example, serial murderers can be either "organized," carrying out planned, premeditated attacks on strangers, or "disorganized," committing unplanned killings and behaving haphazardly.

Other clues—or lack of them—identify organized killers. They often hide their identities by wearing gloves and a mask, and may carry a "toolbox" containing, for example, duct tape and rope for restraint.

## Comfort zone

As well as highlighting personality types, profiling can involve a geographical element. Serial killers first commit crimes in a neighborhood they know well, their "comfort zone," and travel farther as their sense of power grows. An important task of a profiler is to look for the earliest crimes bearing the offender's "signature." A signature is a ritual or behavior pattern that, though unnecessary, fulfils the killer emotionally. Investigations are more successful if they trace this signature back to the earliest crime in a series.

**BUNGLED BURGLARY ▶**
*Inept rifling of a victim's home after rape or murder suggests the criminal does not have past burglary convictions. Experienced burglars would open the bottom drawer first, then work upward to save time.*

# The Milwaukee Cannibal

Picture the most vicious sex killer of horror movies or pulp fiction, add your worst nightmare for good measure, multiply by two, and you may come close to the macabre reality of Jeffrey Dahmer. Though he perfectly fitted the profile of the serial killer, profiling was applied too late to stop him from murdering at least 15 black and Asian gay men.

The neighbors at Oxford Apartments had noticed the smell, but the mild-mannered 31-year-old blond man always had a perfectly sensible explanation. It was "rotting meat," Jeffrey Dahmer said, his excuse made more plausible, perhaps, by the fact that it was only half a lie.

But the police should have been suspicious when they found a 14-year-old boy of Asian descent running naked and drugged around the run-down Milwaukee neighborhood. At his side, Dahmer claimed that the boy was his drunken gay lover. He showed the police some ID and took them back to his apartment. It stank, but everything seemed neat and in order, so the two police officers went away without asking any more questions.

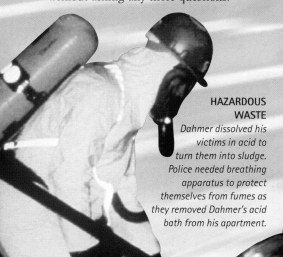

**HAZARDOUS WASTE**
*Dahmer dissolved his victims in acid to turn them into sludge. Police needed breathing apparatus to protect themselves from fumes as they removed Dahmer's acid bath from his apartment.*

### The weird dude

A few months later, around midnight on July 22, 1991, two patrol officers stopped a man with handcuffs on one wrist. It turned out he wasn't a fugitive, as they had thought. He babbled about a "weird dude" who'd tried to cuff him, and led the police to 213 Oxford Apartments.

Jeffrey Dahmer answered the door. He was polite. He was calm. He offered to get the handcuff keys from the bedroom. The police might have treated it as another gay lovers' spat had one of them not followed him and spotted photographs of skulls and horribly mutilated corpses. Dahmer's cool manner evaporated when the cop yelled to his buddy to arrest him. They succeeded in handcuffing him, and started to search the apartment. Then things got rapidly worse.

### Behind the icebox door

"There's a head in the refrigerator!" shouted one of the officers, slamming the door in shock. There were three more in

**MURDERER'S MUGSHOT ▲**
*Even as a teenager Jeffrey Dahmer had murderous fantasies about sex with corpses. He first killed at age 18, burying the body in plastic bags in the woods behind his house.*

the freezer. A cupboard hid two skulls, as well as more photographs of ghastly, murderous horrors, a saucepan containing rotting hands and a penis, and more genitals, pickled in formaldehyde.

The stomach-churning, scarcely credible truth about Jeffrey Dahmer was that he killed for kicks and had sex with the corpses. He would then cut the bodies up, faithfully photographing every slash. He disposed of his victims by dissolving them in acid, but kept parts of them as trophies. On occasions he even ate their flesh.

Dahmer preyed on homosexual men and boys, most of them black, Asian, or Hispanic. Critics of the Milwaukee police suggested after his arrest that this was one reason why his killing spree continued—if the police weren't so racist and homophobic, they would have stopped him earlier. In fact, this overstates the case, for they nearly did. In 1988, when he had already killed five times, he picked up a 13-year-old Asian boy, drugged and groped him, but stopped short of sex or murder. He was arrested for an assault on a child and spent 10 months in prison. However, he was free by day so that he would not lose his job—at a chocolate factory. Dahmer began his murders again almost as soon as he was released, and by the time of his arrest in 1991, he was killing on a weekly basis.

## On the stand

Dahmer's trial was predictably sensational. Sniffer dogs were used to check for bombs in the courtroom, and every court member was scanned with metal detectors and thoroughly searched on entry.

Dahmer's lawyer urged him to plead not guilty, but he ignored their advice and

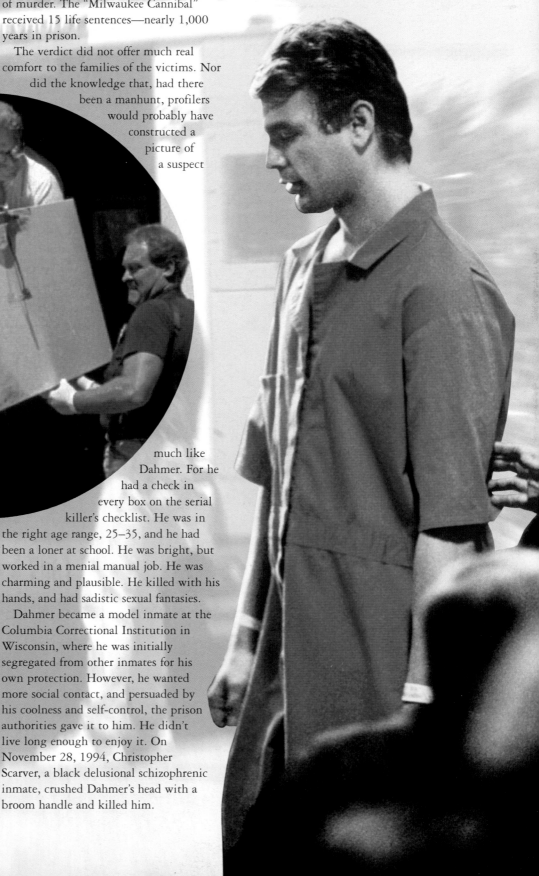

**GRIM EVIDENCE ▶**
*Police cleared the killer's apartment after his arrest, removing evidence such as this refrigerator, in which he preserved the heads and other parts of his victims.*

instead claimed insanity as a defense. This forced the prosecution to establish that he was simply evil, rather than mad. The prosecution's trial strategy drew heavily on the principles of criminal profiling. District attorney Mike McCann directed the jury's attention to the control that Dahmer exerted over his victims: a classic feature of the personality of serial killers. Dahmer picked victims who were intrinsically easy to control, and he heightened his power over them by drugging their drinks. The ritual of their torture, killing, and dismemberment made him feel omnipotent.

## Bad, not mad

McCann's argument was persuasive. The jury rejected the defense plea of insanity, and found Dahmer guilty on 15 counts of murder. The "Milwaukee Cannibal" received 15 life sentences—nearly 1,000 years in prison.

The verdict did not offer much real comfort to the families of the victims. Nor did the knowledge that, had there been a manhunt, profilers would probably have constructed a picture of a suspect much like Dahmer. For he had a check in every box on the serial killer's checklist. He was in the right age range, 25–35, and he had been a loner at school. He was bright, but worked in a menial manual job. He was charming and plausible. He killed with his hands, and had sadistic sexual fantasies.

Dahmer became a model inmate at the Columbia Correctional Institution in Wisconsin, where he was initially segregated from other inmates for his own protection. However, he wanted more social contact, and persuaded by his coolness and self-control, the prison authorities gave it to him. He didn't live long enough to enjoy it. On November 28, 1994, Christopher Scarver, a black delusional schizophrenic inmate, crushed Dahmer's head with a broom handle and killed him.

**COURT APPEARANCE ▼**
*Fearing that Jeffrey Dahmer would be murdered before he could be sentenced, court authorities built a bulletproof screen in front of the public gallery.*

# Criminal identification

Police can be confronted by a dilemma when suspects are identified in lineups, mugshots, and composites. For witnesses are often confident about their memory for faces, and juries trust their evidence. But experience has shown that relying on eyewitness identification alone can lead to wrongful convictions.

**PHOTOFIT COMPOSITES ▲**
*Until recently, investigators built up images of suspects' faces from a jigsaw puzzle of facial features, but the system was inflexible and the result hardly seamless.*

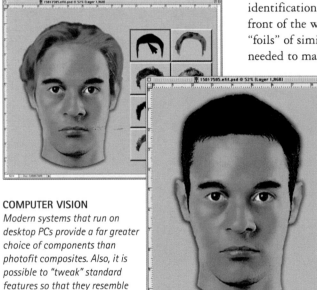

**COMPUTER VISION**
*Modern systems that run on desktop PCs provide a far greater choice of components than photofit composites. Also, it is possible to "tweak" standard features so that they resemble a description more closely.*

It is a familiar story: a convenience store is held up at gunpoint; the robber gets away, but the cashier is convinced she would recognize the man again.

A traditional way of making the identification is to parade a suspect in front of the witness with at least eight "foils" of similar appearance. Care is needed to make sure the choice is as objective as possible. The suspect must be given the opportunity to take any place he wishes in the lineup. It is important that the witness is told that if they are not sure of their identification, they do not have to pick anyone out; otherwise, they may choose the lineup member who most closely resembles the criminal they saw.

## Look in the book
Lineups are an effective way of pursuing a case when investigators believe they know who was involved in a crime. But what do they do when there is no obvious suspect?

A mugshot search is one answer: witnesses try to pick out the suspect from photographs of known offenders. However, this approach has several drawbacks. First, a comprehensive search is possible only in small communities where there are few enough offenders for a witness to view them all. Second, it is a "convicts only" ID parade, so an incorrect choice can steer police attention toward an innocent ex-offender. (By contrast, choosing a foil in a lineup is inconsequential.) Finally, a mugshot search weakens the validity of a later lineup.

If both these approaches fail or are impractical, creating a likeness of the offender can move an investigation forward. Today's police forces are most likely to do this using a painting-by-numbers face-composite system. Witnesses pick facial features and hair from a computer menu, to build up a likeness that can be used in public appeals for information.

**SUSPECTS ON PARADE ▶**
*This mock lineup contains five quite different-looking individuals. In reality, lineup members must be of similar height, build, and race; otherwise, objectivity may be compromised.*

## SKETCHING THE SUSPECT

Though computer composites look slick, forensic artists feel that nothing will ever replace the sketchpad. They argue persuasively that artists are more flexible than software, and that witnesses relax when talking to them, and tell them more. Anecdotal evidence supports this: when a bomb destroyed a government building in Oklahoma City in 1995, a forensic artist used witness descriptions to create a likeness of the man who hired the van used in the bombing, and the picture led to the identification of the bomber, Timothy McVeigh.

**SKETCH SUCCESS**
*A former colleague and a hotel manager both identified McVeigh (right, in a police mugshot) from a forensic artist's sketch (below).*

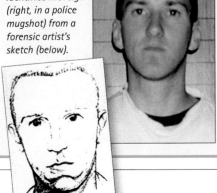

## Fallible memory

Unfortunately, all of these methods of identification suffer from the same handicap: the witness's memory. Everyone overestimates their ability to recognize faces, even in ideal conditions. And in crimes involving violence—whether actual or threatened—victims concentrate more intently on the weapon than on the face of the person holding it. The jury system exacerbates these shortcomings. Jurors may attach great weight to an eyewitness identification, even when there is forensic evidence that contradicts it.

Legal challenges to convictions based on unreliable identification evidence have prompted governments to bring in legislation to tighten up ID procedures, and encouraged police to concentrate on solid forensic evidence.

## Unblinking witnesses

Superficially, CCTV seems to address many of the failings of human memory, but video surveillance is not the objective witness we would like it to be. Video images are often degraded and indistinct, and matching real faces to those on a screen is tricky. In an attempt to make

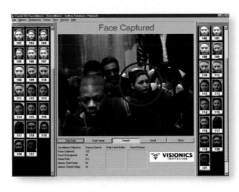

**A FACE IN THE CROWD ▲**
*Facial recognition software helps CCTV camera operators to spot criminals whose faces are stored in a database, and presents them with a "shortlist" of possible matches.*

matches harder to challenge in court, photoanthropometry measures distances between "landmarks" on the faces of suspects captured on film or video, and compares them with the same landmarks on a mugshot. Computerized facial recognition aims to automate this process. The evidential value of video images is likely to improve as technology advances, but rather than "tracking" individuals, it will probably just be used to identify a suspect at a particular location.

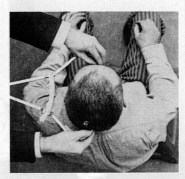

**Alphonse Bertillon 1853–1914**

As a clerk in the Paris police records office, Alphonse Bertillon developed the idea that criminals could be identified by "anthropometry"—measurement of their heads and bodies. He later pioneered the use of the "portrait parlé" (a methodical description of the face) to identify criminals, and photography to document villains and crime scenes. Bertillon's ID systems were very influential in France, but ultimately eclipsed by the fingerprint files, which he dismissed as ineffective.

# Lie detectors

I n pursuit of the truth, crime investigators dream of a foolproof way to spot suspects' lies. The invention of the polygraph in the 1920s promised to make these dreams a reality. Today, however, many people question the value of this "lie detector," and more sophisticated technologies are being explored to supplement or replace it.

In a police station interview room, two detectives question a youth caught loitering in a parking lot. His replies are cool, confident, even cocky, and when the interview moves on to local car crime, his manner stays the same. But his posture changes. He folds his arms. When asked specific questions, he touches his lip. As the interview winds up, he leans back in his chair, crosses his legs, and puts his hands behind his head.

Showing him out, one detective mouths silently to the other: "He's our man." The police covertly keep watch on him, and a week later a CCTV camera catches the same youth stealing car radios.

### Body-language blunders
The two detectives simply used their experience and training to read the suspect's body language. His gestures

said, "I'm not helping you," then "I'm lying," and finally "You won't get me, I'm smarter than you."

Reading a suspect's postures has always been a useful skill, but until the 1960s it was generally regarded as intuition. Then psychologists began research into nonverbal communication, and a 1971 book by Julius Fast popularized the subject. Today, it forms a standard part of interview-technique training.

### Putting faith in the polygraph
Useful though body language is, it is subjective. The polygraph, by contrast, appears to be utterly objective, and produces a permanent record of a suspect's responses. The polygraph measures the body's response to stress. For example, we are all familiar with the "sweaty palm"

Children cover their mouths after lying, but in adults, the gesture is often suppressed into a touch of the chin

Fiddling with the hands, watch, or cufflinks is a "disguised arm-cross" gesture that creates a barrier against ideas

**BODY LANGUAGE ▲**
*It can be easy to read body language; just look carefully at how people sit, and what they do with their hands.*

**◄ TESTING, TESTING!**
*An FBI recruit undergoes a polygraph test. Many US employers use the equipment to test and evaluate staff. In the legal arena, suspects may wish to take the test to prove their innocence.*

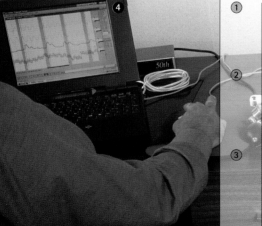

## A POLYGRAPH TEST

① *A pair of plates attached to the subject's fingers measure skin resistance. Lying causes sweating, which lowers this resistance.*

② *A rise in blood pressure and increased pulse rate both indicate stress, so the polygraph examiner wraps a sphygmomanometer cuff around the subject's arm to measure these.*

③ *Heavy breathing also betrays anxiety, and a couple of pneumographs strapped around the chest measure it. Data from this and the other sensors is fed to an interface box.*

④ *A portable computer charts the results of the test and correlates the subject's responses with the questions.*

sensation experienced when under pressure. Perspiration lowers the skin's electrical resistance, and the polygraph gauges this using electrodes on the fingers. The machine also measures depth of breathing, pulse rate, and blood pressure, plotting each of these stress measures on a paper trace or, increasingly, as a graph on a computer screen.

To administer a polygraph test, the examiner must first ask the subject a series of innocent questions. These determine a baseline for each measurement, against which to compare the subject's responses to later questions about the crime itself. In theory, their body will betray them when they answer falsely, leading to a peak on the chart.

## Polygraph problems

In practice, subjects' responses are not so clear-cut. Many physical factors, such as drug and alcohol use, and even hunger, can mislead the machine. Pathological liars can cheat it, and simple techniques such as self-inflicted pain—perhaps by biting the tongue—can send readings awry. Results can also be misinterpreted if the examiner fails to establish a reasonable baseline, due to poor training.

Without supplementary evidence, a polygraph test cannot overcome "reasonable doubt," so it is rarely used as evidence in court. However, suspects fear its reputation, and some change their plea to guilty either after failing a test or in anticipation of one.

## Crime on the brain

Newer technologies may succeed where the polygraph has failed. Some of the most promising use the electroencephalograph (ECG), used by researchers since the 1930s to study the electrical waves that surge through our brains when we think.

Most of the researchers working on this technology concentrate on one wave in particular: the P300, which surges when we see something we recognize.

One organization has worked with the CIA and the FBI to develop and formulate a test nicknamed "Brain Fingerprinting." This test works by monitoring the P300 wave as the suspect looks at images or phrases associated with the crime scene,

and at unconnected images and words. The spark of recognition, so-called "guilty knowledge," triggers a change in the brain wave, which ECG equipment detects. Wrongly accused suspects who were never at the crime scene should show the same response to all images.

Though this test sounds similar to the polygraph, it is not as susceptible to cheating. People with guilty knowledge cannot stop themselves from reacting, so there are no false positives.

## Magnetically minded

ECG is a comparatively old technology, and there are now more sophisticated ways to monitor brain activity, such as magnetic resonance imaging (brain scans or MRI). This highlights areas of the cerebral cortex—the brain's thick, thinking "skin"—where the nerve endings spark most vigorously. This technique may one day allow forensic scientists to probe the criminal mind. So far, however, MRI has defied attempts to untangle

**THE HEADBAND OF TRUTH ▶**
*Brain fingerprinting involves fewer invasive sensors than the polygraph. Terminals on a headband pick up the ECG waves, and the subject's responses are monitored on a computer.*

complex brain activity to produce a standard, easily administered truth test.

Ironically, a simple new lie detection technique may eventually replace the polygraph. Research at the University of Michigan suggests that liars briefly hesitate before responding to a question. Even with training they cannot hide the pause. The technology is still incomplete, but as one researcher puts it, it is a "cheap and easy way of doing the guilty knowledge test: all you need is an ordinary PC, and no electrodes."

**◀ BRAIN ON FIRE**
*This false-color positron emission tomography (PET) scan highlights the areas of the brain triggered during image recognition.*

## A PATTERN OF LIES

Can the sound of your voice betray your lies? That is a question for forensic phoneticians. These experts train for eight years in the field of linguistics and phonetics (language and speech science) before helping to solve legal cases. They have been known to deduce a suspect's age, sex, and race from their voice, as well as matching different recorded telephone calls to a particular caller.

Voice spectrography, popularized in the 1960s, used a graphic representation of sound: a "voiceprint." The voiceprint below shows the sound made by someone saying

"baby." The graph measures amplitude—the strength of sound over time—and shows the two different syllables as bursts of lines on the graph. But forensic phonetics is not solely about voiceprints. Trained experts must use their strong academic background to interpret the prints in combination with phonetic analysis and acoustic measurement.

Experts have argued about the value of voiceprints, but most agree that the psychological stress evaluator, a device that uses tremors in speech as a measure of stress, is not a reliable way of detecting lies.

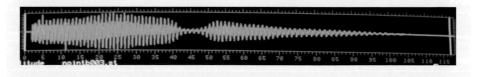

# Ivan the Terrible

**ACQUITTED**

J ohn Demjanjuk was just a retired mechanic to his neighbors in
Cleveland, Ohio. Then a report identified him as "Ivan the Terrible,"
a sadistic Nazi death camp guard. The accusation, which hinged on
identification by Holocaust survivors who last saw Demjanjuk 40 years
earlier, was effectively a death sentence on the 55-year-old Ukrainian.

**FREE AT LAST? ▲**
*The news of his release is broken to Demjanjuk, still
in his Israeli prison clothes, in 1990. But, in
2002, he was once more stripped of his US
citizenship—again accused of war crimes.*

In the Jerusalem courtroom the crowd
chanted "Death! Death! Death!" as the
judge read out the verdict. "It is as if
Treblinka still existed," he said. "Still Ivan
the Terrible poisons and stabs, although
his face has turned into an old man's face.
He still cuts off breasts, slits bellies,
shoots youths, and drills into the living
flesh. In the light of the above, we sign
a punishment of death." From his

wheelchair, John Demjanjuk cried out,
"I am innocent!"

## Gas chamber guard
The crimes of which he was accused took
place during World War II at Treblinka,
an extermination camp in Poland. There, as
many as 900,000 Jews were gassed under
the supervision of hundreds of Ukrainian
guards. One, nicknamed "Ivan the
Terrible" by camp inmates, was notorious

for acts of unspeakable cruelty, and had
personally operated the machinery of death.

John Demjanjuk had emigrated to the
United States in 1951, settling in
Cleveland, Ohio, and working in the
motor industry. He lived inconspicuously
and apparently blamelessly until 1975,
when his name appeared on a list of
suspected Nazi war criminals compiled
by the Soviet Union.

The US Justice Department began
proceedings to strip Demjanjuk of his
citizenship so that he could be extradited
to Israel for trial. The Immigration and
Naturalization Service (INS) studied
Demjanjuk's application for citizenship,
and found that he had claimed to be "a
farmer in Poland in a settlement called
Sobibor" during the war. Soviet records
revealed that Demjanjuk had in fact worked
as a guard at a death camp in Sobibor.

## The Nazi hunters investigate
The INS then supplied Israeli police with
photographs of Demjanjuk taken from his
immigration files. The Israeli police were

**◄ CRIMES AGAINST HUMANITY**
*These starving prisoners escaped death at a Nazi
concentration camp, but more than 15 million others
died at Nazi extermination and concentration
camps. Though acquitted of being Ivan the Terrible
of Treblinka, Demjanjuk is still a war crime suspect.*

investigating another war crime suspect who had worked at Treblinka, and they showed mugshot albums, which included pictures of both men, to Treblinka and Sobibor survivors. However, Demjanjuk's picture, and that of the other accused man, were twice the size of the "fillers" on the page; they were brighter and clearer, too. Several survivors identified Demjanjuk as Ivan the Terrible of Treblinka. Then, at a Treblinka survivors' reunion, witnesses who had already identified Ivan met with fellow survivors, some of whom went on to make the same identification. In spite of these irregularities, other survivors failed to identify Ivan. And there was no hard evidence to suggest that Demjanjuk had ever served at Treblinka. Nevertheless, the INS concluded that he had been positively identified and, in 1981, stripped him of his citizenship. In 1986 he was flown to Israel to stand trial.

## On trial for his life

In the trial that began the following year, the identification evidence of the survivors was crucial to the prosecution. They also produced a certificate (see right) that appeared to prove that Demjanjuk had volunteered as a member of the Nazi SS, and had gassed Jews at Sobibor—

though not Treblinka. The defense questioned the authenticity of the certificate and cast doubt on the identification witnesses, but, despite these arguments, the court found Demjanjuk guilty. He immediately appealed and, when the appeal was heard in 1990, Demjanjuk was able to present witness statements, gathered in the Soviet Union, that identified another man, Ivan Marchenko, as Ivan the Terrible. Demjanjuk's sentence was quashed and he returned to the United States a free man. The case of John Demjanjuk graphically illustrates the hazards of identification evidence, especially when the passage of time has clouded witnesses' memories and changed the physical appearance of the suspect.

**THE "TRAWNIKI" CERTIFICATE ▲**
*Demjanjuk's SS record card showed that he had attended a training camp for death camp guards, Trawniki. Demjanjuk's lawyers insisted that the card had been forged by the KGB (the Soviet secret police) in order to frame their client.*

**IN COURT IN JERUSALEM ▶**
*Demjanjuk sits between guards during the trial. He often had difficulty understanding the proceedings: his Ukrainian translator was also a witness for the prosecution.*

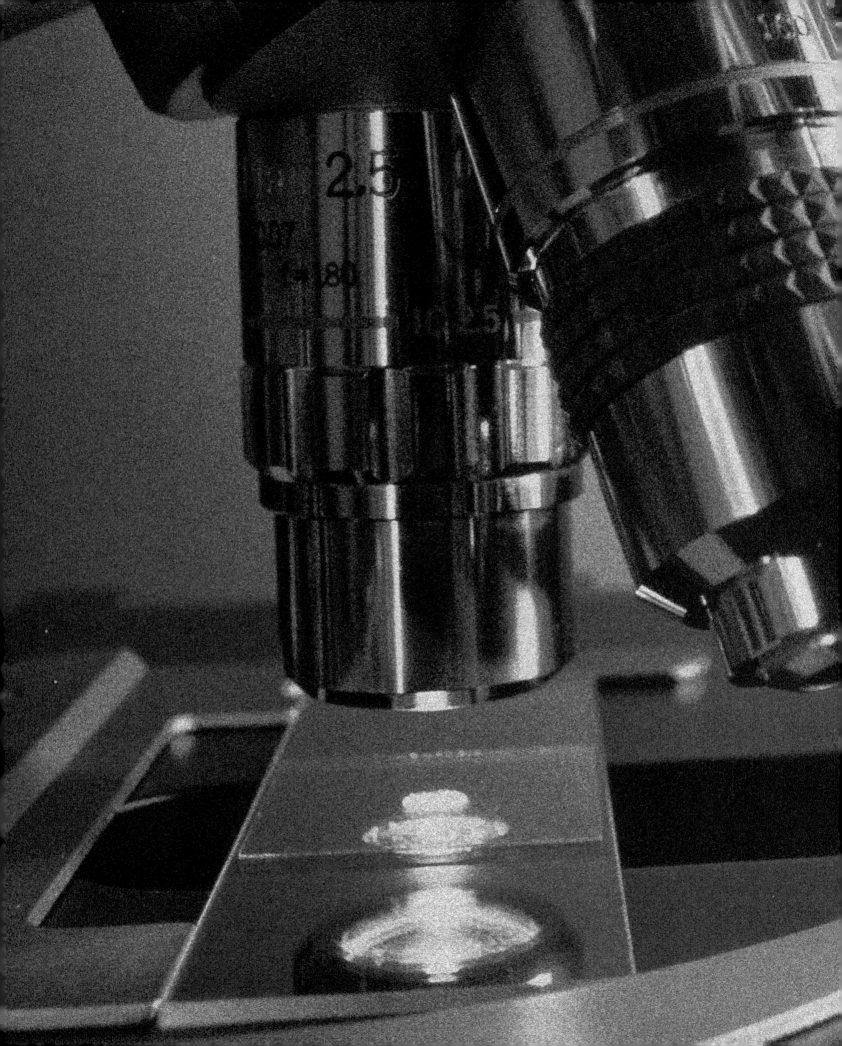

# ANALYSIS OF EVIDENCE

In caricatures of crime investigation, detectives peer at suspicious footprints through an oversize magnifying glass. Though real forensic scientists have not quite abandoned the hand lens, they have supplemented it with a huge selection of sophisticated analytical techniques and diagnostic instruments. Some methods are so sensitive that they can detect incriminating traces diluted a billion times over—quite literally the equivalent of finding a needle in not one haystack, but several.

# The crime lab

Inside the forensic laboratory, mundane evidence yields up vital secrets. An apparently spotless comb identifies its owner. A maggot's gut reveals the poison that killed its human meal. Hidden fingerprints glow clearly beneath ultraviolet lights. Today's crime lab technicians use amazing technology to analyze evidence that connects suspect to crime.

A large national crime lab brings together under one roof almost all the disciplines of forensic science. It may employ multi-skilled technicians, who do a range of jobs, or specialist scientists who focus on complex fields, such as DNA. Some labs are attached to universities or busy police departments; others are independent. A lab serving a small town may be equipped for only the most common tests and may be operated by a lone scientist.

But whatever their size, all crime labs follow similar procedures. Scientists must

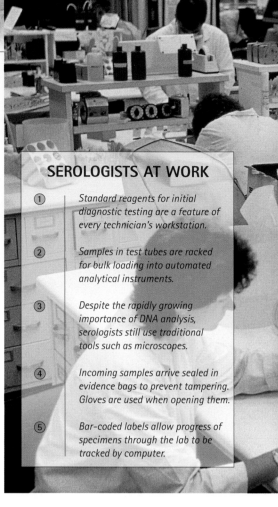

**FBI SEROLOGY LAB ▲**
Serology means the study of blood serum, but forensic serology units, like this one, analyze all bodily fluids, including semen and saliva.

**COMPARING DNA SAMPLES ▲**
Crime labs must use a standardized DNA analysis technique so that their results can be compared directly with national databases.

ensure that an item of evidence entering the lab never comes into contact with anything that could contaminate it. Each item is carefully stored and logged so that its progress through the lab's departments can be traced if necessary.

Testing the evidence brought to the lab usually begins with the most simple diagnosis ("is this stain actually blood?") before continuing to more costly, but

more precise, tests ("whose blood is it?"). Tests that destroy samples are always carried out last of all.

## What's inside?

All crime labs boast an identification unit for revealing and enhancing fingerprints. This is needed because it isn't feasible to perform many of the most sensitive techniques at the crime scene. Fume enclosures, where superglue fumes can reveal hidden fingerprints, line the walls of the lab shown on this page. This lab also houses the special lights needed to reveal developed prints (see p. 46). Tire marks and shoeprints end up here, too.

Similarly, a trace evidence unit also forms a central part of most labs. Staff here look for clues in samples of hair, fiber, fabric, and dust. Their expertise may also be needed for checking forensic dentistry and skeletal remains.

## Chemistry set

Bristling with test tubes and complex analysis equipment, a chemistry unit resembles any general science laboratory. Here, toxicologists test urine and blood samples for poisons, drugs, and alcohol (see p. 82). They also analyze synthetic samples, such as dyes, stains, and medicines. Chemistry labs rely heavily on technology, using gas chromatographs, microscopes, and mass spectrometers to identify telltale chemical signatures (see p. 88).

The serology unit analyzes blood and other bodily fluids. DNA sequencing increasingly dominates this work. Recent advances have brought the most common DNA test, polymerase chain reaction, within the scope of even small labs. The more specialized test on

mitochondrial DNA (see p. 63) is the preserve of larger facilities.

A photography unit is an essential part of any crime lab because photography is so widely used to document evidence. The unit provides resources such as processing and darkroom facilities to other units,

**ELECTRON MICROSCOPE ▲**
Scanning electron microscopes are used to magnify objects, such as hair, fibers, dust mites, and fungal spores, for analysis by the relevant specialist.

## TESTING FIREARMS

Firing suspect weapons gives ballistics experts spent cartridges and bullets to compare with examples in firearms databases, such as the FBI's Drugfire index. It also provides other useful information—the pattern in which cartridges are ejected, for example, can reveal where an assassin was standing to fire a weapon, and the spread of shotgun pellets gives a rough indication of range.

*A bullet fired at a crime scene can be compared with one fired in the lab.*

◀ HAIR TESTING FOR DRUGS
*As a suspected drug abuser's hair grows, it locks up drug residues. By analyzing fragments, toxicologists not only identify the presence of any drugs, but also get a calendar of their use. The same can be done with fingernails.*

*This hair sample is lying on a record sheet, which the technician may sometimes seal with wax to prevent tampering.*

*The hair is cut into half-inch pieces corresponding to specific dates. The drugs and drug metabolites are then extracted by solvents and identified by gas chromatography and mass spectrometry.*

supports crime-scene teams, and gives expert testimony on the authenticity of photographs. Specialists may need to be called in for services such as surveillance and aerial photography.

### Materials, guns, and software
A materials unit analyzes alloys, ceramics, paints and other coatings, soil, and wood to trace the criminal, or to link a suspect to the crime scene. Biological materials, such as seeds, are analyzed by the biology unit.

A firearms unit integrates precision science with the clatter of shooting baths.

Testing weapons means firing them—to study characteristic marks on a target, bullet, or cartridge case. Large labs may also include teams that specialize in arson and explosives, and units that analyze computer data, documents, photographs, and audio and video recordings—though outside specialists are available for the smaller labs to use.

### Collaboration
Every forensic lab needs scientists to do the tests, but they also need support staff to check in,

prepare, and store evidence. They maintain and run the lab, and they help calibrate the complex testing instruments.

Collaboration goes beyond the walls of individual labs. The results of an isolated test may be useful, but comparison with similar tests gives them far greater value. Analysis of marks on a crime-scene bullet, for example, can prove it was fired from a suspect's gun, but matching the marks with records on a national database might link the weapon to a dozen other crimes. So at the elbow of most forensic specialists is a computer that enables them to make these essential comparisons and searches.

SAMPLING BLOOD
*To test dry bloodstains, technicians scrape off samples, or moisten with water and sample with a swab.*

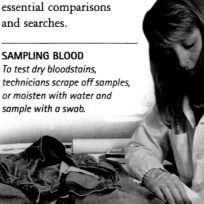

# Toxicology

The sensitive analytical methods that toxicologists use can prove from a few strands of hair that a suspect used illegal narcotics weeks earlier, or detect vanishingly small quantities of poison in one drop of a murder victim's blood. But the bulk of the work in a busy toxicology lab concerns a legal drug—alcohol.

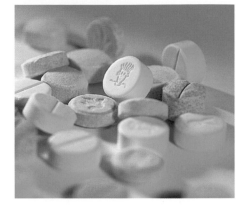

**ILLEGAL DRUGS ▲**
*An immunoassay drug-testing kit for amphetamines would give a positive result if a subject had taken ecstasy (MDMA) tablets like these.*

Though roadside tests roughly measure alcohol in drivers' breath, this test is inadmissible in court. So drunk drivers' samples of blood or urine are tested in the toxicology lab. Because of the number of samples, testing is automated, though it is no less rigorous than other toxicology procedures.

## Drug abuse testing

Testing for other drugs follows a similar pattern: a simple test to establish whether a suspected chemical is present, followed by a more sophisticated procedure that measures quantities and provides proof. The initial test is usually an immunoassay kit, which changes color when drugs in a urine sample combine with antibodies in the kit. If they get a positive result, toxicologists proceed with more sophisticated tests. Drug tests are carried out not only in relation to suspected abusers and athletes, but also on behalf of some employers who have implemented a random testing policy.

## Identifying and measuring

For both drugs and alcohol, these tests are likely to involve chromatography, a method of separating chemicals according to the speed at which they move in gas or liquid. The indispensable tool of the toxicology lab is gas chromatography (GC). At its heart is a narrow tube, usually loosely packed with special solid granules. Through this flows a nonreactive gas, such as nitrogen, which is called a "carrier gas." When a vaporized test sample is injected, every chemical in

**BLOWING IN THE TUBE**
*British police administer more than 200,000 breath tests every year. Around 1 in 25 drivers gives a positive result.*

it passes through the tube at a different speed. By timing when each reaches a sensor at the exit, it is possible to identify the constituents of any mixture. Output from the sensor drives a computer display. Test substances appear as peaks on a graph; peaks matching those of a known drug indicate a positive result. Two other chromatography techniques are often used, depending on what needs to be tested. These are: high performance liquid chromatography (HPLC), which uses

First track on the plate is a control sample containing methadone, which forms the top spot.

The top spot of the suspect sample has risen to the same height as the corresponding spot on the control, suggesting the presence of methadone.

Spraying the glass plate with a reagent, or viewing it under ultraviolet light, makes the formerly colorless tracks visible.

**▲ THIN-LAYER CHROMATOGRAPHY**
*Spots of sample material—usually in liquid form—are pushed up a specially coated plate by an organic solvent soaking up from the base. Components in the sample move up at different speeds and separate.*

## MASS SPECTROMETRY

A gas chromatograph (GC) is often linked to a mass spectrometry (MS) instrument and called GC/MS. This instrument breaks up chemicals into ions (charged particles). Accelerating these ions in a magnetic field and measuring their charge relative to their mass gives a characteristic spectrum that identifies the chemical composition.

a liquid rather than a gas for the carrier phase; and thin-layer chromatography (TLC)—see image at top right.

### Poisoning
Chromatography is also widely used in the other major branch of toxicology, poison. Whether accidental, suicidal, or homicidal, the subject of testing here is not a suspect, but a victim—usually the lab test samples a pathologist has taken at an autopsy. Blood and liver are the most common, but pathologists sometimes send other samples. Bile concentrates antidepressants, morphine, and heroin. Volatile substances such as solvents show up in the lungs, and hair stores a neat chronological record of poisoning in bands along the length of a strand. Toxicologists analyze these samples with techniques

similar to those they use on blood and urine samples from living subjects— usually immunoassay and chromatography.

### Poison sleuth
The popular image of toxicology is of a baffling murder solved by a maverick scientist, but the reality is usually more prosaic. Most poisons leave symptoms pathologists easily spot in the morgue, and poisoning homicides are now rare.

Biohazard emergencies such as the 2001 anthrax attacks in the US are the headline-grabbing exception. In these types of situations, toxicologists are in the spotlight: they take and analyze samples from the scene; they study the effects of the lethal agent on plant and animal life; they advise on how the outbreak might be contained; and they supervise the treatment of victims.

A few murder cases still really do conform to the "poison sleuth" image. In 1979, for example, Georgi Markov, a Bulgarian dissident living in London, felt a stab in his leg. Looking around, he saw a man carrying an umbrella hail a taxi. The tiny wound in Markov's

leg quickly became infected and he died four days later. Pathologists suspected poison but found not a trace of toxin in his body, just a tiny pellet in the wound. Detectives concluded that the man hailing a taxi was a Bulgarian agent who had fired the poisoned pellet from the umbrella. Markov's symptoms suggested the poison was ricin, which is rapidly metabolized by the body and vanishes without a trace.

**BIO ALERT**
*When bioterrorists strike, toxicologists take no chances. The sterile suits they wear to take samples are carefully decontaminated (right), and back at the lab they study specimens in sealed glove-boxes.*

# Bloodstains

At the scene of a murder, bloodstains can literally point to the killer. By analyzing their shape, size, and position, investigators can sometimes figure out not only where an assailant stood, but also their height, how many times they swung the weapon, and whether they are right- or left-handed.

**SCENE OF A SHOOTING**
*Bullets strike a victim with such force that blood is projected at great speed, spraying out in tiny drops. At this scene of a brutal gangland hit, however, the drops are hidden by blood that spurted on to the windshield from an artery.*

Blood can spray everywhere in a violent assault, and it is not easy to remove. Even bleach cannot remove bloodstains totally. This makes blood a valuable aid for forensic scientists trying to reconstruct events.

If a suspect's blood is found at the scene, DNA analysis can identify them (see p. 60). But the blood of the victim is very helpful to investigators, too. The pattern of blood spatters at a crime scene provides important clues to the circumstances of the assault. In the simplest example, a suspect who claims only to have struck once is obviously lying if blood thrown from a weapon has marked the ceiling a number of times. When bloodstains are copious and well-defined, they allow investigators to reconstruct a detailed narrative of an attack.

## Revealing hidden stains

To make full use of bloodstains, though, investigators first have to find them all. A high-intensity light source, filtered

*The UV light is small and maneuverable to reach into awkward places.*

*The investigator's goggles protect his eyes from UV rays, and increase the contrast.*

to produce a violet beam, helps to locate blood spots. If this reveals nothing, or a crime scene has been cleaned, investigators use reagents that make blood visible. Luminol and fluorescin are the most widely used, and have been known to locate blood that has been diluted to 12,000:1. When luminol is sprayed in a completely dark room, it fluoresces on contact with any traces of blood. Flourescin is more sensitive, but only glows when it is illuminated with UV. They both react with the iron found in hemoglobin.

**BLOODY FOOTPRINT ▼**
*Sprayed with reagent and illuminated with UV light, a bloody footprint that was almost invisible in normal lighting stands out clearly enough to photograph as evidence.*

## Meaningful patterns

Bloodstain analysis uses the pattern of spatter to reconstruct the action that originally spread the blood. When a drop of blood hits a surface, the shape of the mark it makes indicates the direction in which the drop was traveling, and the force with which it was projected. For example, blood dripping a short distance forms large, circular drops on the floor; but when blood is projected forcefully it breaks into much smaller drops. As they hit an oblique surface they elongate and can develop a tail that points away from the source.

If a clear pattern of bloodstains has been thrown on to the walls, floor, and ceiling of a room, murder investigators can trace back from each mark to figure out where the victim and the assailant were standing when each

# PATTERNS OF BLOODSTAINS

Scottish professor of forensic medicine John Glaister (1892–1971) was the first to describe bloodstains in the 1930s, and his categories are still in use today. On a crime scene the marks are rarely as neatly defined as those shown here, and rough, porous surfaces may make analysis impossible.

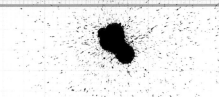

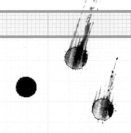

**CIRCULAR MARKS** *form when blood ejected with little force strikes surfaces perpendicular to its path.*

**CRENELLATED MARKS** *result when blood is thrown off at great speed, or falls a large distance.*

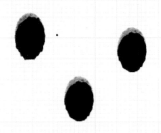

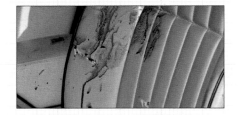

**ELLIPTICAL MARKS** *show drops struck obliquely. A standard formula derives angle from elongation.*

**SPLASHES** *with well-defined tails indicate that blood struck the surface at an angle of 30° or lower.*

**BLOOD SPURT** *forms characteristic marks on surfaces when blood pumps from a cut artery.*

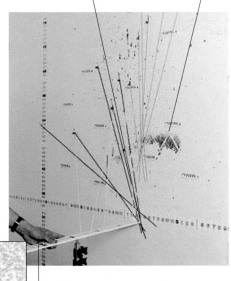

**BLOOD POOLS** *suggest that a victim was static, and still alive, since death stops blood flow.*

**BLOOD TRAILS** *may be surrounded by secondary spatter that shows the direction of movement.*

**BLOOD SMEAR** *suggests that the object pressed against the surface will also be stained.*

blow fell. Traditionally, detectives have assumed that the blood drops fly in straight lines, and used string for reconstruction. Computer programs automate the task now, and allow for gravity, charting the flight path of projected blood as a gentle arc, making the process more precise.

## Use of weapons

Where spatter marks are particularly clear, it is possible to deduce even more information. The pattern of blood flung from the tip of a weapon is particularly revealing. Assailants do not swing weapons in a straight line, and whether the track of blood curves to the left or the right indicates which hand held the weapon. The width of the track hints at the nature of the weapon: a knife leaves a much narrower track than a baseball bat, for example. The cast-off blood also indicates ferocity—multiple, powerfully projected

trails would be compelling evidence of a frenzied and determined attack.

The absence of blood spatter marks can be almost as revealing. A "shadow" that is free of marks suggests that there was an object in between the source of blood and the surface on to which the drops were projected. The intervening object will carry a pattern of spatter marks that fits into the crime scene like the last piece of a jigsaw puzzle.

### ANALYZING BLOOD PATTERNS ▶
*To trace the origin of a blood spatter, investigators first mark the wall with tapes or strings along the axis of each mark. To find how far the source was from the wall, they use the elongation of marks to judge the angle at which drops struck.*

*The shape of the ellipse reveals the angle at which the blood hit.*

Red tapes converge here, showing the position of the source in two dimensions.

A bloody mattress leaning on the wall made this smear.

*Elongation of drops determines the angle of the white strings to the wall, fixing the source in the third dimension.*

# Answers in blood

**SCARS THAT COULDN'T HIDE GUILT ▲**
*Graham Backhouse had been a successful hairdresser before moving to the countryside, but perms and trims did not prepare him for the rigours of life on a farm.*

Defending himself against a vicious knife attack, an English farmer lets fly with both barrels of his twelve-bore shotgun. It seems like the gruesome and tragic climax of a local hate campaign, until investigators take a closer look at the bloodstains on the farmhouse floor, and delve into the case.

Slack-jawed and glassy-eyed, the sheep's head leered from the fence of Widden Hill Farm, in the leafy Cotswolds. Scribbled on a piece of paper fixed to it were two words: "YOU NEXT." To farmer Graham Backhouse it was an unambiguous threat, and he took the grisly emblem straight to the police. He ranted about earlier anonymous letters and phone calls, and a village vendetta against him, but there was little the police could do. Besides, they believed it to be just another village spat.

**◄ BOMB VICTIM**
*Maimed by her husband's bomb, Backhouse's wife divorced him on the incontestable grounds of unreasonable behavior.*

This one, though, turned out to be different. Ten days later, on April 9, 1984, Margaret Backhouse couldn't start her car, so she grabbed the keys to her husband's Volvo station wagon to drive to a nearby village, Horton. When she turned the ignition key, a bomb under the driver's seat blasted off half her thigh.

## Pipe bomb

The police investigation revealed that the bomb had been made from a length of pipe packed with nitroglycerine and the pellets from eight shotgun cartridges. It had been positioned to throw the force of the explosion upward, and it was remarkable that Mrs. Backhouse had not been killed in the blast.

Since it seemed clear that the real target was Graham, the police asked him who he thought might have been responsible. At first he denied that he had any enemies, but when pressed, he singled out two local people who might have borne him grudges. One was a quarry worker with whose wife Backhouse had dallied. He had the motive, and was used to handling explosives. The other was a neighbor, carpenter Colyn

Bedale-Taylor, who had argued with Backhouse over a right of way.

## Self-defense

The police gave Backhouse 24-hour protection, but hardly more than a week later, the farmer suddenly phoned them and ended the arrangement, claiming he was quite able to look after himself. Still concerned for his safety, the police insisted he have a panic button in the house, linked to an alarm at the station.

On April 30, Backhouse triggered it;

**CAR BOMB ▼**
*Backhouse claimed he did not hear the car bomb, or his wife's screams, because he was in a barn some distance away, and was listening to the radio.*

an officer rushed to Widden Hill Farm. There they found Bedale-Taylor dead from two shotgun wounds, gripping a utility knife. Backhouse was bleeding from gashes across his face and chest.

Between frightened sobs, he poured out his story. Bedale-Taylor, he said, had appeared at his door, saying he had come to mend a chair. When Backhouse told him there was no furniture that needed repairs, the carpenter confessed that he had planted the car bomb, then shouted that he had been sent by God, and lunged forward with the knife.

Backhouse claimed he fled from the kitchen to get his shotgun, and had fired twice in self-defense. A search of Bedale-

*"Poison pen" letters that Backhouse wrote himself were all part of his plan to fake a pattern of harassment.*

Taylor's workshop corroborated Backhouse's story: investigators found a piece of pipe matching the makeshift bomb in the Volvo.

## Clues in blood

However, when scene of crime officers began to study Widden Hill Farm, they started to suspect that Backhouse was not telling the truth. The pattern of blood in the kitchen was particularly revealing. If there had been a violent struggle there, as Backhouse claimed, blood would have been thrown off with some force, leaving elongated marks with distinct tails. But on the kitchen floor there were only circular drops characteristic of blood that had dripped from a wound. An upset chair covered some of the marks, suggesting that it had been placed there as an afterthought. More revealing still, there was no trail of blood in the hall leading

from the kitchen—the route that the wounded Backhouse claimed he followed when he went to get his gun.

There were other inconsistencies. The dead man was found gripping the knife, but as the forensic pathologist who carried out the autopsy pointed out, he would have dropped it as he fell. Backhouse's own wounds were curious, too. There were no cuts on his hands, and the continuous slashes from neck to waist suggested he had stood still and offered no opposition as his assailant cut him.

## Insurance scam

Probing further, investigators found out more disturbing facts. Backhouse had huge and growing debts. He was an incompetent farmer, and his crops had failed for two consecutive years. In March 1984, he had doubled the insurance cover on his wife's life. Her death would have cleared his debts.

Police charged Graham Backhouse with the murder of Colyn Bedale-Taylor, and also the attempted murder of his wife. At his trial the prosecution painted a picture of a cynical, scheming killer. Not content with maiming his wife in an attempt to collect the insurance payoff, he was prepared to kill his innocent neighbor in cold blood and mutilate

**SECOND TRY ▶**
*Undertakers carry away the victim of Backhouse's second, more successful murder attempt.*

**SIGN OF A MURDERER ▲**
*Despite the optimistic sign at the gate, Backhouse had run up a $100,000 debt supporting the farm, and this was his motive for murder.*

himself to ensure that he would not be suspected of the bombing.

Detectives were even able to prove that the sheep's head was part of the plan. The writing on the threatening note was crudely but effectively disguised, so it could not be identified as Backhouse's own hand. But faintly embossed on the sheet was a trace of doodle—that perfectly matched a scribble on a pad found at Widden Hill Farm.

Graham Backhouse denied murder, but the jurors were not taken in. The ruthless, ingenious killer received two life sentences on February 18, 1985; he died of a heart attack nine years later.

# Telltale traces

I n the concise motto "every contact leaves a trace," forensic scientist Edmond Locard established a principle that still guides the investigation of every crime. Criminals cannot avoid leaving traces of their presence at a crime scene—and they always carry away with them some evidence that they have been there.

The simplicity of Locard's exchange principle is deceptive. It may seem like an obvious statement, yet its implications are subtle and far-reaching. No matter how much care criminals take, they can never leave a crime scene exactly as they found it. They always leave behind something that may lead to their identification. The reverse is also true: the guilty cannot avoid carrying away traces of evidence that link them to the crime.

When Locard first formulated this idea in 1920, DNA was unheard-of, and he could not have imagined that a nanogram of blood—one forty-millionth of a drop— would be enough to identify a criminal conclusively. The traces he was thinking of were artifacts such as hairs, paint flecks, dust, soil, fibers, and minute flakes of glass— the tiniest of objects that usually pass unnoticed.

Locard demonstrated this exchange principle in his work long before he formulated his famous summary. In 1912, he solved the case of Emile Gourbin, a bank clerk who was suspected of strangling his girlfriend. Gourbin seemed to have a cast-iron alibi for the time of the murder, but Locard's examination of scrapings from his fingernails revealed tiny flakes of skin. More damning still, the flakes were covered with pink dust that matched the face powder on the dead woman's neck. Confronted with this evidence, Gourbin confessed.

Locard's "traces" included all manner of substances, from flakes of skin to gun residue. Today many of these are analyzed in specialized branches of forensic science, such as firearms. The term "trace evidence" now usually refers to just a few categories: fibers, hair, paints and coatings, and soil and botanicals, such as plant fragments.

**SCANNING ELECTRON MICROSCOPE (SEM) ▼**
*By bombarding specially prepared specimens with electrons, the SEM reveals incredible surface detail—as small as one nanometer. That is 100,000 times smaller than a hair's breadth. (With SEM wool fiber inset.)*

## How do we find traces?
The very nature of trace evidence makes it elusive and ephemeral. The clothes a criminal wears collect dirt and fibers from a crime scene, but many of these simply fall off in a matter of hours. Brushing or cleaning clothes removes most of what is left. At a crime scene, trace evidence may be invisible to the unaided eye. So investigators are faced with the problem of finding something they cannot see.

How do they do it? Partly by making a methodical sweep of a crime scene, and partly by making informed guesses about what they are looking for and where they might find it. On garments, for example, seams and pockets retain incriminating fibers even when the rest of the fabric is apparently spotless.

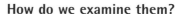

## LOOKING CLOSELY

Microscopes are an essential tool in modern forensic science. Different types are used depending on the nature of the evidence. They range from ones that examine surface details to those that see right through a specimen.

**LIGHT MICROSCOPES ▲**
*Light microscopes allow investigators literally to look inside trace evidence. Their versatility is enhanced by stereo and duplicated optics, and special kinds of illumination.*

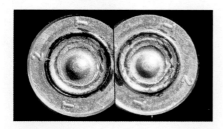

**COMPARISON MICROSCOPES ▲**
*The duplicated optical system of the comparison microscope projects images of two different specimens into a single eyepiece, greatly simplifying comparison of a pair of samples.*

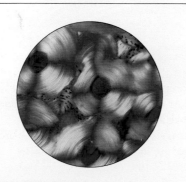

**POLARIZED LIGHT ▲**
*A filter that polarizes light lets through rays vibrating in only one plane, so a pair of crossed filters block all light. Trace evidence placed between them on a microscope scatters and colors the light, creating a vivid image that reveals structure.*

### How do we collect them?

Collecting trace evidence demands as much skill and patience as finding it. Larger fragments can be retrieved by hand—perhaps with the aid of a lens and a pair of tweezers. Forensic vacuums are an effective way of collecting smaller traces: they suck material on to a filter paper for later analysis. Careful and regular replacement of the filter makes it possible to identify where in the crime scene the evidence came from. For small areas, tape lifts are an effective way of removing traces. Investigators also bag up and remove portable objects so that they can recover particles later in the controlled conditions of a lab. There, washing and scraping can reveal trace evidence that might otherwise have escaped notice.

▲ *Forcing an entry creates copious trace evidence. A paint fleck that sticks to clothes has color, composition, and a coat order that make identification simple.*

▲ *The telltale fibers that garments shed are highly distinctive—and are transferred easily. Thousands may stick to the cushions when we sit on a chair.*

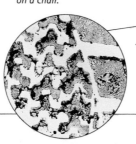

◄ *Shoes do not just leave behind prints: they can also pick up trace evidence such as tiny slivers of glass from the crime scene.*

### How do we examine them?

Close inspection is needed to reveal the secrets of trace evidence, so microscopes are the key instruments in the traces lab. They have several huge advantages over other analytical methods: they are completely nondestructive—a crucial point when evidence is vanishingly small. In most cases, no preparation or treatment of the specimen is required. Finally, microscopy is often the only way to distinguish between different varieties of trace evidence. For example, no chemical test can reveal the order in which paint was applied to a surface, yet the order of layers becomes immediately apparent when placed under a microscope.

◄ *Three or four hairs fall unnoticed from our heads each hour, and microscopy reveals color and structure that can link a suspect to the crime scene.*

Red top coat, badly bonded to original green paint, makes a combination easy to identify.

Paint layers are coated on to rusting body.

**▲ RESPRAYED CAR PAINTWORK**

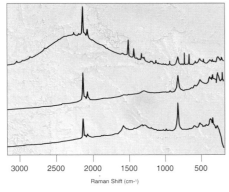

3000    2500    2000    1500    1000    500

Raman Shift (cm⁻¹)

**PAINT COMPARISON ▲**

*A microspectrophotometer can distinguish between two paint samples of virtually the same color. The composition of each sample is analyzed and shown as a line with output peaks on a graph. The graph above shows three samples that are not from the same source.*

# Material witness

To the forensic scientist, tiny particles of glass, fibers, and paint can tell intriguing stories. These manufactured materials add a limitless variety of color and sparkle to our everyday environment. It is this sheer diversity that makes minute traces of them such a powerful aid in linking the crime scene or victim with the suspect.

Open a decorator's color chart, and you will get a glimpse of the rainbow variety of house paints available from just one manufacturer. Multiply this by the number of brands, and you realize that if paint from a crime scene matches a fleck found on a suspect, it strongly suggests a link between the two. But paint is seldom applied in a single layer. If several coats match, the link between suspect and crime is very compelling indeed.

Motor vehicle paints vary widely between makes and models. If a sample from the scene of an accident matches one taken from a suspect vehicle, the odds against a different vehicle being involved may be as high as 16,000:1.

## Looking closely

Even at low magnification, the colors of each coat in a paint fleck are often clearly visible. If simple visual examination is inconclusive, then cutting and polishing paint samples can make the colors and their sequence more obvious. More subtle methods of analysis include microspectrophotometry—an electronic study of the energy wavelengths of light absorbed and emitted by a sample.

In crimes where there are already suspects, paint samples taken from them and from the crime scene can be compared directly, but paint can also help in cases where the criminal's identity is unknown. Police forces maintain databases of vehicle

**TRACING HIT-AND-RUN DRIVERS**
*Road accidents can leave traces on both the victim and the vehicle. Car bodywork retains incriminating clothing fibers, and leaves behind paint, glass, and plastic.*

## TYPES OF FIBERS

Investigators study not only fiber origin but also other identifying factors. These include fiber count, the twist direction in a spun strand, the thickness of a strand, and textile weave.

**◀ ANIMAL FUR** *is usually finer than human hair, and differs markedly between species. Each strand of this cat fur, for example, is covered with distinctive overlapping scales.*

**▶ SYNTHETIC FIBERS** *are less distinctive than natural fibers under the microscope. Their method of manufacture gives them a regular pattern, though texture may vary.*

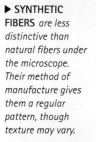

**◀ PLANT FIBERS** *have typical shapes. Cotton (shown here woven) is ribbon-like and twisted. Linen fibers look like knobbly tubes, and are pointed at each end.*

**▶ LEAF MATERIAL** *such as this stinging nettle is easy to distinguish from the fibers of cultivated plants, but only botanists can identify the particular species.*

**◀ GLASS FIBERS** *found together can indicate what they were applied in— aligned in mats, as here, they are widely used to reinforce tough plastic structures, such as boat hulls.*

**BENDING LIGHT ▶**
*Refractive index can link glass pieces to a pane broken in a crime. To measure a shard's refraction, technicians immerse the sample in an oil that changes its refractive index when heated. At the right temperature, the sample all but disappears. For larger pieces of glass, a laser can be used for measurement.*

paintwork, and in a hit-and-run case, this can help narrow down the search to a particular make, model, and even year. It is sometimes possible to fit a paint chip exactly back on to the surface from which it flaked. This physical match would be important evidence.

### Transparently obvious

Flakes of glass can occasionally be matched in a way similar to paint, like pieces of a puzzle. Where this is not possible, investigators see if they can find a match by looking at the refractive index (light-bending ability) and density of the glass sample. Different types of glass bend light to different degrees. The method of measuring refractive index is explained above. Density measurement works by comparing the glass with two liquids that have different densities. Glass floats in the heavier liquid, and sinks in the lighter. Technicians mix the fluids until the glass sample neither sinks nor rises, then work out the glass density from the proportions of the two liquids.

If these two diagnostic methods produce a match for a pair of glass samples, investigators then refer to databases of glass types. This will tell them how common or unusual the glass is.

### Matching fibers

To the unaided eye, most fibers of similar color look broadly alike. But under the microscope, the differences are amazing. Natural fibers vary enormously in cross-sectional shape. Animal fibers have characteristic scales on the surface, and have a varied thickness. There is a much wider variety of synthetic fibers, which can be identified by their solubility and melting point; by optical qualities such

as refractive index; by their shape; and by chemical analysis.

Dyes add yet another dimension— by analyzing their component colors using thin-layer chromatography (see p. 82) or by microspectrophotometry, investigators can distinguish between otherwise similar fibers.

### Common or rare?

Traces of glass, paint, and fibers have provided investigators with important leads in countless cases, and their collection is a routine part of police work. However, it is important to remember that their value as evidence depends on how common they are. Just one fiber of an unusual fabric can be all the evidence that is needed to put a criminal on trial, but undyed cotton is so common that fibers of it found at a crime scene are quickly disregarded.

**LOCK OF HUMAN HEAD HAIR**
*Under the microscope, the cross-section of human hair reveals where it grew. Armpit hairs are oval, beard hairs are triangular, and other head hairs are round. Eyelashes and brows taper rapidly.*

# Riddle of the fibers

When, in the summer of 1979, bodies of strangled children were found in Atlanta, the city police did not suspect a serial killer. As the body count soared toward 30 in just 10 months, terrified parents demanded action. Then, on May 22, 1981, a stakeout trapped a man dumping something heavy into the Chattahoochee River.

Surveillance personnel flagged down Wayne Williams' car a little way from the James Jackson river bridge, and quizzed him. Where was he going at 2:00 A.M. on a Friday? The music promoter's reply was that he had been looking for the address of a young woman he was planning to promote. What had he thrown in the river? "Just trash," he said.

Police became more suspicious when he gave them a nonexistent address and telephone number for his promising young singing talent. However, a search of his car produced nothing incriminating, nor did dragging the river under the bridge. Still not entirely satisfied with his story, the police had Williams followed.

On Sunday, the body of Nathaniel Cater was washed up a mile downstream from the bridge. He had been reported missing a few days earlier. He had been asphyxiated, and he was naked, but in his hair was a single strand of nylon.

### A fiber thread

Some months earlier, trace experts at the Georgia State Crime Laboratory had begun to notice fiber evidence linking the murders. The bodies of the earliest victims had been dumped fully dressed, and studies of their clothing revealed a similar thread stuck to virtually all of them. It was a coarse, yellowish-green fiber. Under the microscope it was clear that the fibers had a lobed cross-section characteristic of furnishing or carpet fabric. Initially, the discovery proved to be a blind alley because forensic experts could not identify the source of the fibers. But when this line of investigation was leaked to the press, the Atlanta killer changed his habits. He continued to strangle or smother his victims, but he began stripping them and dumping them in rivers to remove the telltale textile traces.

The nylon thread in Cater's hair was yellow-green, and had a lobed cross-section. The police got a search warrant.

### Finding a match

On June 3, they combed Williams' car and the house where he lived with his parents, and took away thousands of fiber samples. That night, detective Larry

**CHILD KILLER ▲**
*Wayne Williams' indulgent parents bankrolled his career as a music promoter, but he had little ability for recognising real talent, and he developed a reputation for promising more than he could deliver.*

Peterson worked late at the crime lab, comparing fibers taken from victims with those collected in the search.

He made a remarkable discovery. Hairs found on some of the victims matched hairs taken from the Williams' German shepherd. Most of the victims also had fibers on their clothes that were identical to those taken from a bedspread in the house. And the yellowish-green fibers matched the olive-colored carpet that covered most of the floors. In the early hours of the morning, Larry phoned Hal Deadman, a detective from the FBI's Microscopic Analysis Unit, who was also working on the case:

**RIVER RECOVERY ▼**
*On March 30, 1981, Atlanta police pulled the body of 13-year-old Timothy Hill from the river. He was the last child victim of the killer, who then went on to target young men.*

"I've made some matches…" he said. "You'd better come over here."

Hal dressed and went over to the lab, and together the two men studied the fibers. "Larry and I were convinced that someone in the Williams environment was involved in the murders," he recalled later.

## Combining probabilities

They both knew that the significance of the match depended on how common the fibers were, so they traced the manufacturer: Wellman, Inc. The company had sold the nylon yarn, 181B, between 1967 and 1974. Several carpet manufacturers had bought it, but only one had dyed the fibers yellow-green. In 1970 and 1971 the West Point Pepperell Corporation had woven yellow-green 181B yarn into Luxaire English Olive carpet. They made only 16,397 sq yd (13,710 sq m)—enough to carpet roughly two-and-a-half football fields or about 52 tennis courts. From sales figures and average room sizes, Larry and Hal estimated that the chances of an Atlanta home chosen at random being carpeted with this brand and color were around 7,792 to 1.

But this was just one kind of fiber. Others told the same story. Rayon that matched the carpet in Williams' 1970 Chevrolet was found on the bodies of four victims. Only 680 cars in the Atlanta area had similar carpet. And the odds against a murdered child picking the fiber up by chance were 3,828 to 1. Combining the two probabilities made the case even more compelling: the odds against finding both fibers at random were 29 million to 1. Some of the bodies had 10 different fibers that all matched samples taken from different places in the Williams house. It was virtually impossible that such a match would occur by chance.

## Material witness

Wayne Williams, meanwhile, protested his innocence—with a high-profile press conference at his home.

This proved to be a mistake. In the frenzy of publicity that now engulfed the case, witnesses came forward to say they had seen Williams with some of the victims. Two recording studio staff recalled that they had seen deep scratches on his forearms—the kind strangling victims inflict as they fight for their last breath.

Atlanta prosecutors were hesitant about basing so much of their case on fiber evidence, which they felt was highly technical, and could confuse the jury. But under pressure to get a conviction, they went ahead. Wayne Williams was tried and found guilty of two of the murders. He was sentenced to two life terms.

THE ARREST ▼
*Police had enough evidence to convict Williams, despite the fact that he and his father had cleaned up their house and cars and burned photographs in a backyard barbecue.*

BANKS OF THE CHATTAHOOCHEE ▲
*At his trial, Wayne Williams' defense was that the river water had swept the fibers on to the bodies. But the same fibers were found on victims dumped in streets and woodland.*

# Environmental clues

We brush dirt from our shoes and vacuum dust from our homes, but when a crime is committed, these substances often form valuable evidence. The minerals, fibers, and other particles they contain are the signatures of the outdoor and indoor spaces they came from, and can hint at a suspect's job, hobbies, movements, and habits.

Dust and dirt are so familiar to us that we only notice them as we clean them away. Even then we give scarcely a thought to their significance or composition. In a forensic context, dust and soil can provide direction to an entire police investigation, and may provide crucial evidence to link a suspect to the crime scene. Soil is mostly mineral and plant matter, but can incorporate small quantities of manufactured and building materials, depending on location. Dry, fine soil particles dominate outdoor dust, but indoor dust is mostly fibrous.

## Collecting dust and dirt

At a crime scene, investigators use tape lifts to sample superficial dust, or a forensic vacuum to collect ingrained dust from surfaces such as vehicle seats or carpets. A laboratory provides a more controlled environment for dust recovery from evidence such as clothes. Technicians pick out larger debris with tweezers or tape, and vacuum smaller particles.

A complete analysis of dust or soil is time-consuming, but fortunately, the need to do this is rare. More often, investigators want answers to specific questions, such as "Does the mud on the rape suspect's jeans

### COLLECTING SAMPLES:

① *Sieves in progressively finer meshes grade soil by particle size.*

② *String grid provides measurement baselines in order to locate source of each sample on sketch of site.*

③ *Flags mark location of other evidence.*

④ *Here investigators are retaining large samples, but only a few spoonfuls are needed for soil analysis.*

## CLUES IN THE SOIL

◀ **SOIL COLOR**
*from crime scene and suspect may look similar, but only microscopy can prove they are the same.*

▶ **PARTICLE SIZE**
*is mixed in most soils: the large grains here are silt. Clay is also present, but too small to see.*

◀ **SEEDS**
*and especially pollens resist decay in soil, and can often be identified by their shape and size.*

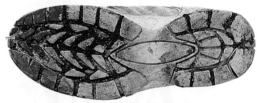

*Shoe treads collect soil easily.*

**A GRAVE FULL OF EVIDENCE ▼**
*Investigators recovering human remains take soil samples to compare with material found on a suspect's clothes, shoes, and vehicle. Pollen traces on the body can confirm whether it was moved, and soil may retain drug or chemical residues from the body.*

To preserve the integrity of soil evidence, it is placed in a clean container that is sealed. Police change clothes between taking samples from crime scene and suspect to avoid compromising the evidence.

**◀ SOIL SAMPLING**
*Investigators often take samples even when there is no reason to believe soil evidence may be valuable: once a crime scene is released, the soil may be contaminated.*

match mud found at the crime scene?"

Forensic scientists answer such questions by directly comparing the two soil samples. They analyze color, pH levels, and types and sizes of the particles the samples contain. Mineral particles have the properties of the rock from which they weathered, such as limestone or quartz. Particle shape can also provide clues; grains of ocean sand and desert sand, for instance, have quite different and distinct shapes. Botanical material, such as leaf debris, seeds, pollen, and fungal spores, may be more important because it can provide copious and highly specific information. In a 1960 abduction case in Australia, for example, investigators identified the culprit because a seed found on the victim's body came from a rare type of cypress tree that grew in the kidnapper's yard. Also, the proportion of different pollen types, a "pollen signature," found on suspects' clothing has been used to narrow search areas for buried bodies. Pollen and seeds can provide chronological information, too. Plants shed them only at certain times of the year, so their presence on clothing not only places a suspect or victim at a particular scene, but also indicates the season that they were there.

**HOUSE DUST**
*These magnified images illustrate how dust from different homes looks nothing alike. So finding a dust match makes for strong evidence. These samples include pet hair, skin flakes, dust mites, and fibers of clothing and carpets.*

## Under the microscope

Initial analysis of dust and soil relies on visual identification, using an optical comparison microscope coupled with a polarizer. More detailed analysis requires a scanning electron microscope. Microscopists need an encyclopedic memory for the many different particles they are likely to find, but they are aided by reference collections of the more common types. (Most labs accumulate such samples over time, but—bizarrely—it is actually possible to buy collections of dust.)

Microchemical analysis and X-ray spectroscopy can be used to provide further information if needed.

## Damning dirt

Most importantly, dust and soil can give detectives new leads to follow. Soil samples may contain minerals from outside the area where the crime was committed, or the seeds and pollen of plants that do not grow locally. In these cases, mineralogists and botanists

may be able to suggest locations where the police should focus their investigation.

Dust can be equally specific. Some house dust, for example, contains particles that are unique to the rooms from which it was collected. Bathroom dust contains talcum powder and cosmetics, and there is often flour and ground spices in kitchen dust. Industrial workers carry with them dust that identifies their employment. Yeast spores cling to brewers and bakers, and printers' clothes are ingrained with ink droplets and paper fibers. A 1960s case demonstrated how valuable industrial dust can be. Dust found on the bodies of murdered London prostitutes contained tiny spheres of paint, which led detectives to the killer. He was a regular visitor to a car paint shop where every surface was covered with brightly colored dust formed by drifting paint spray.

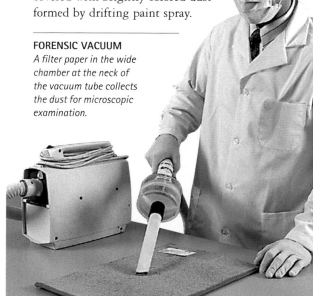

**FORENSIC VACUUM**
*A filter paper in the wide chamber at the neck of the vacuum tube collects the dust for microscopic examination.*

# Festina trial

Racing cyclists from top teams like Festina seemed to have superhuman energy and endurance, yet they rarely tested positive for drugs that might give a competitive edge. It all seemed too good to be true; and it was. The plot started to unravel in 1998 when customs officers stopped a team masseur on his way to the Tour de France.

**WILLY VOET ▲**
*Age 54 at the time of the trial, Willy Voet had once been a promising young amateur cyclist, dropping out only when the pace of training became too much.*

To spectators at a cycle race, the platoon of leading riders is a technicolour streak of lycra and spinning spokes. They are in sight only for an instant, just long enough to grab drinks from their soigneurs—masseurs and minders—before disappearing around the next corner. To see them as anything other than a blur, you have to wait at the finishing line—preferably on a hilltop. Exhausted, the competitors seem suddenly, painfully human. But when they get off their bikes, a different kind of sport begins.

### Passing

The cycling superheroes lope over to the dope-test caravan to see whose turn it is to pee into a bottle. The Union Cycliste Internationale (UCI), cycling's governing

**FESTINA MANAGER ▼**
*Bruno Roussel, the Festina manager, received the harshest sentence for his central role in obtaining the drugs and supplying them to the team.*

body, is vigilant about drugs such as human growth hormone, amphetamines, painkillers, and EPO (see box on opposite page). The chosen few file into the caravan to be tested.

The UCI leaves nothing to chance: the cyclists are observed constantly; and they have to strip, so that they have no clothes in which to hide bogus urine samples. And yet inside the caravan there have sometimes been performances that would befit a conjuror more than a cyclist. A racer with something to hide would wear a condom filled with "safe" urine concealed in his anus; the narrow tube that led down between his legs was dusted with blond fluff to make it less conspicuous. All he had to do was to pull out a cork and clench his buttocks to complete the illusion. The sample was even delivered at body temperature, and the toxicology always came back negative.

There were other tricks for riders who had taken too much EPO. To prepare for the test, their soigneurs put a saline drip in their arms. Within 20 minutes the rider's haematocrit (the proportion of red cells in the blood) would be down below the crucial 50% needed to pass.

### Keeping up

The teams kept this subterfuge to themselves. To the fans and the UCI, cycling was a clean sport.

**WILLY AND RICHARD ▶**
*The relationship between riders and their soigneurs is a close one, and Voet and Virenque were no exception. Here Voet shows off a photo Virenque signed for him.*

And for the riders, there were a dozen ways to rationalize doping. As Willy Voet, soigneur to the Festina team, lucidly explained it, "A champion is not made by the drugs he takes." As long as a few riders took drugs, the reasoning went, everyone had to do it, to avoid losing the competitive edge.

Slipping behind, of course, was out of the question. So Willy Voet would receive consignments of "the latest available technology" from Spain and Portugal. He'd ferry them around in his car as he followed the team. The riders would get their injections along with their massage the night before the race, and drugs to be taken orally were hidden in their water bottles or clothes.

## EPO

Central to the Festina trial was the use of erythropoietin, or EPO, a hormone that occurs naturally in the human body. It's secreted by the liver, and it stimulates the bone marrow to produce the red blood cells that transport oxygen around the body. Extra red cells are a bonus for athletes in an endurance sport such as cycling, because they boost the flow of oxygen to overtaxed leg muscles, keeping them going longer.

Injecting synthetic EPO provides cyclists with this vital boost, with the added advantage that the drug is undetectable. It isn't harmless, though: high levels of red cells literally thicken the blood, raising the risk of thrombosis. In the absence of a test for the drug, the UCI decided in 1997 to test for haematocrit, the proportion of red cells in the blood, setting a level of 50% as the maximum allowed for a rider.

### Caught

This was why, one Wednesday morning in July 1998, Willy Voet had a couple of cold boxes of drugs behind the passenger seat of the Festina team car as he crossed the Belgium–France border. He had taken a minor road, and when a uniformed figure stepped out ahead of him, his first reaction was surprise. Slowing to a halt, he saw a white van parked nearby, and surprise turned to panic. Four more customs men approached, surrounding his car.

CYCLING STAR ▶
*Though the case dented the reputation of Virenque, his popularity meant he was able to return to the sport as a professional in 2001.*

"Anything to declare?" Shaking, Voet replied, "Not really, just vitamins for the riders." One of the officers reached into the box behind the passenger seat, "And these?" Voet squirmed. "I don't know. Stuff to help the riders recover, I think."

They drove to the customs post, and asked him the same question again, this time lining up rows of bottles, vials, and brown balls on the desk in front of him. Voet's answer was the same, so the officers sent the boxes away for analysis in a laboratory.

By Friday, the results had come back: human growth hormone, EPO, testosterone. Willy Voet at first tried to protect his friends and colleagues at Festina by claiming that the drugs were for his own use. When he realized this was ridiculous, the story came tumbling out.

### All the way to the top

Yes, he had supplied drugs, but he wasn't the only one. Everyone knew what was going on—the doctors, the managers, and of course the cyclists, including the team leader and star Richard Virenque. Voet's confession was sensational—the more so because it came at the start of the Tour.

The initial impact on Festina was devastating enough: they were disqualified from the race. Worse was to come. When Voet finally appeared in court to answer charges of supplying the drugs, he was not alone. Also facing the judge were the team's manager, Bruno Roussel, the doctor, Erik Rijkaert, Virenque (the only rider on trial), and six others.

Right up to the start of the trial, Virenque strongly denied taking drugs. But after damning evidence to the contrary he too confessed: "It was not cheating," he said. "It was like a train going away from me. If I didn't get on it, I would be left behind."

### End of the line

Virenque's train derailed when the trial ended, just before Christmas 2000. Though he was acquitted, the UCI barred him from riding. But due to his popularity, this didn't last long, and he was able to become a professional rider again in 2001. The remainder of the defendants did not get off as lightly, receiving fines and suspended prison sentences. The Festina affair rattled the world of cycling, but it is doubtful whether it had any lasting effect. As the Tour weaves through the French countryside each year, the riders still flash past so fast it's difficult to believe they're powered by muscles alone.

DRUG CAR ▼
*Voet suspects customs officers were tipped off, and his team car made him a conspicuous target.*

# LETHAL AGENTS

Filled with a passionate anger, killers reach for the nearest weapon. It may be a gun or a knife, or they may even use their own hands; but increasingly it is the throttle pedal of that most underestimated killing machine, the car. Homicide is not always a spontaneous act, though. Some killers use careful planning, and murder their victims using poison, bombs, or an arson attack. But others may kill inadvertently through negligence, such as in cases of accidental fires, transport disasters, or industrial explosions.

# Firearms at the scene

**G**uns are primarily carried as a status symbol in criminal circles. They indicate a lethal threat and induce fear in enemies and victims. Occasionally they are used with deadly consequences. A bullet, however, creates a trail of subtle but persistent clues linking the victim, the weapon, and the shooter. And the trail begins at the crime scene.

When criminals fire guns, evidence flies in all directions. The first and most lethal is the bullet itself. The second is the spent cartridge case—the jacket that retained the bullet—which usually ejects from the gun. The third is part-burned powder spraying from the barrel, and from gaps in the gun's mechanism and casing. Finally, the sound of the gunshot can be heard by witnesses.

Each of these components can help investigators, and their work at the scene of a shooting is concerned with collecting as many of them as possible. But to understand how they do this, it is necessary to know a little about how a gun works.

## Types of gun

All firearms work in a similar way. Pulling the trigger makes a firing pin strike the back of the cartridge, igniting a tiny pressure-sensitive charge called a primer. The primer in turn detonates the explosive powder in the cartridge, forcing the bullet (or, in a shotgun, the pellets) down the barrel toward the target.

The simplest guns require reloading after firing once or twice. Most, though, have some sort of magazine holding five or more cartridges. In semiautomatic weapons, the force of the explosion that powers the bullet forward also ejects the spent cartridge case, loads a new one, and cocks (pulls back) the firing pin ready for the next shot. In automatic weapons, holding back the trigger fires the gun repeatedly until the magazine is empty.

## Where did the bullets go?

Professional assassins who kill with a single bullet are rare. Most shootings are more hit-and-miss affairs involving several shots. To reconstruct the crime, it is necessary to determine where each bullet went and exactly how it got there.

So an investigator's first task at the scene of a shooting is to figure out how

**THE GIVEAWAYS**
*Loading and firing a semiautomatic pistol leaves a wealth of forensic evidence that can help identify the shooter.*

*Imperfections on breech get stamped on to the cartridge case*

*The firing pin presses a distinctive dent into the primer cup*

*Rifling (spiral grooves in the barrel) scratches the bullet in a unique way*

*The ejector mechanism marks the cartridge cases*

*Gunshot residue can spray from the trigger hole on to the hands*

*Shooter's fingers may pick up traces of soft metals used in ammunition*

*Gun oil traces from the mechanisms can get on the hands*

## SHOOTING SCENE PROTOCOL:

| 1 | Swab suspects for gunshot residues. |
|---|---|
| 2 | Mark the position of cartridge cases. |
| 3 | Account for every shot fired. |
| 4 | Search the scene exhaustively to locate and retrieve all bullets. |
| 5 | Reconstruct bullet trajectories. |
| 6 | Document the scene with photography and video. |
| 7 | Recover any weapons and other evidence and release scene. |

**SPENT CASING ▼**
*The position of a spent cartridge at a crime scene may indicate where the assailant was standing.*

many shots were fired. Witnesses may have counted them, or if the assailant dropped the weapon, it is possible to deduce the maximum number of shots by counting remaining cartridges. Spent cartridge cases are also counted, as explained below.

The next step is to find the bullets. Shooting victims are routinely X-rayed, and lead lodged in their bodies shows up as distinct shadows. Investigators search the crime scene exhaustively for the rest. A bullet found embedded in soft materials is especially valuable, since markings on it can help identify at least what type of weapon fired it. If a weapon has been

## TYPES OF FIREARMS

Guns not to scale

**REVOLVER**
Pulling the trigger turns the cylinder, positioning a cartridge before the barrel, then cocks and releases the hammer.

**SEMIAUTOMATIC**
These are quicker to fire and load than revolvers: a quick-change magazine in the grip holds up to 30 cartridges.

**SUBMACHINE GUNS**
Assault rifles and submachine guns can switch between automatic and semi-automatic fire. Rifles use larger ammo.

**HUNTING RIFLE**
These have a hand-operated lever or slide to eject the cartridge after firing and load a fresh one into the chamber.

**SHOTGUN**
A shotgun fires a handful of small lead pellets that spread, rather than a single bullet. This reduces the need to aim.

done with lengths of rod and string, or by sighting through a succession of holes pierced by the bullet. Lasers may sometimes be used but can only be seen and photographed in certain light conditions.

### Cartridge cases

Scattered around the crime scene, cartridge cases not only help to identify the weapon used, they can also indicate where it was fired from. Most weapons eject cartridge cases to the right, and experimentation with a similar weapon on a range may suggest how far and in what direction the cartridge cases fly. However, the posture and grip of the person firing can affect this. Markings on cartridge cases provide valuable information linking them to the weapon that fired them: impact with the breech stamps a unique pattern on the end, and the ejector mechanism also scratches the metal in a characteristic way.

### Gunshot residue

Investigators look for primer gunshot residues on the victim, in a circle around the bullet wound, and on the suspect, usually on the hands and clothes.

When victims are shot at close range, the entry wound is typically ringed with soot and "tattooing"—stippled marks where partially burned propellant has been driven into the skin. The appearance of the ring can give some indication of range.

Residues found on certain places on a suspect's hand indicate that they have recently fired a weapon, but absence of residues is not proof of innocence. Not all weapons discharge residues, and washing removes deposits. For this reason, investigators sometimes test a suspect's clothes and face as well as their hands.

A suspect may also bear traces of other materials that suggest gun use. Loading a magazine, for example, transfers gun oil and metal on to the fingers.

**TRACING TRAJECTORIES ▲**
*Highly visible string or doweling are used to reconstruct the shooting scene. These are then photographed for use as evidence in a court of law.*

recovered, bullet markings may also prove conclusively that the suspect weapon fired it, as explained on the next page.

Even when bullets are squashed against a hard surface beyond the possibility of analysis, finding the point of impact is important. It enables investigators to trace the trajectory—the path from gun barrel to final resting place. This is traditionally

**SWABBING DOWN**
*Each part of a suspect's hand is individually swabbed because the location of gunshot residue can indicate that a suspect handled a gun, but did not fire it. Below is a highly magnified image of primer gunshot residue.*

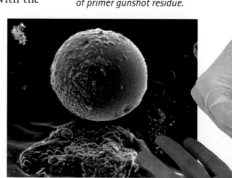

# Firearms in the lab

I n the firearms section of a crime lab, the smell of gun oil and burned powder and the sound of gunfire are never far away. For a firearms examiner needs to be part sleuth and part marksman: it is necessary to have a feeling for guns and ammo that is impossible to acquire without spending time on a firing range.

**BULLET DATABASE ▲**
*In addition to computer databases of ammunition, most firearms sections also maintain a collection of the real thing, for comparison and test firing.*

Though often mistakenly called "ballistics," the forensic department that specializes in guns and ammunition is more correctly described as "firearms identification." For ballistics—literally the flight of projectiles—is peripheral to the job. Instead, firearms examiners spend most of their time studying and comparing the subtle dents, scratches, and marks found on ammunition (see box on cartridge and bullet markings). The testing and firing of suspect weapons to reproduce these marks for comparison, and for other purposes, is also a necessary part of the work.

## Comparing ammunition

When investigators find a bullet, a careful study of the marks on it can reveal what kind of gun fired it. But once a suspect weapon has been found, the firearms examiner can go much further. Loading the gun with the appropriate ammunition, and firing it—into a water tank or a box of gel—marks the test bullet with striation marks that are as unique as a human fingerprint. To compare these scratches and grooves with those on the bullet recovered from the crime scene, or body of a victim, the examiner uses a comparison microscope (see p. 89). A match is positive proof that the same gun fired both bullets.

Microscopic examination of spent cartridge cases can tell a similar story, revealing at least the class of weapon that ejected the case. And

**◀ GROOVE FOLLOWER**
*This instrument uses a stylus to measure the rifling grooves on a spent bullet for comparison with one used in the suspect weapon.*

as with bullets, if a suspect weapon is recovered, a test firing produces a comparison cartridge case that can verify whether the same gun was involved.

## Computerized matching

Bullets found at a scene can also be compared with similar evidence from previous investigations. Using microscopic methods would be impossibly slow, but it is practical to compare hundreds of thousands using computer databases.

One of the best known of these is the FBI's Drugfire system. It works in a way similar to other databases. Firearms examiners mount a recovered bullet or cartridge case on a microscope stage, enter some initial data—such as a case number—into a linked computer, and start a database search. A scanner then automatically creates a digital image of the evidence, and the system looks for similar records for visual comparison.

Like computerized fingerprint searching, this powerful technology saves a lot of time. It also enables firearms examiners to deduce links between otherwise unconnected crimes, and perhaps solve them "cold."

## Testing weapons

Firearms examiners may test a weapon to discover whether it can be discharged accidentally, if this forms part of a defense in a shooting case. And they may dismantle weapons—to find out how a semiautomatic was illegally converted for automatic fire, for example.

Range firing of shotguns reveals the shot spread. The cloud of pellets that a shotgun fires fans out from a tight clump at short range to a scattered cloud farther away. In the past, investigators used rough

## CARTRIDGE AND BULLET MARKINGS

Loading and firing a gun engraves its ammunition with a wealth of marks.

Several different parts of the weapon mark the cartridge case. The magazine scratches it. The impact of the firing pin puts a distinctive dent in the metal cover that retains the primer. The explosion that follows stamps the cartridge case with a mirror image of marks on the breech—the solid block that holds it in the barrel. Finally, the mechanism that ejects the spent cartridge case also scratches it.

Marks on the bullet come from rifling—spiraling grooves inside the barrel that spin the bullet to stabilize it. Scratches on the bullet duplicate the spacing, size, direction (clockwise or counterclockwise), and angle of the grooves. In combination with the caliber (size) of the bullet, this information enables a firearms examiner to identify the class of weapon that fired the bullet, or to match a recovered bullet to a suspect gun.

**◄ RIFLING**
*Firearms examiners use computer databases to match a weapon from the rifling marks it makes on the bullet.*

**◄ FIRING PIN**
*The comparison microscope presents two cartridge cases as one, in a divided image. This makes it easy to see whether the same firing pin dented the soft metal primer cover of each.*

**◄ STRIATIONS**
*Unique to each weapon, striation marks are created from tiny imperfections in the gun's barrel. A close look at two bullets may show an unmistakable match.*

rules of thumb to determine range from the spread of pellets, but research has shown that spread is not easy to predict. It varies between apparently similar weapons, and is affected by the type and batch of cartridges, even by temperature and humidity.

Range firing also has a role in testing the spread of primer gunshot residues (P-GSR) from weapons as they are shot. The area of skin covered by tattooing and soot deposits from a pistol, for example, can corroborate or refute a shooting suspect's statement. Shooting someone at incredibly short range has the hallmarks of a gangland execution, but self-preservation might be a legitimate defense if the victim was slightly farther from the gun, and may drop the charge from murder to manslaughter.

### Who pulled the trigger?

More often it is not the pattern of P-GSR that's incriminating, but its presence or absence. For example, absence of P-GSR on the hands of someone who has apparently shot themselves suggests homicide rather than suicide.

Instrumental testing and microscopy are used to authenticate P-GSR. The atomic absorption spectrophotometer is the most commonly used analytical instrument. It identifies traces of barium, lead, and antimony that are used in primer. Under the scanning electron microscope, particles of primer are easy to spot by their characteristic shape. Energy dispersion X-ray analysis confirms their composition.

**TRIGGER TEST ▼**
*The trigger pressure needed to fire a gun may be a crucial factor in cases where a suspect claims that a shooting was accidental.*

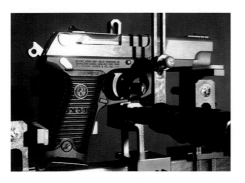

**GUN RACK ▶**
*Revolvers—plain and fancy—form part of the reference collection in the firearms division of the FBI forensic laboratory.*

# Other weapons

In the dispassionate language of the morgue, blunt trauma, sharp trauma, and asphyxiation account for a substantial proportion of homicide. But scientific jargon cannot hide the brutal reality of murder. Improvised clubs, bloody knives, or lengths of cord can bring lives to an end. Though marks from such weapons are not as useful, forensically, as those from guns, autopsy details may nevertheless provide vital clues.

## BODY OF EVIDENCE
*This composite picture of the human body was created using many different imaging technologies. The surrounding images show how some injuries can help to identify at least the type of weapon used to inflict them, and possibly individual characteristics as well. The marks they cause are not always obvious: deep and fatal stab wounds, for example, can close up, leaving a scarcely visible mark on the skin, with little external bleeding.*

## SKULL FRACTURE ▶
*Blows with a broad instrument may fracture the skull, but they do not leave traces that can help identify the weapon. Smaller weapons make marks that are more useful to an investigation. A wrench used as a club, for example, causes a bone impression that suggests its size, and grazing on the skin indicates shape.*

*A depressed fracture typical of an assault with a small, blunt instrument shows up as a Y-shaped shadow in this X-ray*

## ◀ LIGATURES
*Marks on the neck of strangulation victims can provide detailed information about the weapon used, showing through bruising and grazes its size and surface texture, and even suggesting whether or not it was twisted, or applied repeatedly. However, soft material such as panty hose may not leave surface marks. Similarly, bare-hand strangulation does not leave diagnostic marks, causing only nonspecific bruising to the neck.*

## KNIFE WOUND ▼
*Cuts reveal almost nothing about a weapon, but stab wounds do. Their shape can show whether the blade was single- or double-edged (see box), and forcible thrusts can imprint hilt marks on the skin. Dissection of such full-length stab wounds makes it possible to estimate the blade's length.*

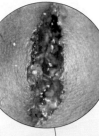

## SKIN INJURIES ▼
*Known as abrasions and contusions to the pathologist, grazes and bruises sometimes show the shape of the weapon with surprising detail. Boots, for instance, can leave prints on the flesh just as they do in mud. More often, though, such marks are less characteristic: a hit from a bar-shaped weapon produces a pair of parallel bruises, indicating its width and the direction of the attack.*

## COLLAPSED LUNG ▲
*A collapsed lung does not in itself provide any clues to the weapon that caused it, but associated wounds may do so. Deeply penetrating stab wounds to the upper body can puncture the lung, and blunt force trauma can have the same effect if a broken rib penetrates the lung. In this picture it is the lung on the right that has collapsed.*

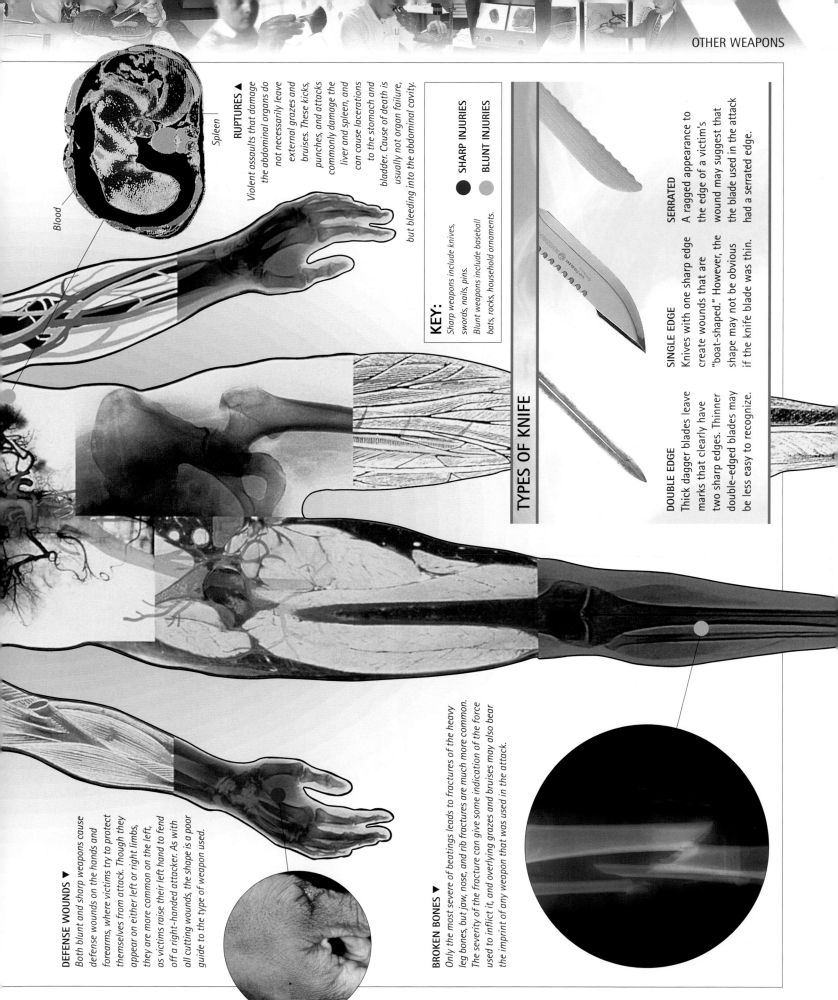

**RUPTURES** ▲
Violent assaults that damage the abdominal organs do not necessarily leave external grazes and bruises. These kicks, punches, and attacks commonly damage the liver and spleen, and can cause lacerations to the stomach and bladder. Cause of death is usually not organ failure, but bleeding into the abdominal cavity.

Spleen

Blood

**KEY:**
Sharp weapons include knives, swords, nails, pins.
Blunt weapons include baseball bats, rocks, household ornaments.

● SHARP INJURIES
● BLUNT INJURIES

## TYPES OF KNIFE

**SERRATED**
A ragged appearance to the edge of a victim's wound may suggest that the blade used in the attack had a serrated edge.

**SINGLE EDGE**
Knives with one sharp edge create wounds that are "boat-shaped." However, the shape may not be obvious if the knife blade was thin.

**DOUBLE EDGE**
Thick dagger blades leave marks that clearly have two sharp edges. Thinner double-edged blades may be less easy to recognize.

**DEFENSE WOUNDS** ▶
Both blunt and sharp weapons cause defense wounds on the hands and forearms, where victims try to protect themselves from attack. Though they appear on either left or right limbs, they are more common on the left, as victims raise their left hand to fend off a right-handed attacker. As with all cutting wounds, the shape is a poor guide to the type of weapon used.

**BROKEN BONES** ▶
Only the most severe of beatings leads to fractures of the heavy leg bones, but jaw, nose, and rib fractures are much more common. The severity of the fracture can give some indication of the force used to inflict it, and overlying grazes and bruises may also bear the imprint of any weapon that was used in the attack.

# Toxic agents

Thanks to advances in forensic toxicology and pathology, poison is too easily detected in the body to be the convenient murder weapon it once was. Rather than the crime-thriller cliché of the impatient heir, today's poisoners are more likely to be terrorists causing urban mayhem, or disturbed doctors with a lust for killing.

**DEATH IN A BOTTLE**
*Morbid symbols on these 19th-century bottles warned of the danger of their contents. A complete lack of regulation made it easy to buy even the deadliest poisons.*

In the bedroom of a palatial hotel in Luxor, Egypt, British industrial chemist John Allan slyly slips a pinch of white powder into his rich girlfriend's gin and tonic. She doesn't notice the faint smell of almonds, but on finishing the drink she immediately suffers a blinding headache and heart palpitations. Her boyfriend watches her agonizing death for ten minutes before calling for help. A tour guide who rushes to the room becomes suspicious when Allan refuses to give mouth-to-mouth resuscitation to his loved one, and a postmortem reveals cyanide in the dead woman's stomach.

It was a classic case of homicide by poisoning: a year earlier the murderer had changed his victim's will in his favor. But Allan's conviction in 2000 made "Death on the Nile" headlines around the world precisely because the crime was so unusually similar to an Agatha Christie plot, and because the murderer was naïve enough to imagine that he could escape justice.

## Unusual weapons

This cynical killing was an aberration: as a weapon of murder, poison is now so rarely used that it hardly features in homicide statistics. Stricter control of poisons is partly responsible, as is the improved sensitivity of postmortem detection.

A century ago, though, it was not difficult for poisoners to escape the hangman. Assassins used toxic plants, metals, and chemicals to end the lives of inconvenient lovers or business partners. Unlike other weapons, poisons require neither strength nor courage. With a slight knowledge of toxins, and careful attention to dose, murderers could simulate natural death. In the absence of forensic tests, only the careless were convicted. Most murderers now use other methods. Medics and terrorists are the conspicuous exceptions.

## Medical murder

While it is very rare for members of the medical professions to harm their patients, for those that do, poison can be easily administered and often goes unsuspected.

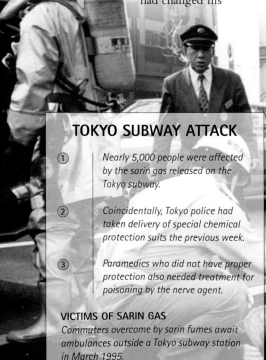

### TOKYO SUBWAY ATTACK

① *Nearly 5,000 people were affected by the sarin gas released on the Tokyo subway.*

② *Coincidentally, Tokyo police had taken delivery of special chemical protection suits the previous week.*

③ *Paramedics who did not have proper protection also needed treatment for poisoning by the nerve agent.*

**VICTIMS OF SARIN GAS**
*Commuters overcome by sarin fumes await ambulances outside a Tokyo subway station in March 1995.*

The culprits have access to poison and professional competence in its use. They are trusted with life—yet they are also intimate with death. Medical poisoners also have frequent opportunities to kill. They favor large doses of drugs that are routinely administered therapeutically. Their motives are diverse. Some simply get a buzz out of killing, or enjoy the sense of power it gives them. Some do it because they will profit from the crime, perhaps through a will. Others may believe that what they are doing is merciful.

### Driven by dogma

Terrorist poisoners, by contrast, are united by their motive. All are fanatical believers in a cause they consider so important that its propagation justifies anything—even mass murder. Some also have a major advantage over the traditional assassin: they are willing to risk sacrificing their own life.

Instead of focusing on a single target, terrorists aim to kill as many as possible; and the only reason for stealth is to give the poison time to spread or take effect.

Terrorists also choose quite different toxins, favoring biological or chemical weapons from the darker side of the military spectrum. Often such toxins are surprisingly easy to make. A chemistry graduate has enough knowledge to synthesize the sarin nerve gas that the Aum Shinrikyo religious sect released on the subway in Tokyo, Japan, in 1995. Fortunately, effective dispersal of chemical and biological weapons is not easy. The Tokyo incident led to only 12 deaths. Fewer still died in the 2001 releases of anthrax in the United States.

### Adapting to terrorism

To limit the impact of similar incidents in the future, the role of forensic science has had to adapt. Toxicologists are developing portable field instruments for rapidly identifying chemical and biological weapons at the crime scene. And in the aftermath of the US anthrax attacks, they are using DNA sequencing to identify the strain of the biological agents involved, in order to trace their source.

## CASE STUDY

To the people of Hyde, near Manchester, England, Harold Shipman was a kindly family doctor. But his benign manner concealed a deadly passion. Shipman was one of the world's most prolific mass poisoners, killing more than 200 elderly women and a handful of men by injecting them with morphine or diamorphine. The doctor himself certified death, giving a variety of apparently innocent causes. For 15 years none of the killings aroused enough suspicion to trigger a police investigation. One of his motives was greed—he was caught in 2000 when he forged the will of a victim—but he was also addicted to killing, and enjoyed playing "God"—the giver of life or death.

## CASE STUDY

## POISONER'S FAVORITES

Until chemical analysis made toxins simple to detect in a corpse, poisoners would use a range of chemical, metal, and plant poisons. Many of these were easy to obtain, acted quickly, and caused symptoms that would not arouse suspicion.

**ARSENIC ▶**
*Almost flavorless white powder popular with Victorian poisoners*
SYMPTOMS
*Include vomiting, weak pulse, blue-green extremities*
AFFECTS
*Stomach and gut*

**◀ CYANIDE**
*Found in garden laurel leaves; extract can kill in five minutes*
SYMPTOMS
*Dizziness, convulsions, unconsciousness, asphyxiation*
AFFECTS
*Blood: cannot carry oxygen*

**◀ ANTIMONY**
*Strong metallic flavor, so often administered in small doses over a long period*
SYMPTOMS
*Vomiting, cramps, sweating, depression, shallow pulse*
AFFECTS
*Heart: causes heart failure*

**LEAD ▶**
*Used as sugar of lead (lead acetate). A fifth of a sugar lump is enough to kill*
SYMPTOMS
*Stomach pain, vomiting, diarrhea, coma*
AFFECTS
*Brain, circulation, and liver*

**◀ THALLIUM**
*As a compound it dissolves invisibly and tastelessly in water*
SYMPTOMS
*Similar to flu; uniquely, thallium causes hair loss*
AFFECTS
*Nerves and cells*

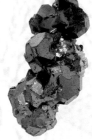

**◀ DEATH CAP MUSHROOM**
*Used to poison Roman emperor Claudius. Symptoms subside after a day, but recur fatally*
SYMPTOMS
*Stomach cramps, vomiting, diarrhea, delirium, coma*
AFFECTS
*Gut, then causes liver failure*

**DEADLY NIGHTSHADE ▶**
*As belladonna, one of the favorite poisons of the Borgias in Renaissance Italy*
SYMPTOMS
*Dry mouth, fever, enlarged pupils, hallucinations, coma*
AFFECTS
*Lungs and heart: paralyzes them*

**◀ STRYCHNINE**
*Intensely bitter-tasting; victims are conscious as they suffer agonizing convulsions*
SYMPTOMS
*Restlessness, then spasms that tear muscle from ligament*
AFFECTS
*Breathing: lung paralysis*

# Arson

Blazing, red-hot flames licking the windows of a burning building seem set on devouring everything. But fire investigators rely on the fact that they do not. Even in a seemingly gutted, charred ruin, some clues will remain intact, and they can prove arson—and even prove intent if the fire has claimed lives, so that manslaughter becomes murder.

**CULT FIRE ▲**
*Swiss investigators search for evidence in charred ruins after members of the Solar Temple Cult torched their headquarters in a bizarre 1994 suicide pact.*

When investigators arrive at a fire, their first job is to question any bystanders. Those who raised the alarm or arrived before the emergency services may be able to provide information about where and how the fire started. They may even have videotaped the developing fire.

Once the fire is under control and the temperature has fallen, making the building safe is a priority. Investigators face some obvious hazards, such as the risk that the building may collapse around them. But there are unseen dangers, too: asbestos, toxic beryllium oxide (used as electrical insulator), and carcinogenic combustion products.

## INSURANCE FRAUD

One of the most common motives for arson is insurance fraud. Typically, an owner of a failing business removes stock, so that he can both sell it and make an insurance claim for it, before torching a warehouse or factory. Investigators sift the ashes for evidence that may contradict a claim. Even when fire consumes clothes in a warehouse, metal zippers and fastenings can survive the blaze, so the absence of any trace of the stock is itself suspicious.

## Take a seat

Investigators first want to know where the fire started and how. Arsonists try to conceal their work, and often start fires in two or more places. By contrast, accidental fires usually start in just one place and, more often than not, the origin, or "seat," of the fire is self-evident.

To the lay onlooker, finding the seat of a fire in a charred, steaming wreck may seem like an impossible task, but investigators are experienced in "reading" the crime scene. Fire travels upward, so they start at the lowest levels. Signs that direct them to the seat of the fire include: residual heat; depth of charring; spalling (splintering or flaking off) of building materials such as plaster and concrete; smoke patterns; distortion of plastic, glass, and metal; ceiling damage; and patterns of structural collapse.

*Glass evidence jars sealed with vapor barrier screw lids to contain volatile accelerants.*

Once they have located the seat of the blaze, investigators comb the wreckage in search of what started it. The basic tools of the arsonist are an accelerant, such as gasoline, that ensures the fire starts quickly, and an incendiary device to light the flames. This can be as complex

**FUEL SNIFFER ▶**
*Called hydrocarbon vapor detectors, they draw in air and feed the samples to a hydrogen flame. A hotter flame indicates the presence of an accelerant.*

as an electronic timer, or as simple as a smoldering cigarette wedged in a match-book. Amazingly, traces of both accelerant and incendiary device often survive the ferocious fires they are intended to start.

You don't need to be a fire expert to smell arson. Unburned hydrocarbon fuels, solvents, and paint thinners all have characteristic odors. Liquid accelerants leave visual clues such as sharply defined, irregular pool marks on the floor. There may also be a characteristic burn pattern along the edges of floorboards, indicating that burning liquid flowed between them.

If none of these indicators is present, investigators use sniffers (hydrocarbon detectors) to find concentrations of accelerants. When they find anything suspicious, they remove the contaminated item for laboratory analysis. The removed

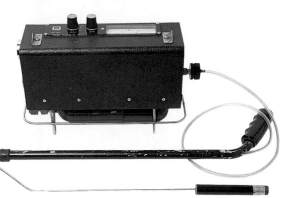

items have to be treated with special care. Accelerants are volatile, and without proper storage the evidence can literally vanish into thin air. Storage containers need secure vapor seals, so screw-cap jars, metal drums similar to paint cans, and polyvinylidine bags ("oven bags") are usually used.

## Conventional sleuthing

A general investigation of the crime scene can reinforce or refute suspicions of arson. Specifically, investigators check whether alarm or sprinkler systems were deliberately disabled. They look for tracks outside the building, and method of entry and exit.

Investigators use the usual grab-bag of tools—written notes, sketches, measurements, photography, and video. They pay particular attention to the position and orientation of unmoved, part-burned objects such as furniture, because the pattern of burning shows which side faced the seat of the fire.

### BRAZEN BLAZE

*Not all arsonists rely on stealth. The Molotov cocktail this Seoul demonstrator hurled into the flames neatly combines accelerant and incendiary device in a handy package.*

## Instruments of detection

Back at the lab, technicians use gas chromatography/mass spectrometry (GC/MS—see p. 82) to identify the accelerants. They generally work not with the evidence itself, but with vapor that it emits when it's heated, which collects in the head-space—the air above the sample in the sealed container.

Volatile compounds in the vapor show up as characteristic peaks on the GC/MS trace, and are identified from a computer database. Infrared spectroscopy is sometimes used in a similar way, especially to identify burned plastics and synthetic materials. Lab work may also include microscopic examination of evidence to search for an incendiary device. If anybody died in the blaze, autopsy reports form part of the investigation (see p. 38). For example, if there is no sign of smoke inhalation, it is clear that the individual was dead when the fire started— suggesting a possible homicide.

## FIRE TOOLS

### CHAINSAW ▶
*Investigators use heavy-duty cutting equipment to remove flooring that has become soaked in accelerant. Chainsaws, though vital, need careful use to avoid fuel spills that could contaminate evidence.*

### FLASHLIGHT ▶
*Simple tools like flashlights are life-savers. Blackened buildings are unlikely to have maintained their electricity supply, and floors are often unsafe.*

### AX ▶
*An ax is used to remove smaller pieces of evidence, without fear of contaminating them.*

### GAS ANALYSIS KIT ▶
*Diagnostic crystals inside a tube change color when there are traces of accelerant in air drawn through it by a bellows.*

## MOTIVES FOR ARSON:

| | |
|---|---|
| 1 | *To kill, or to disguise an earlier homicide as an accidental death.* |
| 2 | *To make a fraudulent insurance claim possible.* |
| 3 | *To hide evidence of a different crime, such as fraud, by destroying business records.* |
| 4 | *To put a competitor out of business.* |
| 5 | *Revenge.* |
| 6 | *For kicks, or to satisfy a compulsive need to create and watch flames.* |

# Explosives

It has never been easier to make a bomb. Fanatical patriots, religious zealots, and plain old-fashioned social misfits can easily find recipes on the Internet, and the materials are widely available. Forensic techniques cannot stop people making bombs, but they can help to catch bombers before they strike, or trace them by analyzing the aftermath of a blast.

The anatomy of a bomb is simple. A timing device or a remote control is needed to start the process. This triggers a primary charge, which is a tiny but easily ignited charge used to spark the explosion. (The timer and the charge combine to be called a detonator). Then a main explosive does the deed – this is a material that reacts violently to the small charge, creating a lot of gas incredibly quickly, producing a pressure shock wave that causes the damage.

## At the bomb scene

An explosion does not completely consume these components. Instead, the blast scatters the pieces, and has been known to destroy as little as 1/20th of the bomb's casing and mechanism. Because so much survives, bomb scenes potentially offer rich pickings for forensic investigators to analyze—if they can find them.

The procedure for finding the remnants of a bomb differs from any other crime-scene search only in detail. The bomb-scene manager first estimates the likely center of the blast, measures how far debris was thrown, then cordons off an area 50% bigger. Measuring and mapping follows, and the scene is divided into grid squares so as to record where the evidence is found.

## Walk-through

The search for evidence typically begins with a walk-through, with searchers moving slowly, line-abreast to recover any obvious evidence. The telltale signs they are looking for are jagged fragments, possibly dusted with soot. Once this search is complete, the debris in each grid square is swept into a heap—using new or sterilized tools, to prevent contamination. Each pile is then literally sieved for evidence.

Clearing the scene reveals the seat of the blast. This is where traces of explosive are most likely to be found, so officers swab the area, carry out a fingertip search, then dig out some of the crater itself for testing.

If the bomb was hidden in a vehicle, its remains are winched on to a tarpaulin, then "gift-wrapped" in another one, so that no evidence is lost on the way to a secure area where it can be examined in detail.

**IRA BLAST ▲**
*In 1993, an IRA truck bomb parked in London's business district killed one person, injured 44, and caused damage estimated at hundreds of millions of dollars.*

## Analyzing the explosive

The search for explosives begins at the crime scene, with reagents that change color on contact with any fuel residues, and sniffers, or vapor analyzers (see p. 108). Nevertheless, bomb scene searches are rather hit-and-miss affairs, and the real work of analysis is done at the lab.

Fragments that may carry traces of unburned explosive are firstly examined microscopically to study the shapes of the residue particles, and then they are washed in water and acetone to get the particles into a testable solution. Any residues extracted from this are then screened and analyzed using reagent spot tests and

*The purpose of casing is to disguise the bomb, but it may also hold metal fragments to wound those nearby.*

*Low-tech bombs often short out a battery across a thin wire. This creates enough heat to start the explosion.*

*The crudest (and most unreliable) of timers rely on the moving hands of a clock closing electrical contacts.*

*Commercial explosives make for compact bombs. Sacks of homemade explosives are needed to produce the same blast.*

**ANATOMY OF A BOMB**

### BOMB SCENE PROTOCOL:

| 1 | *Treat those injured in the blast, put out fires, and make the building safe.* |
|---|---|
| 2 | *Recovery of the dead must preserve evidence: one might be the bomber.* |
| 3 | *Secure and map the scene.* |
| 4 | *Search for larger evidence.* |
| 5 | *Sift debris in grid-squared zones for any remains of bomb.* |
| 6 | *Clear seat of blast, test for explosives, and remove samples.* |
| 7 | *Fingertip search of crater.* |

**OKLAHOMA BOMB SCENE**
*Forensic engineers called to the scene of the Oklahoma bombing were able to estimate the size of the fertilizer–diesel bomb by studying the structural damage that it caused.*

## TYPES OF EXPLOSIVE

There are a number of types of explosive out there for determined people to get hold of—if they have the right contacts. Other types can be made in their kitchens with readily available household products.

**HOMEMADE ▶**
*Gasoline and diesel burn explosively when mixed with an oxidizer, though large quantities may be needed.*

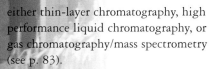

**◀ HIGH EXPLOSIVES**
*Oxidizer and fuel are combined at molecular level in high explosives. When triggered by a small detonating charge, high explosives such as PETN decompose rapidly, creating a large pressure wave.*

**◀ MILITARY EXPLOSIVES**
*Munitions are more tightly controlled than industrial explosives, though identical compounds are used in both kinds.*

**COMMERCIAL EXPLOSIVES ▶**
*Used in quarrying, tunneling, and industry, commercial explosives are stable and often waterproof. Semtex has both military and commercial uses.*

**◀ LOW EXPLOSIVES**
*Gunpowder used in shotgun cartridges is a low explosive, but can still make an effective terror bomb. An extortionist used it to make this VCR bomb.*

either thin-layer chromatography, high performance liquid chromatography, or gas chromatography/mass spectrometry (see p. 83).

Forensic analysts use similar testing techniques to check for the presence of undetonated explosives—perhaps when searching a bomb factory, or testing for the presence of explosives on the hands, clothes, or possessions of a suspected bomber.

### Studying other traces

Though reduced to minute fragments, a casing or trigger mechanism can lead investigators to a bomb's manufacturer. Fragments of bomb components occasionally bear the fingerprints of the bomber, but more often the parts themselves can be traced to their source. A tiny chip of a circuit board, for example, helped trace the Lockerbie bomber (see p. 116). To make this task

easier, the FBI's Explosives Unit maintains a vast collection of commonly used bomb components, including batteries, detonators, and control devices. A database of recovered bomb parts also enables investigators to identify links between blasts.

Determining how a bomb was set off can help security forces devise counter-measures. For example, the discovery that IRA terrorists were using model-aircraft radio controls to detonate bombs led to jamming of the radio frequencies they used. The terrorists responded by switching to radar, triggering the bomb with a radar gun normally used by traffic police. When further counter-measures made this method of triggering impossible, the bombers adopted a light-sensitive "slave" unit normally used by photographers for cordless flash synchronization. When the slave detected a sudden light pulse from a tiny hand-held flash, it closed a circuit, detonating the bomb. The deadly game of forensic leapfrog ended only when a political truce brought the bomb attacks to an end.

**◀ FINGERTIP SEARCH**
*Since debris from bombs is reduced to the tiniest fragments, there is often no alternative to a painstaking hands-and-knees search of the crime scene. Here, a bomb had exploded in a sidewalk trash can.*

# Cars as lethal agents

I t is sometimes hard to remember that a car can be a lethal weapon—until a reckless, drunk, drugged, or simply homicidal driver makes it impossible to forget. Motor vehicles are as dangerous as loaded guns, but proving lethal intent and prosecuting the driver in a vehicle homicide case can involve complex legal arguments.

Through familiarity, we are inclined to think of the family car as a benign, safe form of transport. But as the following three cases show, vehicles can often be the lethal agent in homicide cases.

In London, a drug addict stole a woman's purse and ran to a waiting car. When she pursued him, the driver accelerated over the woman, killing her.

In Hasama, Japan, a carpenter attacked another driver with a crowbar in a fit of road rage after a minor collision, then drove over her body to finish her off.

In Chicago, a driver crushed a cyclist under his wheels after the man banged on the side of his SUV.

To counter attacks like these, many nations have a specific vehicle homicide offense, so that when there is an element of malice, car killings can be treated as murder, rather than fatal traffic "accidents."

## Building a case

In the above examples, the drivers' intention to kill was obvious, but a homicide conviction is not automatic. Prosecutors rely on forensic scientists to help them construct an indefensible case. In less clear-cut cases, forensic investigation plays a still more vital part in establishing what happened. Specifically, investigators look at the crime scene for evidence about the speed and direction of the vehicle, the visibility, and whether the driver was braking. Evidence missed at this early stage is lost forever, but where the crime scene is a busy road, investigators may be under extreme pressure to complete their work quickly so traffic can flow again.

Sketches of the road are particularly important, with exact measurements and locations of skid marks. To a certain

**INTERVIEWING WITNESSES ▲**
*Bystanders can provide useful observations. However, perception is subjective, and eyewitness estimates of speed are often wildly inaccurate.*

extent, photographs can help to fill in any gaps in the information: rectification software can deduce distances of the marks on the road from photographs taken at an oblique angle. Vehicle type and mass are also recorded for later crash reconstruction.

**MARKS ON THE ROAD ▲**
*The length of skid marks, and their radius, are good guides to the speed of a braking vehicle. Cornering at high speed leaves marks with characteristic scuffing where the vehicle slips sideways.*

Once the scene of a fatal crash has been cleared, the vehicles are not just towed away. They are treated with the same care as any other evidence. A forensic engineer will need to study them if there is any suspicion of mechanical failure, or deliberate sabotage such as cut brake lines. Bodywork damage and trace evidence can also help establish facts about the impact, such as the vehicle's speed and orientation.

## Who was driving?

It is not always clear who was driving. Vehicle occupants are sometimes thrown from their seats, and surviving drivers may try to hide their guilt by blaming a passenger who died in the crash.

*Medical care for the injured takes precedence. However, once paramedics have made sure that there is no immediate danger, detectives need access to the survivors. Trace evidence adhering to their clothes and skin, and photographs of injuries, can all help in a prosecution.*

## CRASH SCENE INVESTIGATION:

| | |
|---|---|
| 1 | *Treat crash survivors.* |
| 2 | *Take samples for drug and alcohol tests.* |
| 3 | *Record vehicles and marks on the road.* |
| 4 | *Document vehicle damage.* |
| 5 | *Interview witnesses.* |
| 6 | *Document survivors' injuries.* |
| 7 | *Preserve vehicles as evidence.* |

**DAMAGE TO VEHICLES ▲**
*Vehicles of similar size are built to conform to the same safety standards, so the damage they sustain on impact is a reliable indicator of the combined speed at which they were traveling. But determining the speed of each vehicle is much more difficult.*

**SUSPECTED VEHICLE HOMICIDE ▲**
*Good management of a fatal crash scene is vital for effective investigation. Damaged vehicle parts just thrown into a trunk can destroy useful evidence.*

Trace evidence, with medical and pathology reports, can help establish who was actually behind the wheel. Airbags, for example, retain hair, makeup, and skin traces, and they often cause distinctive facial injuries, too. The vehicle pedals and the soles of the driver's shoes mark each other. If the car occupants were wearing seatbelts, medical and autopsy reports should reveal shoulder bruising, which would indicate the side of the car they were sitting on, and help identify the driver.

## Reconstructing the crash

Determining a driver's intentions and their responsibility for a fatal crash is easier if it can be recreated, with line of sight and reaction times established. Crash modeling packages, such as PC-Crash, work in a way that at first seems upside-down. The operator enters information about the crash scene after the incident, such as the resting position of the vehicles, their mass and type, and the length and radius of the tire marks on the road. The software then works backward, using complex calculations to estimate the speeds and directions of all involved before impact. The final result is an animation of the crash, which the jury can watch at the trial.

**RECREATING THE CRASH ▲**
*Simulation software reconstructs crashes using a variety of information: measurements of the crash scene and skid marks; positions of vehicles and pedestrians; road surface and tire conditions. Vehicle appearance and performance data come from an extensive built-in library.*

**RECORDING DISASTERS IN THE AIR ▲**
*Damage belies the resilience of flight recorders. This one, recovered from Flight 587, which crashed into Queens, New York, in 2001, revealed that turbulence ripped the tail from the aircraft.*

## DISASTER SCENE PROTOCOL:

| | |
|---|---|
| 1 | *Rescue trapped crew and passengers.* |
| 2 | *Make the disaster area safe and secure as quickly as possible.* |
| 3 | *Check bodies for evidence, then remove to morgue for identification.* |
| 4 | *Document and record remainder of scene, and search for evidence.* |
| 5 | *Interview witnesses.* |
| 6 | *Selectively remove vehicle parts for forensic analysis.* |

**ESCHEDE TRAIN CRASH**
*A high-speed train hit a bridge at Eschede, Germany, in 1998 when a wheel failed. The crash killed more than 100 passengers.*

# Major incidents

When ships sink and trains or planes crash, forensic investigators work in harrowing scenes of carnage to locate the cause. Their findings may prevent a repetition of the disaster. They help in prosecutions of negligence or sabotage. And they bring comfort to bereaved families who need to know how—and why—their loved ones died.

Transportation disasters bring death and destruction on an unimaginable scale. Whereas a homicide crime scene may feature several bodies, an air crash can mean hundreds, sometimes scattered over a vast area. The work of investigating such a major incident is often indivisible from the task of locating and identifying victims, since the bodies may themselves be the evidence that pinpoints the cause, or identifies those responsible.

### Cooperation and leadership
Many agencies are involved in these traumatic investigations. There may be specialist police, representatives of the transportation company, accident and safety investigators, and many others. To avoid chaos, the interested parties decide early on which of them will lead the inquiry. If there is any suspicion of criminal activity, the police will take charge.

Regardless of who is leading, the task of investigators is the same: they look for evidence that the incident was caused by human error, by mechanical failure on the vehicle, by the failure of external systems such as signaling, or by deliberate sabotage. Their methodology is determined by the usual imperatives of preserving evidence—except that here, the sheer scale

of the disaster imposes its own rigor. You cannot just "bag and tag" a car ferry.

## Specialists at the scene

Because of the technical nature of transportation investigations, specialists invariably play a major part. In the case of

**HERALD OF FREE ENTERPRISE** ▲
*Nearly 200 died in 1987 when waves swamped this ferry in Belgium's Zeebrugge Harbor. Investigators learned that, under pressure to sail on time, a tired crew set sail before the bow doors were closed.*

a plane crash, individual experts will be responsible for different factors such as the engines, air traffic control, weather, crew performance, and the aircraft's operational record, among others.

## Capturing ephemeral evidence

Once paramedics have evacuated or treated survivors, investigators may urgently need to carry out time-dependent tests, such as measuring engine part temperatures, or carrying out procedures to test braking efficiency.

Investigators then use video and photography to record evidence that cannot be preserved, such as damaged track that must be replaced to restore a train service. Where possible, elements that will prove crucial to a subsequent enquiry, such as locomotive cabs, are removed intact. Air disasters follow a

**FLIGHT 1141 TO SALT LAKE CITY** ▶
*This flight from Dallas crashed on takeoff in 1988 because the crew set wing flaps incorrectly. On retrieving the klaxon (horn) that should have warned of the error, investigators found it did not work.*

well-established routine: every remaining scrap of debris is recovered, and the aircraft is reconstructed in a hangar to try to determine the cause of the accident.

## Mute witnesses

Air crashes are often so destructive that the only witnesses are the data and cockpit voice recorders, and locating them is famously a priority for accident investigators. Commonplace on aircraft since 1960, these boxes are painted high-visibility orange, rather than the eponymous black. Inside are specially toughened tape recorders or solid-state computer data stores. They are capable of withstanding the huge forces of a crash, followed by fire and immersion in water. Those on aircraft record at least 88 parameters each second, including altitude, direction, and condition of the engines, and are capable of storing 25 hours' worth of data. The cockpit recorder stores up to two hours' of speech.

Data recorders are not confined to aircraft: modern trains and some ships also carry them. At the Eschede train crash in Germany, for example, investigators quickly recovered the data recorder. It showed that, on a specific section of track, the train had been traveling at three times the speed limit.

## CASE STUDY

The crew of *Estonia* were used to violent storms on their journeys across the Baltic sea, so they were unconcerned when 20-ft (6-m) waves buffeted their ship on September 28, 1994. But, by 1:15 AM, the ship had developed a heavy list. Two hours later, the ferry was at the bottom of the Baltic. Of the 989 people onboard, 852 died in the freezing water. Inspection of the wreck by divers and two remotely operated submersibles confirmed suspicions that the car deck had flooded when waves tore off the bow door. The investigators blamed poor maintenance and excessive speed for the tragedy.

## CASE STUDY

# The Lockerbie bombing

To Alan Topps, Flight 103 was just another New York-bound "Clipper" when it entered the airspace he controlled on December 21, 1988. But, just after 7 P.M., something happened that he had never seen before: the blip on his radar display, marking the aircraft's position over the Scottish town of Lockerbie, suddenly split into five.

**LOCKERBIE BOMBER ▲**

*The Libyan intelligence officer convicted of the bombing worked for Libyan Arab Airlines. His knowledge of security procedures enabled him to send the bomb as unaccompanied luggage.*

**COCKPIT CARNAGE ▶**

*Amazingly, whole sections of the aircraft survived intact, despite falling from an altitude of 6 miles (10 km).*

Topps made frantic efforts to contact the aircraft by radio, but without success. Minutes later, the pilot of another aircraft reported seeing a fire on the ground, "… as if a gasoline storage tank had blown up." It was the fuel-filled wing of Flight 103, which had hit the ground and exploded with tremendous force, like a small earthquake.

The front section of the aircraft came down in one piece, with the pilots still strapped in their seats. Much of the rest was spread over an area of 1,000 sq miles (1,610 sq km).

## The search for wreckage

The day after the crash, the search for bodies began; then volunteers combed the area for debris. Some had landed in hard-to-reach woodland, and spy satellites and helicopters with infrared cameras had to be used to locate it. Each part of the wreckage was collected and coded for reconstruction. Items of debris were initially bagged and taken to Lockerbie town hall, where investigators entered their details onto a computer database. This eventually swelled to include 200,000 items, some tinier than a fingernail.

The crippled Boeing 747 was virtually rebuilt from recovered aircraft parts. It soon became clear that an explosion had

blown a hole in the fuselage. The blast wave tore the aircraft apart. The pattern of damage suggested that an explosion had occurred in cargo bay 14L. This explained a vital mystery: why had Flight 103 never sent a "mayday" signal? Bay 14L was adjacent to the plane's electricity supply, and the blast would have cut power to the radio. It also brought flight data and cockpit voice recording to an abrupt end, silencing the "black boxes."

## Traces of a bomb

It soon became evident that the origin of the explosion was centered around the baggage compartment. Since it was not possible for this to be linked with the fuel system, a bomb was suspected. Items thought to be from this area were tested, using a GC/MS Instrument (see p. 82), for traces of primary explosive. At the same time, recovered articles were screened for evidence of a timing mechanism. Pieces of a sophisticated trigger device—an altitude-sensitive switch linked to a timer—were discovered. It had been cleverly designed to outwit airport security equipment.

Though the inquiry was exhaustively diligent, it was a stroke of luck that led investigators to the bombers. More than a year after the crash, a man walking his dog found a piece of a gray shirt, missed in the initial search. Detectives traced the manufacturer to the Mediterranean island of Malta (see box).

A minute inspection also revealed a tiny chip of a circuit board, printed with the number "1." From this clue, and other shreds of evidence, the bomb's timer was identified as a Swiss-made MST-13.

## Arab connections

A pattern was beginning to emerge: the timer's makers had sold a batch of them to the Libyan government. And an identical timer had turned up in Senegal two years earlier in a Semtex bomb carried by two Libyan agents.

Other items in the wreckage also suggested an Arab connection. The explosives had been packed into a radio-cassette recorder, and its instruction manual was scarcely singed. It identified the model as a "Bombeat," sold only in North Africa and the Middle East. Piecing together the evidence, investigators identified two Libyan suspects. In 1999, after intense diplomatic pressure, the Libyan government extradited them for trial at a specially convened court in the Hague.

When their trial ended in January 2001, it brought to an end one of the world's longest and costliest criminal investigations. The court found just one of the defendants—Abdelbaser Ali Mohmed Al Megrahi—guilty of the murder of the 259 passengers and crew and 11 people on the ground.

---

**COMBING THE DEBRIS ▼**
*One thousand volunteers joined the air accident investigators in the search for debris. Their brief was simple: "If it's not growing, and it's not a rock, pick it up."*

## EVIDENCE

PP8932 PT/28

The Lockerbie bomb blast shredded a gray T-shirt, which was packed around the bomb, but did not destroy its label. This led detectives to its manufacturer: the Yorkie Clothing Company of Malta. Detectives found out that it had been sold by a small clothing shop called "Mary's House" and, amazingly, the owner, Tony Gauchi, could recall selling it. The purchaser was memorable because he had bought a variety of garments without any consideration of style or size. Gauchi's evidence enabled investigators to close in on two Libyan agents who worked at Malta's airport. Using stolen luggage tags, they were able to send the brown suitcase containing the bomb to Frankfurt, Germany, where it was loaded aboard a flight carrying passengers to London to join Flight 103 to New York.

# CRIMES WITHOUT CORPSES

Murders may make more headlines, but crimes of dishonesty vastly outnumber them. Theft and robbery—plain or fancy—dominate crime investigation, for greed seems as fundamental to human nature as violence and anger. Hunting simple thieves and robbers makes for routine detective work, but the criminal mind is endlessly ingenious: more sophisticated offenses—such as forgery, fraud, and computer or environmental crime—demand inventive solutions.

# Document analysis

From fine calligraphy to ballpoint scrawl, the lines of our handwriting are unique and personal—and more difficult to disguise than you might think. But handwriting analysis is not essential in detecting a forged letter, form, or passport: clues in the paper, ink, and printing style can also help document examiners identify it.

**OUTWITTING THE NAZIS ▲**
*British intelligence services faked these stamps for the French Resistance in World War II, adding a deliberate mistake (see arrow). Used on letters arranging rendezvous, the stamps enabled the resistance fighters to distinguish genuine invitations from the letters of Nazi spies luring them into traps.*

## CASE STUDY

One of the most audacious US con-women forged identity documents and checks in order to steal a fortune in Manhattan's swankiest districts in 1992. In her boldest sting, Lilly Schmidt "bought" an impressionist painting with a cashier's check for $70,000. Since it was a public holiday, verifying the check was impossible, but the gallery owner was reassured by Lilly's credit and ID card. The check bounced. When police finally caught up with Lilly, she was found to be carrying nine ID cards with different names (one of them is shown above). All were forged with a laser printer and an embossing machine. Lilly was jailed for a week, but released when her lawyer posted $30,000 bail—with a check that turned out to be forged.

## CASE STUDY

Writing habits that we learn at school are hard to shake off. We get used to a particular way of holding a pen, shaping letters, and spacing words and lines. These and other persistent qualities are what makes handwriting such a useful diagnostic tool in questioned documents. This is the branch of forensics concerned with comparing and verifying ransom notes, forged contracts and wills, fake passports and ID, and numerous other kinds of written and printed material—mostly on paper. Handwriting analysis is most often used to confirm that the same person wrote two documents.

### Looking at handwriting

Document examiners looking for individual characteristics in handwriting concentrate on four areas: form, line quality, arrangement, and content. The form of the writing is the shape of individual letters: their slant, relative sizes, and how each is connected to the next. "Trademarks"—the use of unusual characters, such as the plus sign or the ampersand (&) instead of "and"—are also examined.

Analyzing the content

**GEORGE IS DEAD**
*Even genuine documents are not above suspicion. When George Harrison died in Los Angeles in 2001, relatives bent the truth on his death certificate.*

of written—or printed—documents highlights similarities of punctuation, grammar, spelling, phrasing, and vocabulary. Computer analysis of long documents, for example, can create "scores" for factors like word frequency and compound word hyphenation that help verify the provenance of questioned texts. Although writers may change these attributes over the years, we usually use them consistently over shorter periods.

*Harrison's family didn't want his place of death to become a fans' shrine, so they listed a false address.*

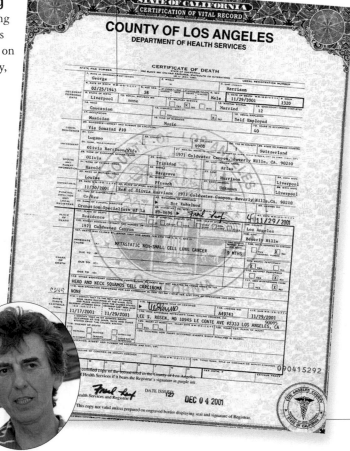

**PASSPORT SCRUTINY ▲**

*Multispectral video microscopes help border police to verify passports and ID. High magnification and UV illumination quickly show up altered information and tampering with security features.*

## Making the comparison

Typically, document examiners compare an unknown sample, such as a ransom note, with a "standard"—the handwriting of a suspect. A requested standard is a handwriting sample that a suspect produces under supervision. Since it can have the same text as the unknown sample, a requested standard makes an exact comparison possible—but gives the suspect the opportunity to disguise his or her handwriting. Collected standards, on the other hand, are casual examples of a suspect's writing. Although undisguised, they can only be compared with the unknown sample where words match, or letter-by-letter.

Examiners make initial comparisons of handwriting with the unaided eye or a hand lens, possibly a low-power stereo microscope. Special lighting helps reveal useful details about how a document was created or altered. Oblique light shows heavy indentation, perhaps suggesting a signature was forged by tracing, and it highlights the roughness that some erasers produce. Backlighting turns erased areas light, and darkens correction fluid. Spectroscopic examination can reveal whether inks of the same color are in fact different by giving each one a unique spectral fingerprint. Forensic examiners may use an infrared microscope to carry out this examination.

## Other clues

Analysis is not confined to handwritten documents. Typed, printed, photocopied, and even faxed documents also carry marks of value to examiners. Worn typewriter letters that incriminate a blackmailer are the mainstay of hackneyed crime-novel plots but, perhaps surprisingly, modern technology has not entirely eliminated the identifying characteristics of individual business machines. A laser printer, for example, accumulates "trash" marks on its light-sensitive drum that appear as tiny black dots on every page printed. Photocopiers, which work in a similar way, also duplicate the marks, and additionally record dirt on the copier glass. Fax headers reveal details of the sending and sometimes also the receiving machines. Even if the information in the header is falsified, the font can be compared with a library of similar headers to narrow down the make and model.

## Paper and ink

Testing the composition of paper, ink, glues, and fastenings can demonstrate the similarity of some questioned documents, and makes the dating of others possible. The pigment titanium dioxide, for example, which was not used in paper until the 20th century, has been discovered in a so-called medieval document.

Document examiners look for distinctive letter formations that appear on both questioned and standard documents. They study the sequence and direction of letter strokes, and note any departures from conventional letter and word construction. The first case in which handwriting analysis played a major part was the kidnapping of wealthy aviator Charles Lindbergh's two-year-old son in 1932. The kidnapper left a note demanding a $50,000 ransom and, 30 months later, Bruno Hauptmann was caught spending the money. Similarities between his signature and the ransom note helped convict him. The example below compares his signature with a composite constructed from letters of the ransom note.

**HAUPTMANN'S SIGNATURE**

**COMPOSITE SIGNATURE**

*Embossed writing is scarcely visible in oblique light ...*

*... but ESDA makes it crystal clear, even when there is also printed text on the page.*

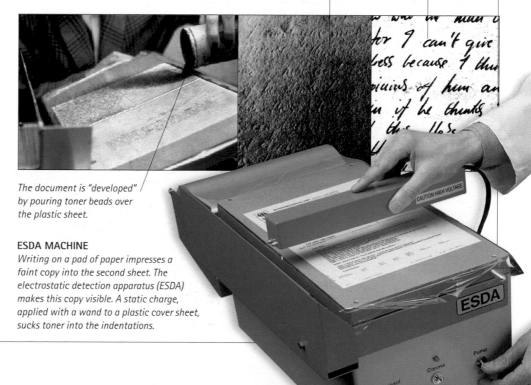

*The document is "developed" by pouring toner beads over the plastic sheet.*

### ESDA MACHINE

*Writing on a pad of paper impresses a faint copy into the second sheet. The electrostatic detection apparatus (ESDA) makes this copy visible. A static charge, applied with a wand to a plastic cover sheet, sucks toner into the indentations.*

# Currency forgery

The crime of counterfeiting is as old as money itself, and it continues despite increasingly sophisticated security features on banknotes. But as the methods of prevention and detection make their trade more difficult, counterfeiters are looking for easier targets, such as credit card fraud and trademark infringement.

*Chinese forgery of Mexican silver dollar, 1930s*

*Gold-plated copper copy of a Greek coin*

*16th-century forgery of a sesterius of Claudius*

**CROOKED COINS ▲**
*Counterfeiting of coins did not end with banknotes–it is still done, but now to cheat collectors.*

Fake currency is at best an irritation to central banks; at worst, it destabilizes economies. Banks characterize the criminals working at these two extremes respectively as "nuisance counterfeiters," who typically use home computers to duplicate notes, and "economic subversives." The first group accounts for only about 5% of false notes, and economic subversion is rare in peacetime.

**SEIZING FILM ▼**
*The 2002 introduction of the euro gave counterfeiters a unique opportunity to hoodwink Europeans unfamiliar with the new currency. Italian finance police who cracked a major forgers' ring also seized film for revenue stamps.*

A bigger counterfeiting problem comes from the middle ground: organized criminals who use multi-million-dollar printing plants to produce convincing currency copies.

## Which currencies are vulnerable?

They pick their targets carefully. Currencies with a wide international circulation are popular, because the notes are easier to pass off outside the issuing country. This is why the US dollar is the most widely copied of all currencies. Easy-to-forge currencies attract counterfeiters, too: the German deutsche mark was heavily copied in 1991 and 1992, until the Bundesbank issued notes with better security features.

## Protection and detection

Traditionally, banknotes have been printed using elaborate engraved designs with hard-to-duplicate watermarking, sequential numbering, and metal threads. But in the late 1980s, high-quality color copiers made further steps necessary. Some of today's notes have "illegal copy" lettering that appears only when a note is heated by a copier lamp. Other features include color-shifting ink that changes from green to black when the note is turned, microprinting visible only with a magnifying glass, machine-readable bar codes, iridescent ink, and holograms (see opposite page).

In the war against counterfeiting, the front line is the cash register. The look and feel, the watermark, and the security thread are the most reliable ways of authenticating notes. Popular but less reliable guides are UV light and iodine pens. These detect fluorescent brighteners and starch, which are not used in genuine banknote paper.

## Finding the forger

In the forensic context, clues in the paper, printing, and ink can help track down the counterfeiter. All paper banknotes are printed on high-quality stock that is impossible to replicate economically.

Optical microscopy, using reflected and back light, is commonly used to identify the substituted paper. Investigators may then be able to trace the supplier. UV illumination reveals security fibers in real notes and simulated features in fakes; X-rays make watermarks clearer. Close inspection occasionally reveals that the paper source is the issuing bank itself. Some counterfeiters clean ink from low-value notes, and reprint them in higher values.

The printing process offers similar detection possibilities. Large-scale counterfeiters typically use offset printing, but may use laser or even inkjet printers. Even at their best, these printing methods are easy to distinguish from the high-quality intaglio method used on genuine banknotes. Chemical analysis of the ink, using chromatography (see p. 83), helps investigators make connections between forged notes, especially if a computer database provides a match for the ink characteristics.

## Flexible fraud

Most criminal use of plastic cards involves fraud rather than counterfeiting—the cards are not copied but stolen. However, making a counterfeit card is not difficult,

**PAYMENT CARDS ▲**
*The IC chips in these smart cards are very much more difficult to copy than the magnetic swipe stripe of older payment cards, which can be duplicated on home computers.*

if the criminal has access to genuine account details to encode in the magnetic stripe. Copying cards is actually easier than copying currency, because there are tens of thousands of different payment card designs. A counterfeiter does not even need to use the graphic identity of a genuine bank. As long as the data in the magnetic stripe is correct, and the card looks authentic, a merchant will suspect nothing. Investigation of payment card counterfeiting focuses on identifying common characteristics, such as defects in the embossing presses used to raise the numerals, and details of the signature strip, the hologram, and the PVC overlays that cover the card's white core.

**◀ COMPUTER GAMES**
*Most games are now on CD, enabling hackers to crack copy protection and sell pirate games—sometimes without vital features such as sound.*

**WRISTWATCHES ▶**
*Major brands such as Rolex are widely imitated, mainly in the Far East. Often openly sold as copies, the watches lack the numbering guaranteeing authenticity, and rarely last more than three years.*

**◀ PERFUME**
*Fake fragrances are advertised on the Internet at a fraction of the price of the real thing, but they rarely smell like it. Some can cause skin reactions.*

**MUSIC ▶**
*Music piracy is a huge problem for record companies. Russia is the counterfeiter's Mecca—just one in ten CDs sold there is genuine.*

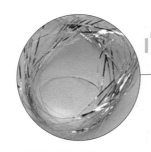

**SECURITY THREAD ▲**
*Faking metal threads in banknote paper is difficult enough, but the newest generation of notes have printed threads for added security.*

**INTAGLIO INK ▶**
*Specially engraved plates printed using the costly intaglio process produce a distinctive raised line that is impossible to reproduce with other printing methods.*

**HOLOGRAM ▶**
*Shiny optical variable devices on notes are not all holograms, but all show color or image changes when turned, and all are difficult to copy realistically.*

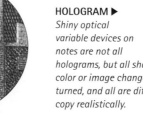

# Art forgery

The brushstrokes of a master artist are surely unmistakable to discerning collectors or museum curators—but how can they be positive? Ingenious forgers have hoodwinked experts for years, creating "priceless" paintings, ceramics, and metalwork. Separating the first-rate from the phony takes more than just a critical gaze.

The crudest forgeries are easy to recognize on stylistic grounds alone. But adept forgers can fool the shrewdest connoisseur, especially when they create works that pander to contemporary taste. Some 19th-century forgers, for example, made their copies more sentimental than the genuine articles because romanticism was in fashion. Sometimes artworks can be exposed by their provenance—or lack of it. This "art pedigree" theoretically allows a buyer to trace back the progress of a work of art through auction rooms, museums, and private collections. But a provenance can be fabricated, too.

Scientific analysis is usually the most accurate, and the most objective, method of authenticating artworks. It compares a suspicious artwork's materials with those of a genuine work by the same artist, or at least from the same period. Laboratory studies also look for the effects of aging, or use instrumental methods to actually measure how old a questioned piece is.

## Looking through varnish

With an oil painting, the simplest method for doing this is microscopic examination. Under a low-power stereomicroscope, it is easier to distinguish genuine from simulated aging of a paint surface. To create surface cracking, forgers roll the canvas, heat and cool it rapidly, or apply a contracting varnish. A stippling brush adds a flyblown appearance.

Other nondestructive testing methods make the difference more obvious. X-ray examination, for example, shows whether cracking penetrates every paint layer. The "Vermeers" painted in the 1930s by Dutch forger Hans van Meegeren (1889–1947) were unmasked by a pattern of cracks on the surface that did not match those on the lower paint layers.

Ultraviolet radiation causes specific fluorescence in materials, depending on their composition and age. A 19th-century varnish, for example, will fluoresce blue-green. Infrared may indicate a paint or ink

**SAMPLING PAINT ▲**
*To identify colors in a paint sample removed with a needle, this lab uses X-ray diffraction. Each pigment's unique crystal structure scatters an X-ray beam in a different and characteristic pattern.*

characteristic to the artist. To an expert eye, familiar with the artist's style, this can help determine if the work is genuine.

If these examinations do not reveal any anomalies, conservators begin a more invasive study. Typically, they cut a paint sample from the edge of a crackle or

*Measuring the quantity of impurities in pigment can make precise dating possible.*

*Binding agents can be identified by mass spectroscopy.*

**◄ INFRARED SCANNING**
*Multispectral analysis of paintings reveals detail invisible in normal light. This IR scanner makes surface layers of paint partially transparent, revealing underpainting or sketching. UV illumination (far left) can detect and identify retouching, overpainting, varnishes, and adhesives.*

damaged area, mount it in cold-setting polymer, polish the edge, and identify the pigments microscopically, using X-ray diffraction (see left), spectrographically (see p. 83), or by chemical analysis.

Since oil painting began in the 15th century, artists have sought brighter, more permanent, or cheaper pigments for their work. The introduction of new colors is thus well documented, and the artist's palette puts an upper limit on a painting's age. For example, Prussian blue was first synthesized in 1704, so a canvas painted with this pigment cannot be more than three centuries old.

The canvas itself is a surprisingly poor guide to age. Though the weave might provide some clues, cunning forgers aiming to simulate the work of old masters may use the cleaned-off canvases of an unknown contemporary. By contrast, panel paintings can be dated using dendochronology, a tree-ring measurement technique that can pinpoint when the wood was cut with single-year precision.

## Metals and ceramics

The incidence of forgery in other art media depends on their value and the labor, skill, or materials involved. Ceramics are hard to copy because success depends on obtaining clay from the same source as the original, and this is usually impossible. Almost all stone statues are authentic because forging them is so labor-intensive. The same is not true of cast metals. As many as half of all archaic Cretan bronze statuettes may be fakes. The tiny figures are easy to cast, and only

**VINCENT'S VASE**
*As many as 10% of modern French paintings may be forged, and the value of Van Gogh's work makes him the most popular target. Some experts even question whether Van Gogh's Sunflowers (left), sold for almost $40m in 1987, is genuine.*

*Under the stereomicroscope, brushstrokes and even the artist's fingerprints stand out in high relief*

the best examples are valuable enough to warrant the same minute scrutiny given to fine paintings.

To spot fakes in these media, curators wheel in some sophisticated technology. They date ceramics, with a precision rate of about 85%, using thermoluminescence. This works by measuring the natural radiation absorbed by the clay since the piece was fired. Unfortunately, the test is

destructive, requiring the removal of around 1 oz (30 g) of material. Dating of metal objects may be possible using nondestructive X-ray fluorescence analysis. Under this test, a piece emits an X-ray spectrum characteristic of the alloy from which it is made. It is necessary only to compare this spectrum with one from a similar artifact that dates from the same period and is known to be genuine.

**FAKE JIAN WARE TEABOWL**
*Stylistic differences identify this supposed 1,000-year-old teabowl as a modern forgery. A close look at the base shows it is roughly joined, the markings are crude, and the glaze too shiny.*

## CASE STUDY

London-born Tom Keating (1917–1984) ranks among the most brazen of modern forgers. During the 1970s he claimed to have painted more than 2,000 works by great artists, including Gainsborough, Degas, Fragonard, Renoir, and Modigliani. Ironically, it was not these big names that caught him out, but his fakes of the work of a comparatively minor 19th-century English artist, Samuel Palmer, who was best known for his illustrations of the works of William Blake. Keating was arrested when he tried to sell 13 "Palmer" watercolors.

## CASE STUDY

**FAKE GOLDEN EAGLE**    **GENUINE ARTICLE**

**NOT-SO-GOLDEN EAGLE**
*Crude fakes are often good enough to take in greedy or ignorant collectors. The 19th-century eagle brooch on the left is made of bronze coated in gold leaf, but was passed off as a valuable Visigoth treasure.*

# The Hitler diaries

The discovery of Hitler's private diaries had historians gasping with anticipation. What was he thinking when he approved plans to gas six million Jews? How did he feel when he faced defeat in World War II? If genuine, the diaries could provide unique insights into the thoughts of the world's most evil dictator.

In April 1945, World War II was drawing rapidly to a close. Sick and demoralized, German chancellor Adolf Hitler was holed up in a Berlin bunker. Not far away, at Schoenwalde airstrip, Major Friedrich Gundlfinger supervised the loading of weighty metal trunks aboard his Junkers 352. Then, just as dawn was breaking, Gundlfinger taxied his plane along the grass runway and opened the throttle.

His mission was part of Operation Seraglio: a desperate attempt to evacuate Germany's command center before Russian troops stormed Berlin. But Gundlfinger's flight did not go according to plan. It's not clear what happened in the icy clouds above Dresden, but by 6 AM the aircraft had crashed in the Heidenholz Forest and burst into flames. The color drained from Hitler's face when he heard the news. "In that plane were all my private archives ..." he gasped. "It is a catastrophe!"

## Diary discovered

After the war, few doubted that Hitler's archive had indeed been incinerated with the plane's crew. So, when a reporter from the Germany magazine *Stern* learned in 1979 that one of the Führer's diary volumes had turned up, he realized he was onto the most sensational story of his career.

Gerd Heidemann had an unhealthy obsession with the Nazis, and it was a fellow memorabilia collector who showed him the first volume of diaries. Written in Gothic script, apparently in Hitler's handwriting, it seemed authentic. A little sleuthing led Heidemann to the source: dealer Konrad Kujau. He claimed he had bought it from an East German general, who was smuggling the volumes across the border that then divided Germany into East and West.

## Buy, buy, buy!

Heidemann's boss was as excited as the reporter himself, and authorized him to buy the diaries—all 62 of them—for nine million German marks

**CONVICTED**

### IMPRISONED

*Forger Konrad Kujau (above) and Stern magazine reporter Gerd Heidemann (left) were sentenced to four-and-a-half years each for their part in the swindle. They repaid some of the money to Stern, but five million marks were never recovered.*

**CONVICTED**

**HITLER'S RISE ▶**
*Adolf Hitler, photographed at a Nazi rally in 1934, on his rise to power.*

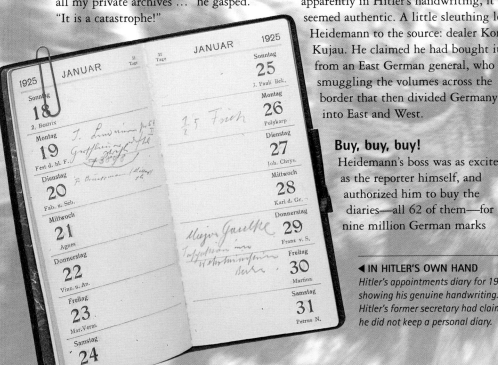

**◀ IN HITLER'S OWN HAND**
*Hitler's appointments diary for 1925, showing his genuine handwriting. Hitler's former secretary had claimed he did not keep a personal diary.*

## DEAD GIVEAWAYS

- The diaries had close parallels with a 1962 book, *Hitler's Speeches and Proclamations*.

- There were diary entries only for dates that appeared in the book. More damning still, the diaries repeated the book's errors.

- Labels supposedly typed in 1943 were as crisp as those dated nine years earlier. If the labels were genuine the typewriter's letters would have worn down.

- The bindings contained threads of polyester, which was not manufactured until 1953.

- The paper contained a fluorescent brightener, blankophor, introduced in 1954.

(equivalent, in 1982, to $3.7 million). In conditions of extreme secrecy, *Stern* editors superficially checked the diaries' authenticity—no experts were consulted—and prepared them for publication. In April 1983 they published extracts in a 356-page special edition, and syndicated them abroad.

## Publication and exposure

The publication was at once disappointing and sensational. The diary entries were surprisingly banal, and added little to knowledge of the period. However, they gave an amazing new insight into Hitler's character, portraying him as kindly and compassionate.

Historians and experts were divided. Some denounced the diaries as obvious fakes, but others leaped to defend them. To end speculation, *Stern* loaned several volumes to the Federal Institute of Forensic Investigation in Berlin.

Their report was damning (see box), and *Stern's* editor, Peter Koch, struggled to defend his magazine's reputation. Still convinced of the diaries' authenticity, he showed them to US handwriting expert Kenneth Rendell. After a day studying them, Rendell announced, "It doesn't look good." The most striking discrepancy was that the capital letters E, H, and K were quite different from genuine examples of Hitler's handwriting. Evidence of fraud piled up on all sides, and just two weeks after publication, Koch was forced to concede that *Stern* had been swindled.

The forger was Konrad Kujau himself. For years he had been making a good living by manufacturing Nazi memorabilia, but with the diaries he had overreached himself. Forging just one at first, he found himself trapped into creating more when *Stern* became involved. Gerd Heidemann, the reporter who "discovered" the diaries, had realized early on that they were fake, but he had

his own motives for making sure the deception continued. As middleman, he was creaming off a percentage of the payments. Also, the diaries' rehabilitation of Hitler provided a veneer of respectability for his own Nazi obsession.

Nor were the editors at *Stern* entirely innocent. Once they had agreed to buy the diaries, they were reluctant to believe that they were forged, and made only half-hearted efforts to check their authenticity.

The Hitler diaries were hardly clever counterfeits, but their place in the history of questioned document analysis is assured, through the enormous sums of money that changed hands, and because the greed and gullibility of all involved made them such enthusiastic dupes.

**SENSATION! ▶**
*Konrad Kujau holding a 1983 edition of* Stern, *in which the faked diaries were published as a "historic sensation."*

**THE FAKE DIARY ▶**
*The first page of Hitler's diary to be made public by* Stern *magazine reads: "Henceforth, I will take note of my political thoughts to leave a record for posterity as does every politician."*

# Computer forensics

Abstracted to a series of ones and zeros, digital information seems elusive and easily hidden. Yet each time it is stored, read, written, transmitted, or printed, data multiplies promiscuously. Solving computer crime can often be a simple matter of tracking down concealed or forgotten copies of incriminating digital information.

Computer forensics, once specialized, is now mainstream due to our total dependence on data. Experts deal not only with computer-related crime, such as hacking, software piracy, and viruses, but also with "conventional" crimes including fraud, embezzlement, organized crime, and child pornography.

The term "computer" extends beyond desktops, laptops, and pocket computers. It applies to anything containing a microprocessor. Cell phones, fax machines, cameras, video recorders—even washing machines—contain chips to process and store data records. All of them are potential sources of evidence.

### Where is that smoking gun?

However, the majority of computer crimes concern conventional PCs. An aid to investigating these crimes is the inherent insecurity of computer hardware and software. For example, deleting a file does not irreversibly remove it from the hard disk. "Deleting" simply changes the file's name, to hide it from the user.

### Data that will not die

Sophisticated criminal computer users are aware of the security loopholes, and use encryption and more secure deletion programs to hide incriminating data.

All computer operating systems use virtual memory to speed programs up. Storing data in RAM (on-chip random access memory) makes software very responsive, but RAM is a scarce resource. The computer's operating system makes RAM work harder by constantly swapping rarely used data from RAM on to a hard disk, which is slower but has a greater storage capacity. This process creates a "swap file" containing as much data as the computer's installed RAM—usually enough to hold the text of 200 novels.

When a file has been securely deleted, its contents may persist in the swap file. However, it does not remain there indefinitely. Each time a computer is switched on and used, new data replaces some of the old contents in the swap file.

This presents the investigator with an interesting problem: evidence may exist on a computer's hard disk, but simply switching the machine on might be enough to erase it.

Fortunately, there is a simple solution. With specialist equipment, it is possible to completely duplicate the contents of a computer's hard disk without switching the suspect machine on. Investigators can then examine files on the copy without running the risk of destroying data on the original. This approach has a secondary advantage—working on a copy avoids

## TYPES OF COMPUTER CRIME:

1   *Software piracy—when computer programs are illegally reproduced and sold.*

2   *Hacking—unauthorized computer access and sabotage, either mischievously or maliciously.*

3   *Computer fraud deals with assets— for example, illegal bank transfers and credit card transactions.*

4   *Computer forgery involves creating false documents using computers, such as laser-printed checks.*

5   *Incidental use of computers in the course of other crimes.*

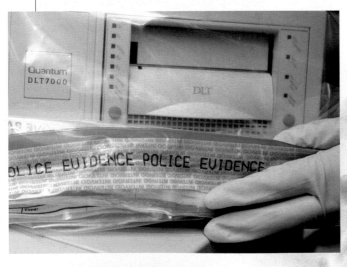

**SEALED AND PROTECTED ▲**
*When investigators seize computers, they must treat them just like any other physical evidence. Careful storage and documentation is essential to avoid defense challenges when a case comes to court.*

**DELVING WITHIN ▲**
*Forensic investigators dismantle and study seized hardware. They identify and photograph each component part before examining the stored data.*

**DIGITAL DATA ▲**
*As well as recovering data, investigators often have to reconstruct the operating system and programs to untangle digital evidence.*

**BOUNCING DISKS ▶**
*Computer hard disks, such as this one, can be remarkably resilient. Even throwing a computer from a second-floor window may fail to damage the data.*

accusations of evidence tampering. It also allows a third party, perhaps an expert working on the suspect's behalf, to repeat and verify any steps that investigators take to recover deleted or encrypted data.

## Internet fraud

Controlling cyber-crime presents investigators with a completely different set of problems. In addition, financial institutions are coy about revealing that they have been the victims of cyber-fraud. Even when they do, tracking down the perpetrators is not easy, as one of the few large cases to be made public illustrates. In 1994, computer hackers broke into the supposedly secure network of the world's largest bank, Citibank, and stole more than $10 million. The thieves used a modem to dial up and gain access to Citibank's payment network, but tracing the rogue calls was far from easy, since the transactions were completed so rapidly. In the end, investigators traced the mastermind of the operation, Russian Vladimir Levin, partly from telephone company records, but also by monitoring the bank accounts into which the stolen money had been electronically transferred.

When one of the cyber-gang tried to cash a multi-million-dollar check, he was arrested, and helped police in exchange for a lighter sentence.

## "Follow the money"

This combination of cyber-sleuthing and tracing financial transactions has also paid dividends in tracking down criminals who use the Internet to exchange pornographic images of children. For example, in spring 2002, British police used special software to monitor Internet chatrooms used by members of a pedophile ring. However, the suspects were eventually identified from credit cards, used to pay for access to child pornography websites.

## Encryption

Criminals may use encryption to try to cover their tracks in computer crime. But, until recently, the commercial password-protection programs they could use offered very weak safeguards against even moderately knowledgeable investigators. Strong encryption is becoming more widely available, but ironically, this may provide little help to cyber-criminals. Whether sent over the Internet as emails or stored on a hard disk, encrypted data has an eye-catching signature that shouts "suspicious." Using encryption can be tantamount to an admission of guilt.

## CASE STUDY

In early May 2000, millions of computer users opened an email headed "I Love You" and got a nasty shock. The message emailed itself to every contact in their address books. By multiplying explosively, this "Love Bug" brought the Internet to a standstill. Investigators found the word "Barok" in the virus code. This word had also appeared in a less damaging virus four months earlier—along with the claim that its author was studying at AMACC, a computer college in the Philippines. The school confirmed that a student, Onel de Guzman, had submitted a similar program as a term paper shortly before dropping out. Manila police raided his apartment and found disks that proved he was one of the authors. However, at that time, the Philippines had no laws against computer hacking. By June, new legislation had been introduced, but it was too late to apply to the "Love Bug" case. So the author of the most destructive virus ever written escaped unpunished.

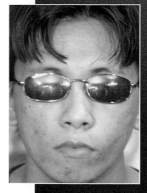

**◀ ONEL DE GUZMAN**
*24-year-old Onel de Guzman denied authoring the virus, but said he may have released it by accident.*

# Environmental crimes

Modern methods of forensic detection make it easier than ever before to track down criminals who trade in endangered species, or who pollute and destroy the natural environment. But the international nature of many of these crimes, the vested interests involved, and lack of political conviction mean prosecutions are rare.

**TOXIC TUBS ▲**
*The "fill and forget" attitude of polluters means toxicologists must identify the contents of rusting, leaking drums in huge and dangerous dumps.*

International agreements and national laws help to protect the environment and endangered species, but pressures to flout them are enormous. Huge sums of money are at stake, and poverty, complacency, and cultural differences make law enforcement difficult. Within both developed and developing nations, greed and corruption can all too easily override concerns for the environment. Governments may also face dilemmas if, for example, environmental protection means closing a polluting chemical plant and losing jobs. If resolving these issues is complex, then at least environmental crime detection is relatively straightforward.

## Pollution control

Analytical techniques can now detect tiny quantities of pollution in water, soil, and air. For example, analysts can spot river pollution diluted a billion times—the equivalent of half a teaspoonful in an Olympic-size swimming pool. Pollution detection and control typically combine remote sensing with automated and manual testing. In water, for example, tests can measure oxygen depletion, as well as levels of nutrients, organic and inorganic chemicals, and other pollutants.

Unfortunately, detecting pollution is only half the challenge. To stop it, the source must be traced, which can be much more difficult. Sampling progressively farther upstream leads eco-detectives to the source of industrial pollution. Other pollutants, however, are more elusive. When it comes to fertilizer or pesticide runoff from fields, the pollutant enters streams and rivers at many points, so proving responsibility may be difficult.

**POLLUTING PIPES ▼**
*Many diagnostic techniques are used to analyze discharges from suspect pipes. Gas chromatography, for example, detects tiny amounts of pesticides.*

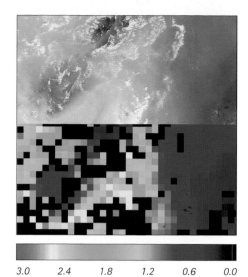

**"HAZE" OVER SUMATRA ▲**
*NASA's* Terra *satellite instruments measure numbers of airborne smoke particles. High values can indicate locations of illegal forest fires set to clear farmland.*

| 3.0 | 2.4 | 1.8 | 1.2 | 0.6 | 0.0 |

## DNA pawprints

DNA analysis is widely used to stop the trade in endangered species. Many animals and birds are in danger of extinction because of the use of their body parts in traditional East Asian remedies, and the demand from collectors. Identifying live animals is not that difficult, but dried or frozen tissue is a tougher challenge. Morphology—studying the shape and structure of bone, fur, beak, and feather—can indicate species. Serology also helps, by using methods similar to the precipitin test for human blood (see p. 59). But as the price of DNA analysis continues to fall, this quick method of positive identification is becoming increasingly favored.

For example, scientists from Hawaii took a portable laboratory to Japan to analyze DNA from samples of restaurant whale meat. Comparing the results with a DNA database revealed that Japanese diners were eating protected species, including North Pacific humpback and North Atlantic fin whales. Similar methods have traced caviar from illegally fished sturgeon, and tiger parts en route to traditional Oriental herbalists.

## Who does it?

Though governments like to favor environmental conservation, proper funding for the detection and prevention of wildlife crime is rare. Many countries have integrated wildlife forensics into their intelligence and policing services, but only the US has a dedicated unit— the National Fish and Wildlife Forensics Laboratory in Ashland, Oregon.

Lack of resources means environmental crime detection is often left to voluntary agencies and pressure groups. Brazil, for example, has a government agency to stop illegal logging, but each inspector polices an area of forest the size of Switzerland. Logging companies use bribes and death threats to stop them from working. In collaboration with the agency, Greenpeace took a ship equipped with aircraft and launches up the Amazon to areas where logging was forbidden. They tagged felled trees with a colorless paint that glowed in UV, and hid electronic tracking devices in log rafts. These undercover methods traced logs to Great Britain and France, and the campaign led to multi-million-dollar fines on loggers in Brazil.

**◄ FEATHERED CONTRABAND**
*X-ray inspection of luggage can detect rare birds packed in tubes. The illegal wildlife trade is worth $10–20 billion annually— only drug and arms trafficking are more lucrative.*

**RHINO PROBLEM ▶**
*Infrared spectroscopy can identify as little as 1% rhino horn in traditional impotence "cures," but the technology is too costly for the countries that need it most.*

## LAB ANALYSIS

The successful prosecution of poachers and smugglers of endangered wildlife usually depends on the positive identification of their prey or contraband. Specialists in birds, mammals, and reptiles can usually use morphology (form and structure) to pin down the specimen to species level—provided they have access to a whole, well-preserved carcass. Incomplete or decayed specimens may limit the identification to the family or genus level. Use of DNA profiles to identify seized wildlife specimens is possible only if the laboratory has access to genetic material known to come from an animal of the same species as the one submitted for testing.

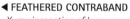

# Shahtoosh trading

In a Hong Kong apartment, wealthy women meet to buy soft shawls with $10,000 price tags. It might seem like any other display of conspicuous consumption, but this party is different. To make each of the garments they are buying, four of the world's most endangered mammals are shot and killed by poachers.

CONVICTED

**SHAHTOOSH TRADER** ▲
*In a landmark case for the Hong Kong authorities, shahtoosh trader Bharati Assomull was fined $40,000 and sentenced to a three-month jail sentence, suspended for a year.*

The Tibetan plateau is a harsh place. It is high—more than 8,200 ft (2,500 m) above sea level—and dry. Thermometers creep above freezing fewer than 60 days each year, and the barren plateau is swept constantly by gale-force winds. To survive these unforgiving conditions, the animals that live here have evolved their own special defenses against the climate. In the case of the chiru, a species of antelope, this protection takes the form of a coat of the finest, softest wool in the world.

Unfortunately, the qualities that make the wool a good insulator for the chiru also make it highly desirable as a garment textile for fashion-conscious humans.

## Fashion victims

Herding and breeding chiru for their wool is out of the question—the beasts are wary, and bolt when they scent humans. The only way to obtain their wool is to kill the antelopes and skin them. In the past, this had little impact on their numbers, because hunters were few and inefficient. However, today's poachers drive fast trucks and use high-powered hunting rifles to pick off chiru that are barely dots on the horizon. The result means chiru numbers have fallen from around a million a century ago to just 75,000 today. Such low numbers mean that the species faces extinction if action isn't taken to halt the killing.

Policing the poachers effectively is impossible—the animals range over an area the size of France. Some 7% of this is inside China's Arjin Shan Reserve, but this offers the chiru little protection, since the reserve's managers have just four vehicles.

## 15K in HK

Demand drives the poaching trade. Fashionable women—and men—wear and collect the shawls, oblivious to the plight of the chiru. Though the fashion for shahtoosh is international, the trade has been especially flagrant in Hong Kong. There, socialites nicknamed "tai-tais" pay $3,000–$5,000 for them, though the largest may fetch $15,000.

Ending the trade should in theory be straightforward. The animals are listed on Appendix I of the Convention on International Trade in Endangered Species of Wild Fauna and Flora (CITES), which ensures that all signatory countries make it illegal to buy or sell products made from chiru.

The Hong Kong authorities had tried repeatedly to stamp out the trade, but a

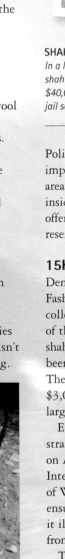

**◄ CARNAGE IN TIBET**
*Poachers skin the chiru they shoot, and leave the worthless carcasses to rot. Each pelt yields about 3.5 oz (100 g) of wool, and 11–18 oz (300–500 g) are needed to weave a single shawl.*

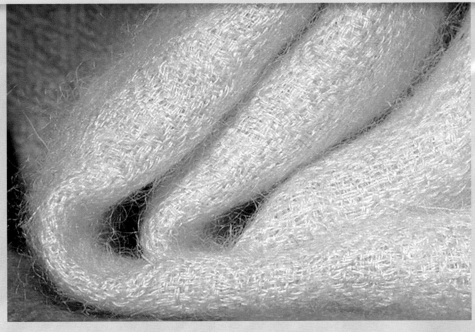

**KING OF WOOLS ▶**

*Shahtoosh is a Persian word meaning "from nature and fit for a king." The fabric, which resembles cashmere, is very soft and light, yet warm.*

loophole in the law has, until recently, enabled traders and collectors to escape prosecution. In 1995, for example, 100 shawls were seized from a tai-tai. The owner's lawyer argued that there was no case to answer, because it would be impossible to prove in court that the wool came from an endangered species. Eventually the shawls were returned.

## Shawl of blood

However, by the following year, opinion was beginning to change. Informants among Hong Kong's elite began to pass on information about clandestine shahtoosh sales to the environmental organization TRAFFIC, which in turn notified the Hong Kong authorities. But there remained the identification loophole. This was finally closed, not in Hong Kong but in the US, at the government's National Fish and Wildlife Forensics Laboratory (NFWFL). A chemist from the Hong Kong Government Laboratory flew to the NFWFL and helped senior forensic specialist Bonnie Yates there to develop a diagnostic test for chiru hair.

**ANTELOPE AT LARGE ▲**

*Chiru can outrun dogs and wolves, but not human hunters. But poachers are not the only threat—a disastrous snowstorm in 1985 decimated the herds.*

## On the merchants' trail

The scientists considered using DNA analysis to identify the source of the wool. However, they discounted this not only due to expense, but also because the shawls rarely contain hair roots, which contain the body tissue needed for analysis. Instead, the scientists looked for morphological clues, studying the shape and size of the hairs.

The chiru's soft, downy wool resembles cashmere, though it is somewhat finer. But the chiru's coat also contains coarser guard hairs, which, though undesirable from the wearer's point of view, are almost impossible to remove. It was these hairs that gave the scientists the landmark they needed. As Bonnie Yates commented, "Guard hairs contain the distinctive microstructure that differentiates hairs of the Tibetan antelope from goat hairs and other closely related ungulates." Best of all, identifying the hairs was easy and quick; the differences showed up even under a conventional optical microscope.

Armed with a test procedure that would stand up to legal scrutiny, Hong Kong police swooped. On December 18, 1997, they raided a private exhibition at the Furama Hotel. They seized 130 shahtoosh shawls and arrested Bharati Assomull. In February 1999, the trader was found guilty of possession of highly endangered species.

Though more prosecutions have followed, the illicit trade in shahtoosh continues in Hong Kong and elsewhere, particularly Western Europe, North America, and Japan. Though police in these areas continue to impound shawls and prosecute those who traffic in them, the trade will end only when the wearing of a shahtoosh becomes as unacceptable as wearing a coat made of panda or tiger fur.

**THE RING TEST ▼**

*Salesmen demonstrate the fineness of shahtoosh fabric to potential customers by gathering a shawl measuring 3 x 7 ft (1 x 2 m) and drawing it smoothly through a man's wedding ring.*

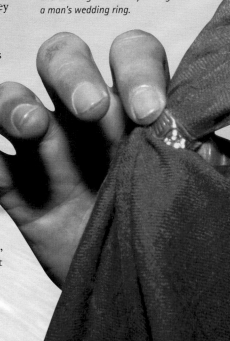

# Breakthroughs in forensic science

## IDENTIFICATION

**1660**
*Italian biologist Marcello Malpighi (1628–94) describes the pattern of ridges on the tips of the fingers.*

**1776**
*Paul Revere identifies the corpse of General Warren by his false tooth, which Revere had made from a walrus tusk.*

**1823**
*Czech physiologist Johan Evangelista Purkinje publishes a description of fingerprint types, identifying whorl, ellipse, and triangle patterns.*

**1843**
*Police in Belgium take the first mugshots of criminals.*

**1850**
*In the US, murderer John Webster's conviction is the first to be made on the basis of medical evidence. Physicians and anatomists tell the jury how they determined the age, sex, and time of death of the victim.*

**1858**
*In India, the chief administrative officer of the Hooghly district, William James Herschel, notices the regular and distinctive patterns on fingerprints, and later requires army pensioners to "sign" with their fingerprints as a receipt for their pensions. This is the first modern use of fingerprints for identification purposes.*

## TRACES, CHEMISTRY, AND DOCUMENTS

**1609**
*In France, François Demelle publishes the first study on handwriting analysis.*

**1670**
*Anton Van Leeuwenhoek invents the first powerful precision microscope. In 1674, he will use it to observe and describe red blood cells.*

**1804**
*German physicist Johann Wilhelm Ritter discovers ultraviolet radiation, the invisible rays that will eventually be widely used to reveal trace evidence that cannot be seen by visible light.*

**1814**
*In Spain, Matthieu Orfila publishes the first scientific paper on the detection of poisons: Traite des Poisons Tires des Regnes Mineral, Vegetal et Animal, ou Toxicologie General. It will earn him the title "father of toxicology."*

**1830**
*In Italy, Giovan Battista Amici invents the polarizing light microscope. By the end of the century such instruments will be widely used to study geological samples.*

**1836**
*Briton James Marsh devises a test for arsenic that is sensitive enough to detect as little as a millionth of an ounce (1/50,000th gram). Earlier tests were not sufficiently reliable to be accepted as evidence in a law court.*

## PATHOLOGY AND MISCELLANEOUS

**44 BC**
*Roman physician Antisius examines the corpse of assassinated emperor Julius Caesar. He concludes that, though Caesar was stabbed 23 times, only one wound, to the chest, was fatal.*

**1247**
*In China, lawyer and death investigator Sung Tzuh writes Hsi Duan Yu, literally "the washing away of wrongs." The book, the first work on forensic science, includes instructions on how to distinguish between suicide, homicide, and natural death, and considers the relative danger of wounds to different parts of the body.*

**1284**
*Chinese writer His Yuan Lu describes how the cause of death alters the appearance of a body.*

**1642**
*In Germany, the University of Leipzig begins to teach a course in forensic medicine.*

**1809**
*In Paris, petty criminal Eugène François Vidocq escapes a further prison term by agreeing to share his knowledge of the criminal underworld. With his help, the French state sets up a security brigade, the Police de Sûreté.*

**1878**
*Scotland Yard sets up Britain's first plainclothes detective force, the Criminal Investigation Department (CID).*

## FIREARMS AND SEROLOGY

**1794**
*The field of ballistics begins with the conviction of murderer John Toms in Lancashire, England. A piece of paper found in the wound of a murder victim matches a section torn from a ballad found in the pocket of the man accused of his murder.*

**1835**
*In England, Bow Street runner Henry Goddard studies the marks on bullets, and demonstrates that a tiny raised area on a bullet could only have been formed by a corresponding imperfection on a bullet mold.*

**1889**
*At the University of Lyon, Alexandre Lacassagne demonstrates that a bullet can be matched to the gun that fired it by comparing grooves on the bullet with the spiral rifling inside the barrel.*

**1891**
*Prussian medical scientist Paul Ehrlich shows that injecting a toxic substance into an animal stimulates the production of antibodies that confer immunity to the toxin. This discovery forms the basis of immunology, and will eventually lead to immunoassay, a key analytical method in toxicology.*

**1898**
*German chemist Paul Jeserich is the first to fire a bullet from a suspect's gun, then compare the markings on it with a bullet recovered from a murder scene. The resemblance between them is used to convict the killer.*

**1859**
The US becomes the first country in which photographs are used as evidence in a court of law.

**1879**
Scottish physician Henry Faulds, working in Tokyo, uses fingerprints to catch a robber. The following year he notices on fragments of ancient ceramics the fingerprints of the potter and writes to the journal Nature, suggesting for the first time that fingerprints could be used to identify people. William Herschel (see 1858) also writes, claiming he thought of it first.

**1882**
Alphonse Bertillon, a clerk at the Paris Sûreté, proposes "anthropometry"—a system of bodily measurements—as a means of identifying criminals. He has his first success in identifying a suspect the following year.

**1892**
In his book, Fingerprints, English scientist Francis Galton proposes a scientific classification of fingerprints based on arches, loops, and whorls. He also demonstrates that fingerprints are not inherited, and that the fingerprints of identical twins are different.

**1892**
In Argentina, fingerprints are used for the first time to convict a murderer. It is a victory for Buenos Aires police officer Juan Vucetich, who was pushing for the acceptance of fingerprints in police investigations. Argentina becomes the first country to adopt fingerprinting in preference to anthropometry.

**1859**
In Germany, physicist Gustav Kirchhoff and chemist Robert Bunsen demonstrate that the color of a flame can be used to identify the substance burning, and use it to build the first spectroscope.

**1861**
German pathologist and statesman Rudolph Virchow, while professor of pathological anatomy in Berlin, is the first to study hair and its value as evidence.

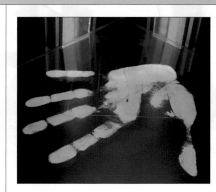

**1877**
At King's College, London, Walter Noel Hartley builds an ultraviolet spectrograph. Developed and automated, his instrument will later become the ultraviolet spectrophotometer, a vital tool for forensic analysis.

**1904**
In Germany, George Popp uses botanical material (soil and plant parts) as evidence for the first time.

**1910**
Victor Balthazard, the medical examiner for the city of Paris, with Marcelle Lambert, publishes Le poil de l'homme et des animaux (Human and animal hair), the first scientific study of hair.

**1893**
Hans Gross, professor of criminal law at Prague University, publishes System der Kriminalstik (Criminal Investigation in the 1907 English edition). It will become a landmark work in forensic science, covering the application of microscopy, serology, fingerprints, and ballistics.

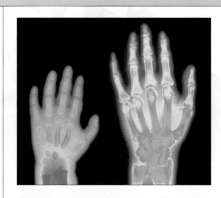

**1895**
Conrad Röntgen discovers X-rays.

**1908**
US attorney general Charles J. Bonaparte establishes the Bureau of Investigation (later the FBI), the first US national force for investigating crime.

**1910**
In France, Edmond Locard starts the first forensic laboratory, and begins to formulate his "contact trace theory," though he will not express it formally until 1920.

**1901**
Austrian pathologist Karl Landsteiner devises the ABO blood-grouping system, and shows that there are at least three types of human blood. In 1930 he will receive the Nobel Prize for Medicine for his work.

**1901**
Paul Uhlenhuth, assistant professor at Greifswald, Germany, devises the precipitin test to distinguish primate blood from that of other animals.

**1913**
Victor Balthazard, professor of forensic medicine at the Sorbonne University, Paris, publishes a pioneering article on the significance of bullet markings, showing that they make each bullet unique.

**1915**
Leone Lattes, lecturer and assistant researcher at the Institute of Forensic Medicine in Turin, Italy, develops a procedure for ABO testing of bloodstains on cloth. He uses saline solution to restore the dried blood to its original liquid state.

**1920**
Physicist John Fisher invents the helixometer to record the interior of gun barrels.

**1920**
In the United States, Charles E. Waite begins to build an international catalog of firearms. When the collection is complete, five years later, it will enable him to judge from a bullet what kind of gun fired it.

# Breakthroughs in forensic science

## IDENTIFICATION

**1902**
*Fingerprint evidence is accepted for the first time in an English court, with the conviction of burglar Henry Jackson.*

**1909**
*US physiologist Thomas Hunt Morgan demonstrates that chromosomes carry inherited information— the basis of DNA evidence.*

**1920s**
*Russian paleontologist Michael Gerasimov devises a way of calculating the thickness of flesh on the face, paving the way for lifelike facial reconstruction.*

**1930**
*The FBI starts the US national fingerprint file.*

**1940**
*Hugh C. Macdonald, head of the Los Angeles Police Department's civilian division, devises the Identikit system.*

**1941**
*In the US, researchers at Bell Laboratories develop voice spectrograms as a means of identifying suspects from the characteristics of their speech. (The technique will be refined by Lawrence Kersta.)*

**1969**
*Photographer Jacques Perry devises the Photo-FIT ID system, capable of creating 15 billion different faces.*

**1975**
*The FBI introduces the Automated Fingerprint Identification System (AFIS), installing 10-print card readers for computerized print matching.*

## TRACES, CHEMISTRY, AND DOCUMENTS

**1910**
*In the US, Albert S. Osborn, the nation's most distinguished handwriting expert, publishes Questioned Documents. It remains a standard work in the field.*

**1924**
*In the US, the killers of student Bobby Franks are convicted on the basis of forensic evidence showing that a typewriter owned by one of them had been used to type a ransom note.*

**1922–1928**
*Arthur C. Hardy builds the first spectrophotometers at MIT. They plot the spectrum from a sample automatically, freeing the operator from tedious and tiring observations. He will strike a deal with GEC to produce them commercially.*

**1925**
*Americans Phillip Gravelle and Calvin Goddard invent the comparison microscope. Their evidence will be used the following year to compare bullets and thus convict anarchists Nicola Sacco and Bartolomeo Vanzetti.*

**1931**
*At the Berlin Technical University, Max Knoll and Ernst Ruska start to build the first transmission electron microscope. Ruska will later help Siemens manufacture them.*

**1938**
*Dutch physicist Frits Zernike builds the first phase contrast microscope, which makes possible the study of cells without staining and killing them. In 1953 he will receive the Nobel Prize for this breakthrough.*

## PATHOLOGY AND MISCELLANEOUS

**1920**
*In the United States, Luke May is the first to study striation marks on tools and use their comparison in the solution of crimes. He is also the first to analyze the results of this work statistically.*

**1921**
*John Larson builds the first lie detector that measures blood pressure and breathing. In 1930, Leonard Keeler will add measurement of galvanic skin resistance, essentially creating the modern polygraph machine.*

**1923**
*In Frye vs. United States, a court rules that polygraph tests are not acceptable as evidence in American courts.*

**1924**
*Los Angeles Police chief August Vollmer sets up the first US crime laboratory in Berkeley.*

**1932**
*The Federal Bureau of Investigation (FBI) creates the Technical Crime Laboratory, its first forensic lab.*

## FIREARMS AND SEROLOGY

**1923**
*Charles Waite and Phillip Gravelle set up the Bureau of Forensic Ballistics in New York. Calvin Goddard, later America's foremost firearms expert, will join the bureau in 1926.*

**1929**
*From machine gun bullets fired at the St. Valentine's Day massacre, Calvin Goddard identifies the weapons used by Al Capone's hit men, leading to the conviction of one of them. Grateful Chicago tycoons fund Goddard's Scientific Crime Detection Laboratory at Northwestern University, Illinois.*

**1930s**
*The first test for gunshot residues on the hands, the dermal nitrate test, is introduced by Tomas Gonzalez, the Chief of Police of Mexico City. It will remain in use until the 1960s.*

**1932**
*Swedish scientist E. M. P. Widmark proposes measuring the quantity of alcohol in human blood as an objective guide to drunkenness.*

**1937**
*Walter Specht first suggests the use of luminol as a preliminary test for the presence of blood.*

**1940**
*At the Vienna Pathological Institute, Austria, Karl Landsteiner, Philip Levine, and Alexander Wiener first describe Rh blood groups, which they name after the rhesus monkey used in their experiments.*

**1977**
At the National Police Agency of Japan, trace evidence examiner Fuseo Matsumur is using superglue to mount hairs on a microscope when he notices that the fumes from the adhesive make his fingerprints much more conspicuous. Superglue fuming will become one of the most important methods for revealing latent fingerprints.

**1980–1985**
The Japanese National Police Agency establishes the world's first fingerprint database that can be searched by computer.

**1986**
Alec Jeffreys, who developed the first DNA profiling test two years earlier, uses it to identify Colin Pitchfork as the murderer of two young girls in the English Midlands. Significantly, in the course of the investigation, DNA was first used to exonerate an innocent suspect.

**1987**
DNA evidence is introduced in the US courts, and faces its first test of admissibility. The case leads to the introduction of accreditation, standardization, and quality controls for DNA laboratories.

**1991**
A team led by Robin Richards at the Medical Physics Department at University College Hospital, London, introduces a laser scanning technique that makes possible the computer simulation of a human face, based on the shape of a skull.

**1999**
The FBI introduces the Integrated Automated Fingerprint Identification System (IAFIS) to store the fingerprints of 65 million people. The system makes possible electronic submission with centralized storage and search facilities.

**1938**
At the University of Kharkov, Russian scientists N. A. Izmailov and M. S. Shraiber develop a simple form of thin-layer chromatography.

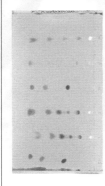

**1941**
As part of his studies of the structure of wool, Archer J. P. Martin develops liquid-column chromatography, and suggests that a similar principle could be used in the analysis of gases. (Gas chromatography will become one of the most important forensic analytical methods.)

**1945–1954**
At the US Department of Agriculture, Justus G. Kirchner and his colleagues perfect thin-layer chromatography as a way of analyzing fruit juices.

**1965**
The first high-resolution scanning electron microscopes are produced as a result of work by Charles Oatley, Dennis McMullan, and Ken Smith at Cambridge University, England.

**1978**
In England, Bob Freeman and Doug Foster invent the electrostatic detection apparatus (ESDA) to reveal handwriting impressions in paper.

**1936**
Alexander Mearns of the Institute of Hygiene at the University of Glasgow uses the life-cycle of maggots to estimate time of death in the trial of Buck Ruxton.

**1938**
Rolla N. Harger develops the "Drunkometer" to measure breath alcohol. His collaboration with Robert F. Borkenstein of the Indiana State Police will produce in 1954 the Breathalyzer, the first easy-to-use roadside instrument.

**1967**
The FBI starts the National Crime Information Center to coordinate information about criminals and stolen goods.

**1949**
Swedish scientist Örjan Ouchterlony improves on the precipitin test (see human ID, 1901) by devising the double diffusion method, which uses agar plates with wells for antigens and antibodies.

**1959**
H. C. Harrison and R. Gilroy develop a color test for the presence of gunshot residue. Swabs taken from a suspect's hands are treated with chemical reagents that change color in the presence of traces of lead, barium, and antimony.

**1968**
At the Scotland Yard forensic laboratories of London's Metropolitan Police, research begins into the detection of gunshot residues using scanning electron microscopy with electron dispersive X-rays (SEM-EDX). It will become one of the principal technologies used for this purpose.

**1992**
The FBI Laboratory commissions the Drugfire database, which stores details of markings on bullets and cartridge cases, and permits rapid searching and computer comparison to establish links between crimes committed with the same weapon.

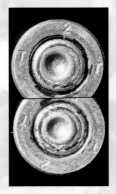

**1996**
At the US Bureau of Alcohol, Tobacco and Firearms (ATF), the IBIS spent ammunition database goes online. Developed by Montreal company Forensic Technology, the system has capabilities similar to the FBI's Drugfire database.

**2000**
The FBI and the ATF begin the merging of their firearms databases to create the National Integrated Ballistics Network (NIBIN), which will eventually replace Drugfire and IBIS.

# Glossary

Words in SMALL CAPITALS refer to other entries in this glossary.

**Abrasion**
A graze

**Accelerant**
Fuel used to make a deliberately set fire burn more vigorously.

**Antibody**
A protein the body produces in response to, and to protect against, an ANTIGEN.

**Antigen**
A foreign, potentially harmful substance in the body, such as a toxin, virus, or bacterium.

**Atomic absorption spectroscopy**
SPECTROSCOPIC analytical method that identifies the elements in an unknown sample—even in very low concentrations.

**Autopsy**
Dissection of a corpse to determine how death occurred.

**Ballistics**
Strictly, the study of how bullets and other missiles fly, but loosely used to mean the study of firearms.

**Capillary electrophoresis**
Method of ELECTROPHORESIS in which the slowing medium is a fine tube.

**Cause of death**
The action that resulted in death, such as a blow to the head, as distinct from the medical condition—such as brain haemorrhage.

**Chain of custody**
The trail followed from crime scene to court by a piece of evidence. Documentary proof that the chain of custody is unbroken guarantees the integrity of evidence.

**Chromatography**
Group of analytical methods that separate mixtures of substances according to their speed of movement through a stationary medium.

**Class evidence**
Evidence that is specific enough to identify overall characteristics—such as the make of a shoe—but too general for a unique identification.

**Comparison microscope**
A microscope with twin optics, to allow side-by-side comparison of similar items of evidence.

**Contusion**
A bruise

**Coroner**
Public official who is responsible for investigating any death that may not have had a natural cause.

**Deoxyribonucleic acid**
Long, spiraling molecule, present in every cell with a nucleus, that carries inherited genetic information unique to each individual.

**DFO**
Abbreviation for 1, 8-diaza-9-fluorenone, a chemical treatment that makes LATENT FINGERPRINTS glow when lit with laser or blue-green light.

**DNA**
See DEOXYRIBONUCLEIC ACID

**DNA profile or fingerprint**
Powerful method of identifying people by analysis of their DEOXYRIBONUCLEIC ACID.

**Dusting**
Brushing of a LATENT FINGERPRINT with a powder to make it visible.

**Electrophoresis**
Analytical method that uses an electric charge to drive substances such as proteins through a stationary medium, thus grading them by size.

**Electrostatic lifter**
Mat charged with static electricity, used to lift and capture PATTERN EVIDENCE such as dusty footprints.

**Fiber evidence**
Evidence provided by human and animal hairs, or synthetic fibers.

**Forensic light source**
A special source of intense light that can be filtered to shine a single-color, ultraviolet, or infrared beam.

**Gas chromatography (GC)**
Method of CHROMATOGRAPHY in which the substance to be analyzed is a gas, and moves through a solid or liquid medium.

**Gas chromatography/mass spectrometry (GC/MS)**
Hybrid analytical technique that produces more specific results than either of the two technologies used individually.

**Gel lift**
A thick sheet of sticky gel used to lift PATTERN EVIDENCE such as footprints from a crime scene.

**Gunshot residue**
Unburned primer powder sprayed on to the hands of someone firing a gun, and possibly on to the target.

**Headspace**
The air above a sample in a sealed container, in which volatile compounds (for example of ACCELERANT) collect.

**High performance liquid chromatography**
Method of CHROMATOGRAPHY in which a solid medium slows and separates components of a (usually organic) liquid pumped through it.

**Histology**
The microscopic study of the tissues of the human body, usually undertaken as part of a POSTMORTEM examination

**Immunoassary**
SEROLOGY analysis method that relies on the human body's self-protecting response to ANTIGENS.

**Infrared spectroscopy**
SPECTROSCOPY using infrared radiation. Commonly used to determine the class of synthetic compounds.

**Inquest**
A CORONER'S inquiry

**Iodine fuming**
Method of revealing LATENT FINGERPRINTS by the action of iodine vapor.

**Landmark**
A tissue-depth measurement point on the human face, used when visualizing facial features from a skull.

**Latent fingerprint**
An invisible or inconspicuous mark left by the ridges on the fingertips.

**Lie detector**
See POLYGRAPH

**Ligature**
Any cordlike object used for strangulation.

**Lividity**
Darkening of the skin caused by blood pooling in the lower parts of a body.

**Luminol**
Reagent that makes blood traces glow faintly. A PRESUMPTIVE TEST for blood.

**Manner of death**
Legal classification of how someone died—suicide, natural, accidental, or homicide—determined by the CORONER.

## Mass spectrometry
Versatile analytical method that breaks substances into charged particles, using their deflection in a magnetic field to gauge their size and abundance.

## Medical examiner
Trained medical practitioner who devotes some or all of their time to forensic work.

## Microchemical analysis
Analytical techniques carried out on microscopic samples of evidence, using methods adapted from conventional chemical analysis.

## Microspectrophotometry
Method of SPECTROSCOPY typically used to identify microscopic samples of dye or pigment.

## Microtome
Planelike device for paring very thin slices of tissue for microscopic analysis.

## Mitochondrial DNA (mtDNA)
Special form of DEOXYRIBONUCLEIC ACID found in the mitochondria of cells. MtDNA survives very much longer than ordinary DNA and is inherited maternally, making it ideal for determining family realtionships.

## Ninhydrin
Reagent that turns LATENT FINGERPRINTS purple.

## Odontology
Forensic dentistry

## Pathology
In a forensic context, the study of the causes and consequences of disease and injury in relation to crime and the law.

## Pattern evidence
Evidence in which the shape or distribution of a substance, such as blood or dust, provides information—rather than the substance itself.

## Peroxidase
Enzyme found in blood that is commonly detected by PRESUMPTIVE TESTS.

## Physical development
Method for revealing LATENT FINGERPRINTS on wet surfaces by depositing metallic silver from solution.

## Polygraph
Device that measures the sweating, pulse, and breathing of a suspect under questioning, to try to detect whether they are lying or to encourage a confession.

## Polymerase chain reaction
Method of "amplifying" a DEOXYRIBONUCLEIC ACID sample to a size sufficient for analysis and identification.

## Postmortem
Literally "after death," but loosely used to mean the examination of a corpse, including an AUTOPSY.

## Postmortem interval
The time since death

## Precipitin test
Test that confirms whether the source of a blood sample is a primate.

## Presumptive test
Cheap, simple test that shows that a sample probably contains the substance the test aims to identify.

## Profiling
Also called psychological, criminal, or offender profiling: a method of analyzing common factors in associated crimes to help understand the perpetrator and narrow the suspect list.

## Refractive index
Light-bending power of (for example) glass.

## Rifling
Raised, spiraling pattern in the barrel of a firearm.

## Rigor mortis
The stiffness of a corpse: a rough measure of POSTMORTEM INTERVAL.

## Scanning electron microscope
Instrument that reveals surface detail, often at very high magnification, by scanning a beam of electrons across a sample.

## Serial killer/rapist
Offender who commits three or more crimes with a cooling-off period in between.

## Serology
The study of blood

## Short tandem repeats
Repeated pattern of base pairs commonly identified in a DNA profile, and typically used to match samples from suspect and crime scene.

## Sniffer
Hydrocarbon vapor detector device used to reveal the presence of accelerant at a suspected arson scene.

## Spectroscopy
Method of identifying unknown substances from the characteristic spectra they absorb or emit.

## Spectrophotometry
See SPECTROSCOPY

## Spot test
Identifying test in which (typically) a color change occurs when a drop of reagent is applied to a small area.

## Superglue fuming
Method of revealing LATENT FINGERPRINTS using superglue vapor.

## Suspect
An individual who might possibly have committed the crime under investigation, as distinct from an offender or perpetrator, where guilt is presumed or has been proven.

## Taping/tape lift
Lifting fingerprints from a surface using adhesive tape.

## Thin-layer chromatography
Method of CHROMATOGRAPHY in which (typically) a liquid flowing up a gel-coated plate separates components of a mixture.

## Tool mark
Mark on a surface that can identify the individual tool that made it, or at least its class.

## Toxicology
The study of drugs and poisons

## Trace evidence
Evidence in minute quantities transferred unknowingly by contact.

## Vacuum metal deposition
Method of revealing LATENT FINGERPRINTS by evaporation of metal in a vacuum.

## Vital reaction
Reddening that occurs around damage to live skin, distinguishing such wounds from damage after death.

## Voiceprint
Representation of the sound of speech in graphic form.

## X-ray spectroscopy
SPECTROSCOPIC analysis made in a scanning electron microscope, which identifies elements in a sample from the energy of X-rays emitted.

# Index

Page numbers in **bold** type denote the main reference to a spread title. Page numbers in *italic* type indicate an illustration or its caption.

# Acknowledgments

**Dorling Kindersley would like to thank the following people for their assistance:**

Leyla Ostova and Carey Scott for editorial assistance; Chris Bernstein for the index; Alyson Lacewing for proofreading; Dean Price for jacket design; Darren Holt and Bradley Round for modeling; Catherine Goldsmith for additional design; Dave King for photography; Guy Harvey, Robin Hunter, John Kelly, and KJA-Artists.com for digital artwork; Dudley Crossling, developer of the Treadmark system, for information about the case study on p. 21; Bruce Grant, Brian Rice, Dave Field, and John Bunn of the Metropolitan Police, New Scotland Yard, for their time and help concerning the case study for pps. 48–49; Michelle Pettigrew and Elizabeth Stein of the Department of Forensic Medicine and Science, University of Glasgow, for their unending help, time, and patience concerning pps. 56–57; Elizabeth McClelland, Forensic Phonetician, for information and help regarding voiceprints for p. 75; Andrew McNeill, Institute of Alcohol Studies, for his help with pps. 82–83; DC Chris Soteriou and DC Paul Anderson of City of London Police, Data Recovery Unit, for their help with pps. 128–129; Rosemary Lomas, Urvashi Dogra, and Jabaduojie from the International Fund for Animal Welfare for the images for p. 132; Bonnie Yates for her help with information for pps. 132–133.

**Picture Credits**

The publisher would like to thank the following for their kind permission to reproduce their images:
(Position key: b=bottom; c=center; l=left; r=right; t=top)

**Page borders:** Federal Bureau of Investigation cl, cr, tl, Metropolitan Historical Police Museum cr; 2: H.K. Melton: cr; Popperfoto r; 2: Science Photo Library/Colin Cuthbert cl; 2–3: Pascal Goetgheluck r; 3: Katz/FSP/Demange François r; PA Photos/EPA European Press Agency cl, Science Photo Library/Dr. Jeremy Burgess cr, /James King-Holmes l; 4: Masterfile UK/Gail Mooney t, /Green Project tr; Science Photo Library/Costantino Margiotta b; 5: Corbis/Steve Prezant bc, Masterfile UK/Pinto bl, Popperfoto br, Science Photo Library/Dave Parker b; 6–7: Science Photo Library/TEK Image; 8–9: Topham Picturepoint; 9: Katz/FSP trb, PA Photos tr, Rex Features b, David White cra, Greg Williams cr, Science Photo Library/Dr. Jurgen Scriba crb; 10: Masterfile UK/Gail Mooney c; 10–11: Masterfile UK/Green Project; 11: Popperfoto cra, Rex Features br, Science Photo Library/Sheila Terry tr; 12: Rex Features/Kenneth Lambert tr, Star Telegram b; 13: Associated Press AP/Jennie Zeiner, Stringer c, Corbis t, Getty Images/Eyewire b; 14: Popperfoto b; 15: Katz/FSP, PA Photos bl, br, Rex Features tl; 16: PA Photos t, John Giles b; 17: Corbis Ron Slenzak c, Rex Features tr, 19: Corbis Ed Kashi tr, Katz/FSP Demange François Gamma/Frank Spooner c, Science Photo Library/James King-Holmes tl; 20: Associated Press AP/Denis Poroy tc, Corbis/Richard Hamilton Smith bl, Federal Bureau of Investigation/FBI Laboratory Division cr, Rex Features/Stewart Bonney tr; 21: Associated Press AP tl, tr, Corbis/Nogues Alain/Sygma bl, Pictures courtesy of Foster & Freeman Ltd c, br; 22: alamy.com r, Science Photo Library/Sheila Terry l; 23: Associated Press AP tl, Custom Medical Stock Photo/Rowan cr; 24: Associated Press AP/LAPD, Handout tl, tr, /Sam Mircovich, Corbis/Sygma bl; 25: Associated Press AP/LAPD, Handout tr, /Myung J. Chun br; 26–27: Science Photo Library/Costantino Margiotta; 27: Photos crb, Science Photo Library/Custom Medical Stock Photo br, /Pascal Goetgheluck cra: 28: Custom Medical Stock Photo: Shout Pictures b, PA Photos/EPA European Press Agency c; 28–29: Science Photo Library/Pascal Goetgheluck; 29: PA Photos cb, Rex Features/Sam Morgan ca, Science Photo Library/Simon Fraser tr; 30: Katz/FSP br. 31: Katz/FSP tl, PA Photos b, 32: CMSP tl, Science Photo Library/Dr. Arthur Tucker cl; 33: Corbis/John Bartholemew bl; 34–35: Science Photo Library/Custom Medical Stock Photo; 35: The Design Works, Sheffield tr, Science Photo Library/Custom Medical Stock Photo br; 36: Custom Medical Stock Photo/Miller bl, Mediscan t, Science Photo Library/Dr. P. Marazzi br; Scott Camazine cl; 37: Custom Medical Stock Photo/M. English tl, /Wilson b, Mediscan cr, Rex Features tr; 40: Associated Press AP/Al Behram bl, Corbis/Bettmann tr; 41: Bernard Greeberg l, Associated Press/Al Behram br; 42–43: Science Photo Library/David Becker; 43: Associated Press AP/Alexander Zemlianichenko cr, /Freddy Martin cra, Science Photo Library/Chemical Design cr, Jerry Young crb; 44: Rex Features tr, bl, 45: Corbis/Steve Chenn, Forensic Science Laboratory/Courtesy of Elaine M. Pagliaro, CT Department of Public Safety cr, Mediscan tc, Science Photo Library/Dr. H.C. Robinson tl, /Françoise Sauze br; 46: Rex Features/David White tl, Science Photo Library bl /James King-Holmes tr; 46–47: Science Photo Library/Mehau Kulyk; 47: Metropolitan Historical Police Museum tl, Popperfoto br, Rex Features/Action Press tr, Science Photo Library/David Becker bl; 48: Metropolitan Police Service c, Rex Features/Photo News Service tl, Photo News b; 48–49: PA Photos/David Giles; 49: PA Photos/Tony Harris r, Rex Features/Photo News cl; 50: Mary Evans Picture Library br, Popperfoto bl; 51: Freddie Martin tl, bl, br; 52: Associated Press AP/Alexander Zemlianichenko b, Science Photo Library/Peter Menzel tr; 53: Associated Press AP tr/cra/cr, Science Photo Library tl, /Alfred Pasieka br; 54: Associated Press AP/STR bl, Novosti (London) tr, University Of Manchester/Faculty of Medicine, Dentistry, and Nursing tl; 55: Jerry Young; 56: Prof. Attardi and Silvano Imboden bl, br, Forensic Pathology, Sheffield University: cl; 57: Prof. Attardi and Silvano Imboden: tl, cl, cr, bl, br. 58: Custom Medical Stock Photo/©SHOUT b, Science Photo Library tr; Chemical Design c; 59: Science Photo Library tr; 60: Science Photo Library/A. Barrington Brown tr; 61: Custom Medical Stock Photo tl; 62: Science Photo Library/David Parker bl; 62–63: Corbis/Duomo; 63: Corbis/Quadrillion tr, Science Photo Library br, t; 64: Associated Press AP bl, Corbis/Paul Thompson/Eye Ubiquitous br, Newspix Archive/Nationwide News tr; 65: Newspix Archive/Nationwide News tr, br; 66–67: Masterfile UK/Pinto; 67: Corbis/Anna Clopet b, Rex Features tr, /Greg Williams crb; 68: Corbis/Bettmann bl, Science Photo Library/Jim Varney tr; 69: Rex Features br, Science Photo Library/Jim Varney t; 70: Rex Features/Sipa Press tr, bl; 71: Associated Press AP/Joe Picciolo l; Mark Elias l; 72: Associated Press AP/Noble County Jail, Handout br, Commissioner for the City of London Police tl, Federal Bureau of Investigation bl; 73: Identix Incorporated www.identix.com tl, Rex Features/Greg Williams b, Science Photo Library/Stanley B. Burns, MD & The Burns Archive, N.Y. tr; 74: Corbis/Anna Clopet bl; 75: Brain Fingerprinting Laboratories, Inc cr, Science Photo Library/Hank Morgan br, Wellcome dept. of Cognitive Neurology t; 76: Associated Press AP/Nati Harnik tl, b, Ira Nowinski tr; 77: PA Photos tr, Corbis/David Turnley b; 78–79: Science Photo Library/David Parker; 80: Corbis/Tom & Dee Ann McCarthy cl, Science Photo Library/Colin Cuthbert br; 80–81: Peter Menzel; 81: Custom Medical Stock Photo/Rowan br, Federal Bureau of Investigation tc, Science Photo Library/Dr. Jurgen Scriba cl, /Michel Viard, /Peter Arnold Inc. tr; 82: Science Photo Library/Jim Varney b, /TEK Image tr, tr; 83: Custom Medical Stock Photo cl, Dr Brian Widdop of the Medical Toxicology Unit Laboratory: photo: Gary Ombler t, PA Photos/EPA European Press Agency bc, bc, br; 84: Esther Neate br, Katz/FSP/A. Morvan/Gamma bl, L'Est Republicain t, PA Photos/EPA European Press Agency c; 85: www.bloodspattersoftware.com/A L Carter Phd. tl, tr, cla, ca, cra, cl, c, br, bl, Rex Features/Argyropoulos cr, Science Photo Library/Peter Menzel c; 86–87: Topham Picturepoint tr, bl, br; 87: Topham Picturepoint tr, cl, br; 88: Science Photo Library/Andrew Syred tl, /Colin Cuthbert tr, Roger Viollet bl; 89: Corbis/Lester V. Bergman tr, Science Pictures Limited/David Spears tl, Leica Microsystems, Inc. cl, Rex Features/Clare Dickson br, Anthony Ise/Getty Images/PhotoDisc tc, Science Photo Library/Dr Jeremy Burgess cb, Innerspace Imaging bl; 90: Science Photo Library/Dr Jeremy Burgess tl, Mark Thomas b; 91: Rex Features/PNS tr, Science Photo Library/Dr Jeremy Burgess clb, Eye of Science cla, cl, bl, Volker Steger tl; 92: Corbis/Bettmann tr, b; 93: Associated Press AP/John Bazemore l, Corbis/Bettmann br, Dr Brian Widdop of the Medical Toxicology Unit Laboratory/Gary Ombler tr; 94: Katz/FSP/photo: G. Bassignac b; 95: Katz/FSP tl, br, Gamma/G. Bassignac tr, Science Photo Library/Custom Medical Stock cr, M. Kalab/Custom Medical Stock Photo cl; 96: Corbis/Ruet Stephane bl, PA Photos br, /European Press Agency tr; 97: Corbis/Sygma br, Getty Images/Mike Powell bl, Nick Laham tl; 98–99: Corbis/Steve Prezant; 99: Corbis/Ruet Stephane/Sygma cr, Getty Images cr, Topham Picturepoint/Image Works crb; 100: Rex Features br; 100–101: Getty Images; 101: Associated Press AP cl, Michael V. Martinez, MSFS, Senior Forensic Scientist, Bexar County Criminal Investigation Laboratory bc, Science Photo Library/Michel Viard, Peter Arnold Inc. br; 102: Katz/FSP bl, Rex Features tr; 103: Federal Bureau of Investigation tc, r, Katz/FSP c, bl; 104: Custom Medical Stock Photo/Willoughby tr, Mediscan cb, b, Science Photo Library/PHT tl; 104–105: Science Photo Library/Mehau Kulyk; 105: Custom Medical Stock Photo/Willoughby bl, Science Photo Library br, /GJLP tl; 106: Rex Features/Sipa Press b, www.antiquebottles.com tr; 107: Rex Features tr, Science Photo Library/Astrid & Hanns-Frieder Michler bc, Klaus Guldbrandsen clb, /Richard Megna/Fundamental bl; 108: Assistant Divisional Officer Derek and the Fire Investigation Unit at Acton Fire Station c, br, PA Photos/EPA bl, Rex Features/Action Press t; 109: Corbis/Sung-Su Cho/Sygma b; 110: Corbis/Sygma tr, Getty Images/Image Bank bl; 110–111: Topham Picturepoint/David Giles; 111: Getty Images/Eyewire tc, /Photodisc tr, /Taxi c, Topham Picturepoint cr, /Malcolm Croft br; 112: Associated Press AP b, Federal Bureau of Investigation tl, Corbis tr; 113: © 2003 21st Century Forensic Animations br, Corbis/Ruet Stephane/Sygma cr, Getty Images/Taxi tr; 114: Rex Features/Ron Sachs (CNP) tl, /Sipa Press b; 115: Rex Features/Sipa Press tl, tr, Topham Picturepoint/Image Works b; 116: Rex Features tl, /Bryn Colton b; 117: PA Photos tr, Rex Features/Tom Kidd b; 119: Picture courtesy of Foster & Freeman Ltd cra, PA Photos cr, Science Photo Library/Volker Steger cb; 120: Katz/FSP/Rotolo-Liaison b, H. K. Melton tl, PA Photos bl, Rex Features/Judy Totton b; 121: Corbis/Bettmann cr, Picture courtesy of Foster & Freeman Ltd tl, br, cbr, Federal Bureau of Investigation cbl; 122: PA Photos/EPA b; 123: ECB cr, Rex Features/Martti Kainulainen br; 124: Science Photo Library/Volker Steger tr, bl, bc, br; 125: © Christie's Images Ltd tl, Getty Images cb; 126: Corbis/Bettmann cr, PA Photos tr, /EPA r, Rex Features br; 127: Topham Picturepoint bl; 128: PA Photos bl, Corbis bc, Getty Images/The Image Bank c; 129: Associated Press AP br, Getty Images/The Image Bank tr; 130: Corbis/Jim Richardson bl, /Mug Shots tr, Science Photo Library br; 131: Corbis/Sharna Balfour, Gallo Images br, Jim Chamberlain – U.S. Fish & Wildlife Service cr, Rex Features/Profile Press cl; 132: International Fund for Animal Welfare cl, bl, Wan Kam-yan/South China Morning Post tr; 133: Corbis/Earl & Nazima Kowall br, Jim Chamberlain – U.S. Fish & Wildlife Service tr; 133: Nature Picture Library Ltd bl; 134: Katz/FSP b Science Photo Library cl; 135: Katz/FSP ca, Science Photo Library cb, b, /Stanley B. Burns, MD & The Burns Archive, N.Y. t; 136: Associated Press AP cl, Science Photo Library/Michel Viard, Peter Arnold Inc. b; 137: Dr Brian Widdop of the Medical Toxicology Unit Laboratory, photo: Gary Ombler tl, Leica Microsystems, Inc. b, Science Photo Library/Colin Cuthbert cr, /Jim Varney crb.